10 — 23 - 85

nuremberg

German Views of the War Trials

nuremberg

German Views of the War Trials

Edited by

WILBOURN E. BENTON
GEORG GRIMM

SOUTHERN METHODIST UNIVERSITY PRESS
DALLAS:

PRINTED AND BOUND IN THE UNITED STATES OF AMERICA
BY BOOK CRAFTSMEN ASSOCIATES, INC., NEW YORK

Preface

For many years there has been much interest in the development of an international penal or criminal law, as well as the establishment of an international criminal court. The persistent search for the juridical formula is noticeable in the numerous conferences and the literature on the subject. Some of the thinking on the matter of an international criminal jurisdiction envisages a world criminal code, applicable alike to states and to individuals, and effective in times of peace and war. Such is the nature of the proposed criminal statute ("Plan For a World Criminal Code") prepared by Professor V. V. Pella of Rumania and published by the International Association of Criminal Law in 1935.[1] Other efforts have been concerned with specialized phases of the problem—such as terrorism,[2] genocide,[3] human rights,[4] and the crimes enumerated in the Charter of the Nuremberg Tribunal (crimes against peace, war crimes, and crimes against humanity). Hence, an analysis of the Nuremberg trials represents only one phase of the problem of an international criminal jurisdiction.

The Nuremberg trials have been a subject of much discussion throughout the world. In the United States there has been a voluminous literature, in the form of books and articles, on the topic. Nevertheless, the editors believe that an analysis of the trials, as presented in selected articles by German professors and lawyers, will be of special interest to readers in this country. Most of the articles and statements were taken from German journals, and, except as otherwise indicated, were translated into English by Dr. Georg Grimm.

The contribution by a particular individual in no way implies agreement or disagreement, in whole or in part, with the views of others included in the study. Therefore, an exchange of ideas has been attempted—rather than a debate—upon an important topic of our time.

The editors wish to express their appreciation for the splendid co-operation of the individual contributors and publishers, and for the financial support made available by the Graduate Research Fund of Southern Methodist University.

Heidelberg and Dallas
December 23, 1954

W. E. BENTON
GEORG GRIMM

Contents

Introduction

WILBOURN E. BENTON

HISTORY, as it has unfolded itself thus far, has revealed various types of wars. For example, writers often have referred to just and unjust wars, aggressive and defensive wars, as well as legal and illegal and hot and cold wars. As a consequence of the important role of war in the drama of mankind, it became necessary at an early period to formulate rules of warfare. This development of the laws and customs of war—which in modern times found expression in the Hague Conventions—has raised important questions. Does the existence of the laws of warfare imply that the tribe or sovereign always had the right to make war? If so, the initiation of war has been a legal right from the dawn of civilization. Hence the doctrine of the irresponsibility of the individual or state for the initiation of war. On the other hand, has civilization been realistic in recognizing the probability of war, as well as the need for regulation, and therefore developed rules of conduct which in no way imply that *all* wars may be legally initiated? It is at this point that history is a little confusing, since the concept of the *illegality* of aggressive war evolved concurrently with the rules of warfare. Historically speaking the two ideas are interrelated and represent a limitation on the sovereign power of states. Consequently another question may be asked: Does

1

the transformation of the concept of the *illegality* of aggressive war to *criminality*—in the sense that penal sanctions may be applied against those who wage such a war—represent a modern refinement of the age-old limitation on sovereignty in the matter of waging war (laws of war)? Regardless of how one may answer this question, history does afford ample evidence of the concurrent development of the rules of war and the *illegality* of aggressive war.

One of the earliest codes of warfare was the Indian Code of Manu, believed to have been compiled about 500 B.C. This code appears to have been inspired by a genuine regard for the "rights of humanity." Humane treatment for both combatants and noncombatants was recommended in the code.[1] Despite evidence of a higher moral law restraining on occasion the ruthlessness with which war was generally waged, the Assyrians, Babylonians, Medes, Persians, Phoenicians, Carthaginians, and Jews continued to wage war under few restraints.

In the Greek period an attempt was made to regularize and humanize the conduct of hostilities. Even though in actual practice the Greeks frequently engaged in war as if bound by no rules, the foundation was laid in this period for the development of the *jus bellicum* by the Romans. This law, which regulated the actual conduct of war, was derived in part from religion and the universal law of nature. The Greek wars, generally speaking, did not produce the excesses or brutalities which characterized the oriental wars. Wars in Greece were not undertaken "without the belligerents' alleging a definite cause considered by them as a valid and sufficient justification therefor, and without their previously demanding reparation for injuries done or claims unsatisfied."[2] The concept of a "just war" *(bellum justum)* underwent a more extensive development in the Roman period.

In Plato's *Republic* Socrates and Glaucon discussed what acts should be forbidden in a quarrel or disorder between Greek states.[3] Socrates suggested that such quarrels should be conducted solely with a view to reconciliation; that friendly correction should be the objective rather than the enslavement or destruction of one or more of the parties involved.

And as they are Hellenes themselves they will not devastate Hellas, nor will they burn houses, not even suppose that the whole population of a city—men, women, and children—are equally their enemies, for they know that the guilt of war is always confined to a few persons and that the many are their friends. And for all these reasons they will be unwilling to waste their lands and raze their houses; their enmity to them will only last until the many innocent sufferers have compelled the guilty few to give satisfaction.[4]

A similar view was expressed by Polybius when he declared:

The purpose . . . with which good men make war is not to destroy and annihilate the wrongdoers, but to reform and alter the wrongful acts; nor is it their object to involve the innocent in the destruction of the guilty . . .[5]

At least some of the early philosophers thought in terms of punitive action which could be taken against those individuals who made war.

The Ancient College of Fetials *(Collegium Fetialium)*,[6] which conducted Roman relations with foreign nations, performed a variety of sacerdotal, diplomatic, and judicial functions. Among its more important judicial functions was the determination of whether or not a war was a just war.[7] The fetials not only considered the legality of the preliminary proceedings, but also made a determination whether or not there existed a just cause for war. The decision of the fetials in this matter had a great influence on the action taken in the Senate.[8]

The doctrine of the "just war" *(bellum justum)* was recognized by Roman law. Therefore, in the conduct of this type of war certain specific rules and ceremonies had to be followed— for such war was a legal institution involving both rights and duties.[9] According to Professor Oppenheim, Roman law recognized four just causes of war: "(1) violation of the Roman dominions; (2) violation of ambassadors; (3) violation of treaties; (4) support given during war to an opponent by a hitherto friendly State."[10] Even in the case of a just cause for war, the resort to armed force was justifiable only after satisfaction had been demanded and refused. In case of refusal, war was formally declared by a varying number of fetials who proceeded to the Roman frontier; there, after making a formal declaration of war, the fetials hurled a spear into the enemy's territory. Such action symbolized the existence of hostilities.

Embedded in the fetials' demand for satisfaction or justice *(res repetere)*, in the event Rome had a grievance against a foreign state, was the early concept of an international criminal jurisdiction. For example, "In 320 B.C. envoys were sent to the Samnites to demand the surrender of the author of the war which the latter had waged against Rome."[11] The Romans, like the Greeks, were aware of such concepts as "acts of aggression" (especially when committed against Roman territory) and the doctrine of "criminal liability." In other words, a punitive war could be waged in order to punish those guilty of such acts of aggression.

It is true that the fetiale procedure, as a means of determining the existence of a just cause for war, did reflect certain weaknesses. Rome was not only a party to the dispute, but also judge of its own cause. Also, it may have been that at times the College of Fetials was under the complete domination of the Roman Senate—exercising little or no independent power. Furthermore, that part of the fetiale procedure concerned with the formalities preliminary to a declaration of war was, on occasion, dispensed with by the Romans, or used by them as cover for waging an unjustifiable war. Nevertheless, the Ancient College of Fetials, the *jus fetiale*, and the fetiale procedure made a rather significant contribution to the development of international law. The doctrine of the "just war" had a profound influence on the Catholic school of international law, on Hugo Grotius, and on other writers in the field of international jurisprudence.

Rome did not have a well-developed *jus belli* (law of war), but she did develop certain rules which did much to regularize and humanize the actual conduct of hostilities. These rules, known as the *jus bellicum*, were derived from religion and the universal law of nature. This law created certain rights and obligations which resulted from an actual state of war. Therefore, the *jus bellicum* was related to, but not synonymous with, the *jus fetiale*. The latter was more concerned with the regularity of the proceedings preliminary to a declaration of war than with the actual conduct of hostilities. Certain practices during war, e.g., acts of treachery, use of poisoned weapons, and assassinations, were condemned by the *jus bellicum*. It is true that the Romans, like the Greeks, did not always feel themselves bound by the law; nevertheless, their efforts did contribute to the development of the modern law of war.

One of the outstanding contributions made by the Middle Ages to the development of international law was the revival of the Roman doctrine of the just war. The resuscitation of the doctrine, as modified by Christian principles, was due to the writings of certain of the early Church Fathers—especially St. Augustine (354-430) and St. Thomas Aquinas (1225-74). The just war doctrine became a topic of great importance in the Middle Ages because of certain objections and questions which had been raised concerning the participation of Christians in war and military service. Tertullian (160-230) and other early Church Fathers objected to such participation by Christians. Furthermore, certain of the Scriptures appeared to make pacifism an essential part of the Christian doctrine. On the other hand, certain other passages from the Holy Writ seemed to support Christian participation in war. It is little wonder that so much doubt and confusion existed in regard to the matter of Christian participation in war, especially at a time when the church was being undermined by pagan and Gnostic doctrines.

St. Augustine, "who presented perhaps the first great synthesis of Christian ethical and political ideas of the post-apostolic age . . . ,"[12] firmly believed that Christians could participate in war. Nevertheless, he qualified his position by the requirement that the war be just.

Those wars are described as just wars which are waged in order to avenge a wrong done, as where punishment has to be meted out to a city or state because it has itself neglected to exact punishment for an offense committed by its citizens or subjects or to return what has been wrongfully taken away.[13]

In other words, there was neither cause or justification for war unless a wrong had been committed previously. War was for the redress of injury and the protection of rights rather than for conquest. Such action for the redress of injury received would require some sort of vengeance or punishment. Even a defensive war "could not," according to St. Augustine and his followers, "be waged satisfactorily, were no vengeance taken on enemies who have done or tried to do a wrong," for the reason that they would "only be emboldened to make a second attack, if the fear of retribution did not keep them from wrongdoing."[14] But the end and aim of war, which likewise must be just, was something higher than the recovery of property or avenging a wrong; it was "the peace and security of the State."

St. Augustine realized that the conditions existing in Italy and the provinces created certain grave dangers. Since the empire had lost its power, various groups would challenge the authority which remained; on the other hand, the development of heresies would tend to undermine Christian unity. Therefore, wars could be made in order to protect the social order against destruction. If the social order could be maintained, the civil arm of the state could be employed against heretical sects, thereby removing a positive danger to the survival of the church. Thus, the maintenance of secular unity was necessary for the preservation of the Christian faith.

This led St. Augustine to justify certain kinds of war for the sake of peace, so that an important distinction was made between just and unjust wars. St. Augustine had no sympathy for what today would be classified as imperialistic wars; nevertheless, wars were just when their aim or end was to repel attacks on law. The unjust state should not be allowed to attack with impunity those states which strive to maintain the social order and promote the good life. Such action by the unjust state could be forcefully suppressed. War in this sense "may become necessary to prevent disorder, arising from unrighteous resistance to just laws."[15]

"Unfortunately," to quote Professor Thomas I. Cook, "the mere admission that war might be used on behalf of the true faith laid a foundation for the support of war by the later church against heretics." Thus the Crusades against the Albigenses and Mohammedans could be justified by the church authorities. As a result, "the essential pacifism of Christianity was forced into the background, and the papacy could without inconsistency give its moral aid to participants in earthly struggles."[16] Therefore, the application of St. Augustine's doctrine by the church had a tremendous impact upon the course of history.

Nevertheless, St. Augustine was one of the first to classify wars as just and unjust. Henceforth it became important for an interested party to show, or at least allege, that the proposed use of force was just; likewise, the party attacked could declare that such a war was unjust. The growth of the idea that war needed justification and of the establishment of criteria of judgment became an important topic—especially after the Reformation when St. Augustine's doctrine of the just and unjust war was reapplied and expanded by both Catholic and Protestant writers.

St. Thomas Aquinas, the greatest of the medieval philosophers, was, like other early Church Fathers, confronted with the question "whether it is always a sin to wage a war." Christian participation in warfare was firmly established by Aquinas ("I, indeed, rejoice that there are wars in defence of the state"[17]). Nevertheless, important limitations were placed upon the right to make war. In the first place, the making of war was proper for the king or public personage but not for a private individual. In the second place, there must be a *justa causa* of war. In regard to the latter the Angelic Doctor declared

that, with respect to these three points,—namely, avenging itself upon its enemies, recovering its property, and punishing its enemies, —the state possesses the same power over its enemies as that which it possesses over its subjects. And if the state has this power, so also has the prince; for he draws his power from the state.[18]

Thus, there are three just causes for waging war: (a) the recovery of property, (b) vengeance, and (c) the punishment of one's enemies. In short, for a just war, "there must be a just cause," that is to say, "some fault must deserve the attack."[19] This implies that war should be made for some reasonable cause rather than out of a desire to do harm. Also one notes the parallelism between individuals and states, since "the state possesses the same power over its enemies as that which it possesses over its subjects." Thus, it was unnecessary to apply to the conduct of states rules of appraisement different from those applied to the conduct of individuals.

Aquinas also considered various questions relating to the actual conduct of war; that is, the action which the belligerents could and could not take during and after the conflict *(Summa Theologica,* Question 40: On War). One is impressed by the great emphasis placed upon the doctrine of "military necessity" which then, as now, has provided the basis for the justification of various types of action deemed necessary in the war effort. However, the Angelic Doctor did declare against certain excesses in war, e.g., the killing of women and children, on the theory that war against them would not be just. Furthermore, he was opposed to lies and the violation of promises in war. In short, the war must be just—a *justa causa* of war—and not unjustly waged. This part of his theory of war had considerable influence on the application and development of the *temperamenta* of warfare by later writers.

In the writings of St. Augustine and St. Thomas Aquinas the

just war doctrine was conceived as a norm of theology. Hence, during the twilight period of its existence the doctrine was hardly distinguishable from morality or justice. It came, therefore, within the jurisdiction of the church. The result was that during the early years practically all topics of international law fell within the orbit of theology and the just war doctrine, because a prince could declare that the infringement of territorial sovereignty, the violation of treaties or of the right of embassy, as well as the violation of other rights, constituted a just cause for war. This left the determination of the justness or unjustness of war to each individual prince—a procedure which, of course, was subject to abuse. Nevertheless, imbedded in the just war doctrine was the embryonic concept of the illegality of certain types of war, since punishment could be assessed against those princes or states that waged an unjust war. The world continues to search for some equitable means of translating this theory into practice.

The just war doctrine of St. Augustine and St. Thomas Aquinas, as well as the right to take punitive action against those who wage such a war, had a tremendous influence upon later writers, as for example Francisco Vitoria (1480-1546), Hugo Grotius (1583-1645), Christian von Wolff (1679-1754), Emmerich de Vattel (1714-67),[20] and others. Many of the writers of the sixteenth, seventeenth, and eighteenth centuries made elaborate classifications of just and unjust wars, attempted to establish norms or criteria of judgment, and gave some consideration to the matter of punitive action. Hence one may conclude that the concept of aggressive war, as well as of the right to take punitive action against those who wage such a war, has been in the process of development for many centuries. During the formative years the principle was interwoven with the doctrine of the just war *(bellum justum)*. The latter was in the nature of "a reaction against a wrong, a procedure either in tort (restitution, reparations, guarantees) or in criminal law (punishment, sanctions)."[21] Such a doctrine was of "Catholic origin, anchored in natural law, [and] a theological, . . . [rather than] a legal concept."[22] Yet "international law, or the law that governs between states," as Mr. Justice Cardozo put it, "has at times, like the common law within states, a twilight existence during which it is hardly distinguishable from morality or justice, till at length the 'imprimatur' of a court attests its jural quality."[23] Many rules of positive law were, at their inception, based upon theology or natural law. Yet the latter did have certain deficiencies. For example, the determination of the justice of the cause was left to the rulers themselves, who were expressly recognized as judges in their cause. In fact, little effort was devoted to devising criteria and means by which a more impartial judgment could be obtained. The problem is still with us—of developing a valid technique for determining in a given case whether an act of aggression has been committed by a state.

The writings of Vitoria, Grotius, Wolff, Vattel, and others helped to establish the notion of the *illegality* of aggressive war rather than its *criminality* in the sense of penal law. Nevertheless, the moral and juridical aspirations of jurists and commentators, however noble, "are resorted to by judicial tribunals, not for the speculations of their authors concerning what the law ought to be, but for trustworthy evidence of what the law really is."[24] It is in this spirit that the "teachings of the most highly qualified publicists of the various nations" may be considered "as subsidiary means for the determination of rules of law" (Art. 38(d), Statute of The International Court of Justice). In short, recognition of the *illegality* of aggressive war by many of the early writers did not create a rule of law. Hence, the jurists and statesmen of the twentieth century were confronted with the difficult task of translating the concept into positive law.

The Covenant of the League of Nations did not completely outlaw war. Rather, members were forbidden to go to war only under certain conditions.[25] "The obligations not to go to war were presented in the Covenant only as exceptions, and once the exceptions were complied with, it could be argued that

recourse to war was not unlawful."[26] As Hans J. Morgenthau
put it, "Even if the members had lived up to the provisions of
the Covenant, they would have found in the fundamental law
of the League an instrument for the prevention of some wars
and for the legalization of others."[27] Hence, the Covenant
seemed to assume that war remained the normal means of
settling international conflicts. However, a number of treaties
which did outlaw aggressive war were ratified in the post-World
War I period. For example, the Briand-Kellogg Pact (the General Treaty for the Renunciation of War) was signed on August
27, 1928, "and was ratified by the largest number of states ever
to accept a multilateral political instrument."[28] The Briand-
Kellogg Pact did not make all wars illegal, since the signatory
nations recognized the inherent right of self-defense. As a result
of this understanding, each nation was competent to decide
when it might go to war in self-defense. Since war in self-defense was recognized as legal and since each nation had the
right to interpret the treaty for itself, every nation engaged in
war could declare itself engaged in a war of self-defense. Consequently, there were those who questioned the practical effect
of the Pact. On the other hand, there were those "who claimed
that no state could unilaterally interpret a treaty in such a way
as to free itself from contractual obligations."[29] It is difficult,
if not impossible, to resolve this conflict of views in the absence
of some generally accepted definition of aggression.

There was no machinery provided in the Briand-Kellogg Pact
for action in the event its provisions were violated. Nevertheless, many thought the Pact would play an important role,
since it would mobilize world public opinion. Prentiss Gilbert,
the American "observer" who was authorized to attend the
meetings of the League Council when the Manchurian question
was under consideration, declared that the Briand-Kellogg Pact
"represents to us in America an effective means of marshalling
the public opinion of the world behind the use of pacific means
only in the solution of controversies between nations."[30] In a
memorandum to his Cabinet, President Hoover said, "The

Nine-Power Treaty and the Kellogg Pact are solely moral instruments based upon the hope that peace in the world can be held by the rectitude of nations and enforced solely by the moral reprobation of the world. . . ."[31] On August 11, 1932, in his speech accepting renomination, President Hoover declared,

> . . . . We have given leadership in transforming the Kellogg Pact from an inspiring outlawry of war to an organized instrument for peaceful settlements backed by definite mobilization of world public opinion against aggression. We shall, under the spirit of the Pact, consult with other nations in times of emergency to promote world peace. We shall enter into no agreements committing us to any future course of action or which call for the use of force to preserve peace. . . .[32]

The Pact was invoked by the United States as grounds for the nonrecognition of the Japanese puppet state of Manchukuo during the Manchurian crisis in 1931. The American government contended the puppet state was established contrary to the principles of the Pact. This method of enforcing the Pact was endorsed by the League Assembly by its resolution of March 11, 1932, which declared that the members of the League should not recognize any action contrary to the Briand-Kellogg Pact. Russia's failure to observe the Pact—as well as certain other agreements—resulted in her expulsion from the League following the attack upon Finland (Assembly and Council Resolutions of December 14, 1939).

Wars of aggression were condemned by those nations of the Western Hemisphere which ratified the Anti-War Treaty on Non-Aggression and Conciliation, signed at Rio de Janeiro, October 10, 1933. The purpose of the Treaty, according to the Preamble, was to condemn "wars of aggression and territorial acquisitions that may be obtained by armed conquest, making them impossible and establishing their invalidity through the positive provisions of [the] treaty, and in order to replace them with pacific solutions based on lofty concepts of justice and equity."[33] This principle was reaffirmed by the nations of the Western Hemisphere in the Act of Chapultepec of March 3,

1945.[34] Many contend that such treaty provisions as those noted above are merely declaratory, since no specific penalty or enforcement machinery is included in the treaties.

It was within this historical framework that representatives of the United States, France, Great Britain, and Russia had to consider what action should be taken following the termination of World War II. On August 8, 1945, the Four Great Powers signed the Declaration of London for the prosecution and punishment of the major war criminals of the European Axis. The organization, procedure, and jurisdiction of the Court to be established were provided in the Charter of the International Military Tribunal, which was annexed to, and formed an integral part of, the Declaration of London. Under the agreement the Tribunal had power to try and punish the major war criminals, either as individuals or as members of organizations, for the violation of the crimes mentioned in the Charter.

It appears that the Nuremberg Judgment was based on both the conventional element and customary rules.[35] Considerable emphasis was placed on the Briand-Kellogg Pact and various other documents. Since the Charter of the Tribunal made "the planning or waging of aggressive war" a crime, it was "not strictly necessary to consider whether and to what extent aggressive war was a crime before the execution of the London Agreement." Because of the importance of the questions involved the Tribunal attempted to show that "the Charter [was] not an arbitrary exercise of power on the part of the victorious nations, but . . . [was] the expression of international law existing at the time of its creation; and to that extent [was] itself a contribution to international law."[36] Hence, the Charter represented a codification of existing law on the subject and was accepted by the four powers concerned. The American prosecutor admitted the lack of judicial precedent in the matter of crimes against peace yet declared that "unless we are prepared to abandon every principle of growth for international law, we cannot deny that our own day has the right to institute customs and to conclude agreements that will themselves

become sources of a newer and strengthened international law."
The law of nations "grows, as did the common law, through
decisions reached from time to time in adapting settled principles to new situations."[37] In the words of the Tribunal: "The
law of war is to be found not only in treaties but in the customs
and practices of States, which gradually obtained universal
recognition, and from the general principles of justice applied
by jurists and practised by military courts." International law,
like other systems of law, is progressive, and as a federal district
judge in the United States has observed, "Its principles are
expanded and liberalized by the spirit of the age. . . . Cases,
as they arise under it, must be brought to the test of enlightened
reason and of liberal principles. . . ."[38]

In the matter of sentences the Tribunal did not find that the
"supreme crime" against peace deserved the most severe punishment. Hess, the only one convicted on counts one and two
alone, was given life imprisonment, while those who were
condemned to death were those found guilty of war crimes and
crimes against humanity. Raeder, Von Neurath, and Dönitz,
although guilty of other crimes in addition to those against
peace, were sentenced to life, fifteen years, and ten years
respectively.

A number of serious charges have been directed against the
Charter and Judgment of the Nuremberg Tribunal. For instance, some contend that war has always been a natural
phenomenon which existed outside of law; that is, an institution
neither legally authorized nor outlawed. In this sense, at least
technically speaking, the Briand-Kellogg Pact, by which the
contracting parties condemned "recourse to war for the solution of international controversies" and renounced it "as an
instrument of national policy in their relations with one another" was illogical, since the Pact presupposed an existing
legality of war. Regardless of this inconsistency, the Pact was
never abrogated by any subsequent treaty among the signatory
states. Nevertheless, there are those who believe the treaty
inconclusive in that: (a) war was not defined and no machin-

ery was provided for the determination of its occurrence; (b) waging war was not declared a crime, since no penal sanctions were included; and (c) the treaty did not provide for the punishment of individuals for the nonfulfilment of obligations assumed.

Many offenses are punishable although undefined. For example, some of the American state constitutions are silent as to what constitutes impeachable offenses; neither do they prescribe the mode of impeachment except to stipulate that the power of impeachment shall be vested in the House of Representatives and that trial shall be before the Senate sitting as a High Court of Impeachment. Yet, some state officials have been impeached and removed from office by the fact that "impeachable offenses" are designated by the term impeachment. The same is true of high treason, which in some countries is punishable but undefined. In fact, many constitutional and statutory definitions of crimes are incomplete, since they are subject to interpretation by the local courts. The Hague and Geneva Conventions which embody the laws and customs of war do not define their violation as "war crimes," nor are penal sanctions provided in the event the treaties are violated. Nevertheless, the conventions have been recognized and applied by the nations. The Paris Pact implies the belief that those who plan and wage a nondefensive war commit a crime in so doing. But the criticism that the Pact did not provide for the punishment of individuals is a more serious charge, since under orthodox international law the nonfulfilment of treaty obligations was a matter of condemnation perhaps sounding in damages—in the nature of state responsibility—rather than a crime for which individuals could be punished. Herein lies the real innovation of the Charter, in that individuals could be held responsible for the crime of war and the common plan of aggression and domination.

Professor Jahrreiss, counsel for defense at Nuremberg, placed considerable emphasis upon contemporary state practice in the interwar period. In a notable address to the court he maintained that the prohibitions and condemnations of war contained in the Covenant of the League of Nations and the Briand-Kellogg Pact, as well as various other treaties, some of which were unratified, formed a part of the collective security system which collapsed prior to the commencement of World War II. Furthermore, according to Professor Jahrreiss, "this collapse was acknowledged and declared expressly, or shown by unambiguous actions, by three world powers." Evidence to support this argument may be found in the unpunished acts of aggression committed by Italy, Japan, and Russia in the 1930's. In fact, many nations showed their acquiescence in matters of aggressive wars and recognized their consequences. For example, many members of the League made neutrality declarations in the Italo-Abyssinian conflict and later recognized Abyssinia's conquest by Italy. The United States, by its neutrality legislation of 1935, recognized the existence of war between certain powers with whom she lived in peace. Although the American legislation was modified in time for political reasons in favor of the Allies, the fact remains the United States did recognize the existence of war, regardless of whether she considered the Axis cause just or unjust. Certainly Russia, as one of the prosecuting powers at Nuremberg, with two nationals as judges, did not contribute to the prestige of the court—especially since the Soviet Union shared in Germany's aggression against Poland, later went to war against Finland, and in time annexed three Baltic states with which she had concluded nonaggression treaties. In the case of Russia, it was a matter of treaty violation; while with the other nations it was a matter of nonapplication of the treaties by the signatories. Nevertheless, it may be contended with considerable force that the Briand-Kellogg Pact was inapplicable as a result of the breakdown of the collective security system.

Closely associated with the above contention is the doctrine of *Rebus Sic Stantibus* and the plea of condonation. By the doctrine of *Rebus Sic Stantibus,* or the lapse of treaties by reason of change of circumstances, it might be reasoned that the Pact of Paris and other nonaggression treaties to which Germany was a party were concluded on the basis of the collective security system which the nations attempted to establish after the conclusion of World War I. Hence, the failure of the collective security system caused these treaties to lose their binding force. Yet one may question whether the above doubtful rule should be applied to those nations largely responsible for the failure of the collective security system. Under the plea of condonation some maintain "that the other signatories lost the power subsequently to punish acts which they themselves sanctioned by their recognition or by an agreement at the time they were committed." The plea of condonation should, according to Dr. C. A. Pompe, "indeed be admitted for such actions as the annexation of Austria, the seizure of Sudetenland after the Munich Agreement, the aggression in Manchuria and the wars, if wars they were, between Japan and Russia, each of which was followed by recognitions, treaties or agreements with the Powers concerned." The Nuremberg Tribunal did not invoke the principle of condonation since it held that the acts in question did not have the character of wars. Even if one admit condonation as a question of fact, the doctrine of the illegality of aggressive war, as provided in the Paris Pact and other instruments, "was not nullified by the temporary failure of the Governments to draw from the illegality practical consequences. The Powers acted late to forestall the outbreak of the Second World War, but they acted finally."[39]

In reply to the proposition that frequent breaches of the law result in its abrogation, the British chief prosecutor, Sir Hartley Shawcross, raised certain questions:

But what is the relevance of the fact that the system designed to enforce these treaties and to prevent and to penalize criminal recourse to war failed to work? Did the aggressions of Japan and Italy and the other states involved in the Axis conspiracy, followed by the German aggressions against Austria and Czechoslovakia, deprive those obligations of their binding effect simply because those crimes achieved a temporary success? Since when has the civilized world accepted the principle that the temporary impunity of the criminal not only deprives the law of its binding force but legalizes his crime?

The British chief prosecutor concluded

that in the case both of the Japanese and Italian aggressions, the Council and the Assembly of the League of Nations denounced these acts as violations both of the Covenant and of the [Paris Pact] ... and that in both cases sanctions were decreed. It may be that the policemen did not act as effectively as one could have wished them to act. But that was a failure of the policeman, not of the law.[40]

Despite the argument of prosecution, there is some question whether or not the latter adequately met the contention of the defense which was, for the most part, based on contemporary state practice.

The implied reservation of self-defense in the Paris Pact did not free the signatories of the legal obligation not to resort to war. Otherwise the Paris Pact would be nothing more than a scrap of paper devoid of any meaning. Neither the Pact of Paris nor any other treaty could take away the right of self-defense. This did not mean that the state acting in self-defense was the final judge of the legality of its conduct. Each state acted at its own peril. Japan alleged that events in Manchuria justified resort to force in self-defense. Yet an impartial inquiry by the League found there was no justification for action in self-defense. Under Article 51 of the United Nations Charter the inherent right of individual or collective self-defense is recognized. Nevertheless in Article 2(4) of the Charter we read, "All Members shall refrain in their international relations from the threat or use of force against the territorial integrity or political independence of any state, or in any other manner inconsistent with the Purposes of the United Nations." Hence, the right of self-defense, whether expressly reserved or implied by treaty, does not prevent the treaty from creating legal obligations against resort to war.

If the Pact of Paris and various other treaties established the notion of the illegality of aggressive war which has been transformed into criminality by action of the Nuremberg Tribunal, certain vital questions remain to be answered. For example, wherein does the primary responsibility for aggressive war reside—in the collectivity, that is the state, on whose behalf the acts were committed, or in the human agents who represent the state? In short, where should the primary criminality be located and what should be the nature of the punishment? The philosophical basis of this question may be found in the works of the great classical writers. Thus, Christian von Wolff, an eighteenth-century German scholar, declared, as had others before him, that "he who wages an unjust war is a robber, an invader, and a bandit."[41] Yet he was of the opinion that

nation is bound to nation for the penalty for a wrong, in so far as satisfaction is to be given for the wrong. For it is self-evident that there is no place here for penalties, either capital, or those affecting the person, or those which consist in infamy, such as are inflicted in a state by the sovereign upon those committing crime, but only for those which consist in payment and therefore have the character of a fine. Therefore, infamy does not attach to these penalties as to civil penalties.[42]

Thus, a fine or reparations, charged to the nation as a whole, could be inflicted upon a state for injury resulting from the use of unjust force. Again,

Those things which are done in war by unjust force are charged to the nation as a whole, and not to the individuals as individuals. Therefore, although we assume that the act of the corporate body deserves punishment, nevertheless, since no one can be punished for the act of another, and since any one of those who share the punishment with each other is punished for his own act, by which he concurs in the act of another, individuals cannot submit to that punishment which the corporate body deserves. . . . Therefore, although an unjust belligerent may be a robber and a brigand, and robbery and brigandage may be chargeable to the nation which the ruler of the state represents, nevertheless on this account it is not to be said that any one of the individual persons is guilty of robbery and brigandage . . . nations cannot be punished for using unjust force in war in the way in which it is customary for robbers and brigands to be punished or as has been introduced by a positive law. By the right to punish provision is made for security in the future, and from this purpose in the existing circumstances is to be determined how much is allowable to attain that purpose.[43]

On the other hand some of the classical writers, as for example Emmerich de Vattel (1714-67), the disciple of Wolff, believed that the sovereign who waged an unjust war was answerable for all the evils and all the disasters of the war.[44]

On the basis of the "act of state" plea immunity is said to exist for acts committed on behalf of the state. If the leaders of a defeated nation could be tried and punished such action, it is asserted, would be in violation of the "fundamental principle of international law prohibiting the unauthorized interference by force of one national legal order in the jurisdictional sphere of validity of another national legal order."[45] A similar view was expressed in the reservations presented by the representatives of the United States to the *Report of the Commission on Responsibilities,* April 4, 1919. The American memorandum —in supporting the exemption of the sovereign and of the sovereign agent of a state from judicial process—declared:

This does not mean that the head of the State, whether he be called emperor, king, or chief executive, is not responsible for breaches of the law, but that he is responsible not to the judicial but to the political authority of his country. His act may and does bind his country and render it responsible for the acts which he has committed in its name and its behalf, or under cover of its authority; but he is, and it is submitted that he should be, only responsible to his country, as otherwise to hold would be to subject to foreign countries, a chief executive, thus withdrawing him from the laws of his country, even its organic law, to which he owes obedience, and subordinating him to foreign jurisdictions to which neither he nor his country owes allegiance or obedience, thus denying the very conception of sovereignty.[46]

The American position was based upon the existence of the German state following the termination of World War I. Yet, could such a principle be applied to a nation that had unconditionally surrendered and was within the jurisdiction of the victorious Powers?

The French prosecutor considered the Nuremberg trial a municipal proceeding. Since the German state had been dissolved, only its former agents could be held criminally responsible for various criminal acts they had committed on behalf of the German state. The idea of the primary criminality of the state may also be found in the remarks made by the British chief prosecutor, who placed the responsibility for crimes against peace on the defendants since they counseled and carried out a crime committed by the state. The Tribunal, however, rejected the "act of state" plea, since its acceptance would have made prosecution impossible by providing a cover of immunity for both the former agents of the state and the state itself. Such dual immunity would have resulted from the fact that the former agents of the state could not be held criminally responsible because they acted on behalf of the state, while the latter would have enjoyed immunity because of its sovereign capacity. Again, the immunity of the state presupposed the continued existence of the German state which the French prosecutor denied. As observed elsewhere, state criminality was admitted prior to 1939—for example, international tribunals had awarded penal damages against states for undermining the sovereignty of other states—and the League sanctions, although ineffective, were of a penal nature.

International law, in the opinion of the Tribunal, is concerned not alone with the actions of sovereign states, but "imposes duties and liabilities upon individuals as well as upon States." In conformity with Article 7 of the Charter, the Tribunal, in rejecting the act of state plea, declared:

It is the very essence of the Charter that individuals have international duties which transcend the national obligations of obedience imposed by the individual State. He who violates the laws of war cannot obtain immunity while acting in pursuance of the authority of the State, if the State in authorizing action moves outside its competence under international law.

Hence the Tribunal concluded that "the principle of international law, which under certain circumstances protects the representatives of a State, cannot be applied to acts which are condemned as criminal by international law." Although the Tribunal accepted the principle of immunity of state agents, nevertheless it did say that the proposition was subject to qualifications. It should be noted "that although the Tribunal considered the principle applicable only under certain circumstances, it restricted its nonapplication to the case of violations of the laws of war, to which it assimilated crimes against peace."[47]

According to the Nuremberg Judgment, "Crimes against international law are committed by men, not by abstract entities, and only by punishing individuals who commit such crimes can the provisions of international law be enforced." This statement has evoked considerable discussion in the United States and elsewhere. Dr. Hans Ehard, in his scholarly article, "The Nuremberg Trial Against the Major War Criminals and International Law," supports "the allegation advanced several times, that crimes are always committed by individuals." This, he says,

is undoubtedly correct, but it is a truism. It applies to every human act and of itself proves nothing with regard to criminal responsibility in the individual case. . . . International military tribunals also are made up of human beings, conventions also are entered into by human beings, a charter also is created by human beings, the indictment is brought by individual human beings—and nevertheless the indictment [is in the name of the Four Powers] . . .

Others who question the extension of international law to individuals contend that states are the only proper subjects of the law. Since the law of nations provides no sanctions for individual offenses, the authors of such offenses cannot be proper subjects of the law. The subject-object theory of the law has found considerable support in the United States. Again, it is worth noting that the Hague Conventions on the Laws and Customs of War applied to individuals and contained no sanctions, yet they were recognized and enforced by the nations of the world. Nevertheless, one must admit that with few exceptions, as in matters of piracy, breach of blockade, and ordinary war crimes, traditional international law, as it existed prior to 1939, did not extend to individuals. On the other hand some take the position that "the final object of the law of nations is not the protection of the impersonal interests of juridical entities termed states, governments, or sovereigns. It is the protection of the ordinary common interests of 'peoples.' "[48] In any case, the protection of the latter interest may or may not be promoted by establishing criminal responsibility in the case of individuals. The fact that Article 4 of the Weimar Constitution provided that "the generally accepted rules of international law are to be considered as binding, integral parts of the law of the German Reich" could in no way alter the general rule among nations that only in exceptional cases did international law apply to individuals.

The part of the Nuremberg Judgment concerning the plea of "superior orders" has stimulated some comment. Article 8 of the Charter which restricted the plea of "superior orders" was, according to the judgment, "in conformity with the law of all nations." The Court considered the "true test" of responsibility "not the existence of the order, but whether moral choice was in fact possible." In the case of Dithmar and Boldt (Germany, Reichsgericht, July 16, 1921) it was held that "the subordinate obeying [an illegal order in war] is liable to punishment, if it was known to him that the order of the superior involved the infringement of civil or military law." The liability of subordinates for the execution of an illegal order of a superior during war was recognized not only in the German Military Penal Code, but in the military codes of other nations as well. Yet there are mitigating circumstances; that is, the evidence of each particular case must be weighed to determine "whether moral choice was in fact possible."

There has been some criticism of the composition of the Nuremberg Tribunal in that no neutral or German judges were included in the personnel of the court. No doubt the prestige of the court would have been enhanced in the eyes of public opinion if judges from neutral countries and Germany had been included on the bench. Nevertheless, the exclusion of such judges was—legally speaking—irrelevant, because the judges, whatever their nationality, would have been obligated to accept the law of the Charter as the basis for the trial. It would appear that a more valid criticism could be directed at the enactment of the Charter, its substantive and procedural provisions, as well as its interpretation and application by the court.

The phrase "victors' justice" has played a prominent role in the discussion of the Nuremberg trials. For many the expression has become a legal and an emotional symbol of injustice. The determining factor was not the existence of a court established by the victors, but whether or not the proceedings were, in fact, arbitrary from the standpoint of the law applied, the sufficiency of evidence to convict, and appropriate trial safeguards for the accused. There could have been injustice in an all-German court or a mixed court composed of Allied, German, and neutral judges. In short, the development, interpretation, and application of law by the victor may or may not be synonymous with judicial arbitrariness. The justice or injustice of Nuremberg must be determined by an objective analysis of the facts and circumstances involved in the trial itself. In all criminal prosecutions, whether at the local or international level, criminals are apprehended, tried, and punished by the victor—the latter being represented by the power of the individual state or international community. No doubt as international criminal law becomes a more mature law both substantive and procedural machinery will be devised by which a more impartial judgment may be obtained in determining when an act of aggression has been committed by a state. International criminal law—if compared with established standards of local penal law—may be considered an instrument of pioneer justice. In a sense, "these are pioneer days in world law."[49]

International criminal law, as it has developed to the present, "is very much in the state that common law was in Blackstone's time."[50]

The United Nations Charter has been invoked to show that the victorious Powers did not subject themselves to the same rule of law that they formulated for the defeated nations. Individual responsibility for crimes against peace, war crimes, and crimes against humanity was not included in the San Francisco Charter. Also it should be noted that according to Article 34(1) of the Statute of the International Court of Justice, "Only states may be parties in cases before the Court." This provision of the Statute of the Court, as well as the absence of the Nuremberg Principles, has been interpreted by some as evidence that the London Charter was a temporary derogation from the general principles of international law. However, the planning, preparation, initiation, or waging of a war of aggression would be in violation of Article 2 (4) of the United Nations Charter ("All Members shall refrain in their international relations from the threat or use of force against the territorial integrity or political independence of any state, or in any other manner inconsistent with the Purposes of the United Nations"). The Charter contains no definition to guide the Security Council in determining the existence of a "threat to the peace, breach of the peace, or act of aggression" (Article 39). It would appear that the Charter does, at least by implication, make a distinction between legal and illegal wars—an illegal war being one not waged in self-defense or to maintain international peace and security. Of course the reservation of the veto makes impossible the application of sanctions to the Prosecuting Powers. Hence, it would take a drastic revision of the United Nations Charter to bring it into harmony with the principles of the Charter and Judgment of Nuremberg.

One may ask whether the "forces of history" were adequately considered at Nuremberg. It is true that many deep-rooted economic and political factors—both local and international—contributed to the development of the Nazi regime. For example, restrictions on foreign trade by many countries, the world-wide economic collapse in the early 1930's, the threat of communism in western and eastern Europe, as well as factors deeply rooted in the past of the German state, created a fertile environment for the establishment of a strong military government. Hence it was impossible for Germany, caught in this web, to make the necessary adjustments by peaceful means. The history of Germany, as of other nations, is a fabric, the pattern of which is conditioned by the "roaring loom of time." Many nations faced with similar internal and external threats of the period met the challenge through peaceful procedures. The "forces of history" proposition is in the nature of a justification for action taken, rather than a matter of important legal significance.

After considering the pre-Nuremberg developments, as well as the Charter and Judgment of Nuremberg, one must conclude —so it seems to the author—that two significant innovations resulted from the War Crimes Trials: (1) The concept of the *illegality* of aggressive war was transformed into *criminality*, in the sense that penal sanctions may be applied against those who wage such a war. This was accomplished by assimilating "crimes against peace" with the violations of the laws of war in which the immunity of state representatives does not exist because such acts are considered criminal under international law. Such an expansion of the notion of the illegality of aggressive war indicates again the concurrent development of the concept with the rules of war, both developments further restricting the sovereignty of nations in the international field. (2) This transformation, together with the new rule recognizing individual responsibility for the crime of war, provided the connecting link between Article 6a of the London Charter and the Kellogg Pact. Hence, the search for juridical techniques by which aggressive war may be outlawed and punishment assessed against those who wage such a war, as a part of the past, "is not something that we have left behind us . . . it is something that moves along with us."

Motion Adopted by All Defense Counsel

19 November 1945

Two frightful world wars and the violent collisions by which peace among the States was violated during the period between these enormous and world embracing conflicts caused the tortured peoples to realize that a true order among the States is not possible as long as such State, by virtue of its sovereignty, has the right to wage war at any time and for any purpose. During the last decades public opinion in the world challenged with ever increasing emphasis the thesis that the decision of waging war is beyond good and evil. A distinction is being made between just and unjust wars and it is asked that the Community of States call to account the State which wages an unjust war and deny it, should it be victorious, the fruits of its outrage. More than that, it is demanded that not only should the guilty State be condemned and its liability be established, but that furthermore those men who are responsible for unleashing the unjust war be tried and sentenced by an International Tribunal. In that respect one goes now-a-days further than even the strictest jurists since the early Middle

Reprinted from Trial of the Major War Criminals Before the International Military Tribunal (Nuremberg, 1947), I, 168-70.

[The Tribunal rejected this motion November 21, 1945, ruling that insofar as it was a plea to the jurisdiction of the Tribunal it was in conflict with Article 3 of the Charter.]

Ages. This thought is at the basis of the first three counts of the Indictment which have been put forward in this Trial, to wit, the Indictment for Crimes against Peace. Humanity insists that this idea should in the future be more than a demand, that it should be valid international law.

However, today it is not as yet valid international law. Neither in the statute of the League of Nations, world organization against war, nor in the Kellogg-Briand Pact, nor in any other of the treaties which were concluded after 1918 in that first upsurge of attempts to ban aggressive warfare, has this idea been realized. But above all the practice of the League of Nations has, up to the very recent past, been quite unambiguous in that regard. On several occasions the League had to decide upon the lawfulness or unlawfulness of action by force of one member against another member, but it always condemned such action by force merely as a violation of international law by the State, and never thought of bringing up for trial the statesmen, generals, and industrialists of the state which recurred to force. And when the new organization for world peace was set up last summer in San Francisco, no new legal maxim was created under which an international tribunal would inflict punishment upon those who unleashed an unjust war. The present Trial can, therefore, as far as Crimes against Peace shall be avenged, not invoke existing international law, it is rather a proceeding pursuant to a new penal law, a penal law enacted only after the crime. This is repugnant to a principle of jurisprudence sacred to the civilized world, the partial violation of which by Hitler's Germany has been vehemently discountenanced outside and inside the Reich. This principle is to the effect that only he can be punished who offended against a law in existence at the time of the commission of the act and imposing a penalty. This maxim is one of the great fundamental principles of the political systems of the Signatories of the Charter of this Tribunal themselves, to wit, of England since the Middle Ages, of the United States since their creation, of France since its great revolution, and the

Soviet Union. And recently when the Control Council for Germany enacted a law to assure the return to a just administration of penal law in Germany, it decreed in the first place the restoration of the maxim, "No punishment without a penal law in force at the time of the commission of the act." This maxim is precisely not a rule of expediency but it derives from the recognition of the fact that any defendant must needs consider himself unjustly treated if he is punished under an *ex post facto* law.

The Defense of all defendants would be neglectful of their duty if they acquiesced silently in a deviation from existing international law and in disregard of a commonly recognized principle of modern penal jurisprudence and if they suppressed doubts which are openly expressed today outside Germany, all the more so as it is the unanimous conviction of the Defense that this Trial could serve in a high degree the progress of world order even if, nay in the very instance where it did not depart from existing international law. Wherever the Indictment charges acts which were not punishable at the time the Tribunal would have to confine itself to a thorough examination and findings as to what acts were committed, for which purposes the Defense would cooperate to the best of their ability as true assistants of the Court. Under the impact of these findings of the Tribunal the States of the international legal community would then create a new law under which those who in the future would be guilty of starting an unjust war would be threatened with punishment by an International Tribunal.

The Defense are also of the opinion that other principles of a penal character contained in the Charter are in contradiction with the maxim, *"Nulla Poena Sine Lege"*.

Finally, the Defense consider it their duty to point out at this juncture another peculiarity of this Trial which departs from the commonly recognized principles of modern jurisprudence. The Judges have been appointed exclusively by States which were the one party in this war. This one party to the proceeding is all in one: creator of the statute of the Tribunal and of the rules of law, prosecutor and judge. It used to be until now the common legal conception that this should not be so; just as the United States of America, as the champion for the institution of international arbitration and jurisdiction, always demanded that neutrals, or neutrals and representatives of all parties, should be called to the Bench. This principle has been realized in an exemplary manner in the case of the Permanent Court of International Justice at The Hague.

In view of the variety and difficulty of these questions of law the Defense hereby pray:

That the Tribunal direct that an opinion be submitted by internationally recognized authorities on international law on the legal elements of this Trial under the Charter of the Tribunal.

On behalf of the attorneys for all defendants who are present.

/s/ DR. STAHMER

Statement Before the Nuremberg Tribunal

DR. HERMANN JAHRREISS

M<small>R.</small> President and Gentlemen of the Tribunal, the main juridical and fundamental problem of this Trial concerns war as a function forbidden by international law; the breach of peace as treason perpetrated upon the world constitution.

This problem dwarfs all other juridical questions.

The four chief prosecutors have discussed the problem in their opening speeches, sometimes as the central theme of their presentation, sometimes as a fundamental matter, while indeed differing in their conceptions thereof.

It is now up to the Defense to examine it. The body of Defense Counsel have asked me to conduct this examination. It is true that it is for each counsel to decide whether and to what extent he feels in a position to renounce, as a result of my arguments, his own presentation of the question of breach of the peace. However, I have reason to believe that counsel will avail themselves of this opportunity to such an extent that the intention of the Defense to contribute materially toward a technical simplification of the phase of the Trial which is now beginning, will be realized by my speech.

This statement by the counsel for Defendant Jodl is reprinted from Trial of the Major War Criminals Before the International Military Tribunal *(Nuremberg, 1948), XVII, 458-94.*

I am concerned entirely with the juridical question, not with the appreciation of the evidence submitted during the past months. Also, I am dealing only with the problems of law as it is at present valid, not with the problem of such law as could or should be demanded in the name of ethics or of human progress.

My task is purely one of research; research desires nothing but the truth, knowing full well that its goal can never be attained and that its path is therefore without end.

I wish to thank the General Secretary of the Tribunal for having placed at my disposal documents of decisive nature and very important literature. Without this chivalrous assistance it would not have been possible, under the conditions obtaining at present in Germany, to complete my work. The literature accessible to me originated predominantly in the United States. Familiar as I am with the vast French and English literature on this subject, which I have studied during the last quarter of a century—I am, unfortunately, not conversant with the Russian language—I believe, however, that I can fairly say that no important concept has been overlooked, because in no other country of the world has the discussion of our problem, which has become the great problem of humanity, been more comprehensive and more profound than in the United States.

This very fact has enabled me to forego the use of legal literature published in the former German sphere of control. In this way even the semblance of a *pro domo* line of argumentation will be avoided.

Owing to the short time at my disposal for the purpose of this speech, and at the same time in view of the abundance and complexity of the problems with which I have to deal, it will not be possible for me to cite all the documents and quotations I am referring to. I shall present only a few sentences. Any other procedure would interrupt the train of argument for the listener. I shall therefore submit to the Tribunal the documents and literary references in the form of appendices to my juridical arguments. What I am saying can thus quickly be verified.

The Charter threatens individuals with punishment for breaches of the peace between states. It would appear that the Tribunal is accepting the Charter as the unchallengeable foundation for all juridical considerations. This means that the Tribunal will not examine the question whether the Charter, as a whole or in parts, is open to juridical objections; yet such a question nevertheless continues to exist.

If this is so, why, then, have any discussion at all on the main fundamental legal problems?

The British chief prosecutor even made it the central theme of his long address to examine the relationship of the Charter, where our problem is concerned, to existing international law. He justified the necessity of his arguments by saying that it was the task of this Trial to serve humanity and that this task could be fulfilled by the Trial only if the Charter could hold its own before international law, that is, if punishment of individuals for breach of the peace between states was established in existing international law.

It is, indeed, necessary to clarify whether certain stipulations of the Charter may have created new laws, and consequently laws with retroactive force.

Such a clarification does not serve the purpose of facilitating the work of the historians. They will examine this, just as all the other findings in this Trial, according to the rules of free research; perhaps through many years of work and certainly without limiting the questions to be put and, if possible, on the basis of an ever greater wealth of documents and evidence.

Such a clarification is indispensable, if only for the reason that the decision as to right and wrong depends, or may depend, thereupon, all the more so if the Charter is considered legally unassailable.

Let us assume for the sake of argument that the Charter does not formulate criminal law which is already valid but creates new, and therefore retroactive, criminal law. What does this signify for the verdict? Must not this be of importance for the question of guilt?

Possibly the retroactive law which, for instance, penalizes aggressive war had not become fixed or even conceived in the conscience of humanity at the time when the act was committed. In that case the defendant cannot be guilty, either before himself or before others, in the sense that he was aware of the illegality of his behavior. Possibly, on the other hand, the retroactive law was promulgated at a time when a fresh conscience was just beginning to take shape, although not yet clear or universal. It is then quite possible for the defendant to be not guilty in the sense that he was aware of the wrongfulness of his commissions and omissions.

From the point of view of the European continental conception of penal law, the fact that a person was not aware of doing wrong is certainly a point which the Tribunal must not overlook.

Now the question as to whether the penal law contained in the Charter is *ex post facto* penal law does not present any difficulty as long as the stipulations of the Charter are unequivocal and the prescriptions of international law as applying to date are uncontested.

But what if we have regulations capable of different interpretations before us or if the concepts of international law are the subject of controversy? Let us take the first: A stipulation of the Charter is ambiguous and therefore requires interpretation. According to one justifiable interpretation the stipulation appears to be an *ex post facto* law; according to another, which can be equally well justified, it does not. Let us take the second: The regulation is clear or has been clarified by interpretation of the Court, but experts on international law are of different opinions as to the legal position applying to date; it is not certain whether we are not concerned with an *ex post facto* law. In both cases it is relevant whether the defendant was conscious of the wrongfulness of his behavior.

I intend to demonstrate how important these considerations are in this Trial, and shall now begin the examination.

The starting points of the British and French chief prosecutors are fundamentally different.

The British chief prosecutor argues as follows, if I understood him correctly:

First, the unrestricted right of states to wage war was abolished in part by the League of Nations Covenant, later as a general principle of the Kellogg-Briand Pact, which continues to be the nucleus of world peace order to this very day. War, thus prohibited, is a punishable violation of law within and toward the community of nations, and any individual who has acted in a responsible capacity is punishable. Secondly, the indictment of individuals for breach of the peace, although novel, not only represents a moral necessity, but is in fact long overdue in the evolution of law; it is quite simply the logical result of the new legal position. Only in outward appearances does the Charter create new law.

And if I understood the British chief prosecutor correctly, he is asserting that since the conclusion of the Pact of Paris there exists a clear legal order based on the entire world's uniform conviction as to what is right. Since 1927 the United States have negotiated first with France, then with the remaining Great Powers, with the exception of the Soviet Union, and also with some of the smaller powers concerning the conclusion of a treaty intended to abolish war. Secretary of State Kellogg stated (in a note to the French Ambassador, 27 February 1928) with memorable impressiveness what the Government in Washington were striving for, namely:

The powers should renounce war as an instrument of national policy, waiving all legal definitions and acting from a practical point of view, plainly, simply, and unambiguously, without qualifications or reservations.[1] Otherwise the object desired would not be attained: To abolish war as an institution, that is, as an institution of international law.[2]

After the negotiations had been concluded, Aristide Briand,

the other of the two statesmen from whose initiative springs
that pact which in Germany is often called the "Pact to Outlaw
War," declared, when it was signed in Paris:

Formerly deemed a divine right and remaining in international law
as a prerogative of sovereignty, such a war has now at last been
legally stripped of that which constituted its greatest danger: its
legitimacy. Branded henceforth as illegal, it is truly outlawed by
agreement. . . .[3]

According to the conception of both leading statesmen, the
Paris Pact amounted to a change of the world order at its very
roots, if only all, or almost all, nations of the world—and particularly all the great powers—signed the pact or adhered to it
later on, which did actually happen.

The change was to be based on the following conception: Up
to the time of the Kellogg-Briand Pact, war had been an institution of international law. After the Kellogg-Briand Pact, war
was high treason against the order created by international law.

Many politicians and scholars all over the world shared this
conception. It is the definite basic conception of that unique
commentary on the League of Nations Covenant by which
Jean Ray, far beyond the borders of France, stirred the hearts
of all practical and theoretical proponents of the idea of preventing war.[4] It is also the basic conception of the Indictment
at Nuremberg.

Diplomacy and the doctrine of international law found their
way back into their old tracks after the first World War, after
a momentary shock from which they recovered with remarkable rapidity. This fact horrified all those who were anxious to
see the conclusions—all the conclusions—drawn from the catastrophe.

Mankind had a "grand vision of world peace" then, as Senator Bruce called it when the Pact of Paris was before the Senate for ratification.[5] I know how much the personality and the
achievements of Woodrow Wilson are a subject of dispute.
But the more detachment we achieve, the clearer it becomes

that he—by making fortunate use of his own preparatory work and of that of others[6]—finally conceived and presented to the humanity of the time an entirely brilliant train of thought which is as right today as it was then, and which can best be condensed as follows:

It is necessary to start afresh. The tragic chain of wars and mere armistices termed peace must be broken. Sometime humanity must have the insight and the will to pass from war to real peace, that is, to peace which is good in its essence, founded on existing legal principles, without regard to victory or defeat; and this peace, which is good in its essence, must be maintained—and maintained in good condition—by an organized union of states.

These aims can only be achieved if the most frequent causes of war are eliminated, namely excessive armaments, secret treaties, and the consecration—detrimental to life— of the *status quo* as a result of lack of insight on the part of the possessor of the moment.

Humanity did not follow this path. And it is not to be wondered at that among those who fought against the instruments of Versailles, St. Germain, Trianon, Neuilly, and Sèvres, be it in the camp of the vanquished or in that of the victors, were the very ones who strove after real, lasting peace. When the Governments of the South African Union and Canada, in their replies to Secretary of State Hull's Principles of Enduring Peace of 16 July 1937, indicated in unusually strong language that a revision of unjust and forcibly imposed treaties was an indispensable precondition for real world peace, they took up one of the basic views of the great American President.[7]

Humanity did not follow Wilson.

Even for the members of the League of Nations war remained a means for settling disputes, prohibited in individual cases, but normal on the whole. Jean Ray,[8] as late as 1930, said:

The League of Nations did not prove to be a guide to the true order of peace, indeed it did not even prove to be a sufficient brake to prevent a complete backward movement into the former state. For the world did in fact slide back entirely.

For this is the all-important factor in our problem of law. Before the commencement of the second World War the whole system of collective security, even in such scanty beginnings as it had made, had collapsed;[9] and this collapse was acknowledged and declared expressly, or by equivalent action, by three world powers—and, in fact, declared with full justification. Great Britain clearly stated this at the beginning of the war to the League of Nations. I shall show this immediately.

The Soviet Union treated the German-Polish conflict simply according to the rules of classical international law concerning *debellatio*. I shall explain this shortly.

The United States declared their strict neutrality. I shall also explain the import of this declaration.

The system of collective security has been the subject of much dispute. In this matter involving the world's conscience, which is of fundamental importance in this very Trial, it cannot be a matter of indifference that the system, rightly or wrongly, appeared in 1938 to such a prominent specialist on international law as the American, Edwin Borchard, to be absolutely inimical to peace and the offspring of the hysteria of our age.[10] The collapse may have had various causes; it is certain that the above-mentioned three world powers testified at the beginning of September 1939 to the collapse—the complete collapse—and that they did not, in fact, do so as a consequence of the German-Polish war.

To begin with, on 7 September 1939, the British Foreign Office told the Secretary General of the League of Nations[11] that the British Government had assumed the obligation, on 5 February 1930, to answer before the Permanent International Court of Justice at The Hague whenever a complaint was filed against Great Britain, which would include all cases of complaints which other states might lodge on account of conduct whereby Great Britain in a war had, in the opinion of the plaintiff, violated international law. The British Government had accepted this regulation because they had relied on the functioning of the machinery of collective security created by the League of Nations Covenant and the Pact of Paris—because, if it did function properly, and since Britain would certainly not conduct any forbidden wars, her opponent on the contrary being the aggressor, no collision between Britain and those states that were faithful to the security machinery could possibly be caused by any action of Britain as a seapower.[12] However, the British Government had been disappointed in this confidence: Ever since the League Assembly of 1938 it had no longer been possible to doubt that the security machinery would not function; on the contrary it had, in fact, collapsed completely. A number of members of the League had already declared their strict neutrality before the outbreak of war: "The entire machinery intended to maintain peace has broken down."[13]

I will proceed to show how right the British Government were in the conclusions they drew. It should not be forgotten that the British Premier, Mr. Neville Chamberlain, had already proclaimed, on 22 February 1938 in the House of Commons, that is, before the so-called Austrian Anschluss, the complete inefficiency of the system of collective security. He said:[14]

At the last election it was still possible to hope that the League might afford collective security. I believed it myself. I do not believe it now. I would say more: If I am right, as I am confident I am, in saying that the League as constituted today is unable to provide collective security for anybody, then I say we must not delude ourselves, and, still more, we must not try to delude small weak nations into thinking that they will be protected by the League against aggression and acting accordingly, when we know that nothing of the kind can be expected.

The Geneva League of Nations was "neutralized," as Noel Baker politely expressed it later in the House of Commons.[15]

Secondly, in view of the correct conclusions drawn by the British Government and expressed in their note of 7 September 1939 to the League of Nations, it is no wonder that the Soviet

Union treated the German-Polish conflict in accordance with the old rules of power politics. In the German-Russian Frontier and Friendship Pact of 28 September 1939 and in the declaration made on the same day in common with the Reich Government,[15a] the Moscow Government bases its stand on the conception of the *debellatio* of Poland, that is, the liquidation of Poland's government and armed forces; no mention is made of the Pact of Paris or the League of Nations Covenant. The Soviet Union takes note of the liquidation of the Polish state machinery by means of war, and from this fact draws the conclusions which it deems right, agreeing with the Reich Government that the new order of things is exclusively a matter for the two powers.

It was therefore only logical that in the Finnish conflict, during the winter of 1939-1940, the Soviet Union should have taken its stand on classical international law. It disregarded the reactions of the League of Nations when, without even considering the application of the machinery of sanctions and merely pretending to apply an article of the Covenant referring to quite different matters, that body resolved that the Soviet Union had, as an aggressor, placed itself outside the League.[16] The report of the Swiss Federal Council of 30 January 1940 to the Federal Assembly endeavored to save the face of the League which was excluded from all political realities.

Thirdly, the President of the United States stated on 5 September 1939 that there existed a state of war between several states with whom the United States lived in peace and friendship, namely, Germany on the one hand, and Great Britain, France, Poland, India, and two of the British dominions on the other. Everyone in the United States was required to conform with neutrality regulations in the strictest manner.

Since the time of the preliminary negotiations, it was a well-known fact in the United States that Europe, and particularly Great Britain and France, saw the main value of the Pact to Outlaw War in the fact that the United States would take action in case of a breach of the pact. The British Foreign

Secretary stated this on 30 July 1928, that is, 4 weeks previous to the signing of the pact. During the deliberations of the American Senate on the ratification of the pact, Senator Moses drew particular attention to this.[17] Senator Borah affirmed at the time that it was utterly impossible to imagine that the United States would calmly stand by.[18] After the discredit resulting from the failure of the policy of collective security in the case of Manchuria and Abyssinia the world had come to understand the now famous "quarantine" speech of President Franklin D. Roosevelt on 5 October 1937 and his "Stop Hitler!" warnings before and after Munich to mean that the United States would act on the next occasion. The declaration of neutrality of 5 September 1939 could therefore only mean: Like Great Britain and the Soviet Union, the United States accepts as a fact the collapse of the system of collective security.

This declaration of neutrality has often been looked upon as the death blow to the system. The Washington Government would be entitled to reject such a reproach as unjustified. For the system had already been dead for years, provided one is prepared to believe that it was ever actually alive. But many did not realize the fact that it was no longer alive until it was brought into relief by the American declaration of neutrality.

By 1 September 1939 the various experiments, which had been tried since the first World War with a view to replace the "anarchic world order" of classical international law by a better, a genuine, order of peace, were over, that is, to create in the community of states a general statute according to which there would be wars which are forbidden by law and others which are countenanced. These experiments, in the opinion of the major powers of the time, had failed. The greatest military powers of the earth clashed in a struggle in which they pitted their full strength against one another. For the proponents of a materialistic conception of history this meant the second phase in a process developing according to

inexorable laws, whereby history swept away all diplomatic
and juridical artifices with supreme indifference.

The majority of international lawyers throughout the world
maintained that in universal international law as at present
applied, there exists no distinction as to forbidden and non-
forbidden wars.

Hans Kelsen set this forth in 1942 in his paper *Law and
Peace in International Relations*, which he wrote after pains-
taking research into literature. He himself belongs to the
minority who are prepared to concede a legal distinction
between just and unjust wars, so that his statement carries all
the more weight.

Now we must ask: Are we in point of fact right in speaking
of the collapse of the system of collective security? This
would presuppose that such a system at one time existed.
Can that really be maintained? This is a question of the
greatest importance for this Trial, in which the existence of
a world-wide consciousness of right and wrong is taken as
the basis for the indictment for breach of the peace.

Let us recall the tragedy of the Kellogg-Briand Pact, that
tragedy from which all those have suffered so much who rejoiced when the pact was concluded and who later, after
a first period of depression, hailed the Stimson Doctrine as a
long overdue step essential for the achievement of real peace
and as an encouraging omen of fresh progress.

The United States had a great goal in view in 1927 and
1928, as I already mentioned. In the League of Nations the
problem had been tackled only half-heartedly and with half
measures, and this had perhaps done more harm than good
to the cause of real peace. The Geneva Protocol had failed.
Kellogg now wanted to overcome all the difficulties inherent
in the problem and bring the world round by vitality and
determination. The pact as published, with its two articles
containing the renunciation of war and the obligation of peaceful settlement, seemed to still the yearning of humanity eager
for some deed.

But the difficulties it was desired to surmount are in part rooted in the problem, and no rules laid down by any legislator will ever fully eliminate them. For even if unambiguous criteria existed, who among fallible mankind would have the authority to give a decision in case of dispute? We do not even possess unambiguous criteria for aggression and defense.[19] This holds good both for the so-called political concept, which is in a way natural, and for the legal concept or concepts of aggression and defense.

Yet these were not the only difficulties pointed out, explicitly and implicitly, by the French Government in the preliminary negotiations for the pact; they did so with the full title[20] of one who knows Europe and its ancient historical heritage just as the United States Government knows America and its vastly different history.

When the world came to know the notes exchanged during the preliminary negotiations with all their definitions, interpretations, qualifications, and reservations, it became manifest to what extent the opinions of the governments differed behind that wording. One saw the Soviet Government's frank—even scathing — criticism of the refusal of the Western Powers to disarm and thus create the essential precondition for an effective policy of peace and generally of the vagueness of the treaty;[21] but especially of the famous British reservation of a free hand in certain regions of the world, that reservation which has often been called the British Monroe Doctrine or the Chamberlain Doctrine;[22] and one knew that in reality there existed only formal agreement behind the signatures and that no two powers were implying exactly the same thing by the treaty. Only on one thing did complete agreement exist: War in self-defense is permitted as an inalienable right to all states; without that right, sovereignty does not exist; and every state is sole judge of whether in a given case it is waging a war of self-defense.

No state in the world at that time was prepared to accept foreign jurisdiction concerning the question of whether its decisions on basic questions of its very existence were justified or not.

Kellogg had declared to all the nine states participating in the negotiations, in his note of 25 June 1928:[23] ". . . The right of self-defense . . . is inherent in every sovereign state and is implicit in every treaty. Every nation . . . is alone competent to decide whether circumstances require recourse to war in self-defense."

The friends of peace were cruelly disappointed. What was the use of such a treaty anyway? They were only too right. Very soon afterward they heard with even greater grief of the course of the discussions in the American Senate. The ratification was, it is true, passed with 85 votes against 1, with a few abstentions; but if, behind the signatures of the contracting states there was no material agreement, there was even less behind the result of the vote in the Senate of that world power which was, as far as the conception and initiative was concerned, the leading one.

The discussions in the Senate, which will remain memorable for all time because of their earnest and profound character, showed — and several senators expressly said so — that the opinions of the senators were oscillating between two poles which were worlds apart. For some the treaty really meant a turning-point in world history; to others it appeared worthless, or at best a feeble or friendly gesture, a popular slogan, a sort of international embrace; to yet others as fertile soil for all the wars of the future, a gigantic piece of hypocrisy, as the legalization of war or even of British world control, or as a guarantee of the unjust *status quo* of Versailles for France and Great Britain.

Some senators criticized the utter vagueness of the stipulations of the treaty even more bitterly than the Russian note. And if Kellogg's declaration about the right of self-defense, which, according to the will of the signatory states, was an integral part of the treaty, was taken literally: What kind of war was then forbidden?[24] Sarcastic and ironical words were used in the Senate.

Nothing was gained by this Paris Pact if everything were to remain as at its conclusion. In the opinion of the great American expert on international law, Philip Marshall Brown, the pact unwittingly engendered by its ineptness the horrible specter of "undeclared war."[25]

Those, Germans or non-Germans, who fought against Versailles because progress was blocked, and those, Germans or non-Germans, who criticized the League of Nations because it did more harm than good to the will toward progress, had all rejoiced for nothing at the end of August, 1928. The decisive step had not been taken.

But above all the one thing which, though not sufficient in itself, is indispensable if a guarantee of peace is really to be created, the one thing that is necessary in the unanimous opinion of all who reckon with human frailty, was never tackled: To create a procedure by which the community of states, even against the will of the possessor, can change conditions that have become intolerable, in order to provide life with the safety valve it must have if it is to be spared an explosion.

The individual state, if at all, can avoid revolutions only by good legislation and an early adjustment of order to changing conditions; and the same is true of the community of states. Wilson also had this fundamental principle in mind, as we saw. One of the great British experts on international law, one of the enthusiastic, unconditional, and progressive adherents of the Paris Pact, McNair, took this into account too when, in 1936, he wanted to see placed beside collective force the collective and peaceful revision of conditions which had become dangerous.[26] And it was also taken into account by the American experts on international law, Borchard[27] and Fenwick,[28] in their warning illustration of the situation as regards international law shortly before the second World War. The Reich Government, by the way, had pointed out quite rightly refrained from justifying them as consistent with neutrality. On the contrary, they took their stand on the Pact of Paris as interpreted by the Budapest Articles.[49] As we saw, this would, according to Viscount Sankey's indisputably correct conception of the sources of international law, have been wrong as far back as 1935.

After the developments which had taken place since Italy's victory over Abyssinia, such discussions were entirely outside the field of legal realities. Their purpose was to resolve internal dissensions in America and for that very reason could not have been of direct importance for international law. Even had these discussions taken place between states, they could at most have helped to create law. But is it actually necessary to assert or prove that such discussions could not have created, in the midst of the great struggle, a law to attain which so many efforts—efforts which were proved to have been Utopian —were made in vain in peacetime?

In this Court many ways of legal thinking meet—ways which are in part very different. This leads to a number of ineradicable differences of opinion. But no manner of legal thinking anywhere on earth, from the most ancient times to the most recent, could or can make possible arguments which contradict the very nature of law as a social order of human life arising out of history. If several governments accept articles about whose contents they are of different opinions and if these articles then find no real application in the practice of these governments—which is not to be wondered at considering the circumstances under which they arose—and if logicians then interpret these articles, while the practice of governments rejects these interpretations either expressly or tacitly, then one will simply have to resign oneself to this, inasmuch as one proposes to keep to the task of legal appreciation, however much the goal may seem worth striving for, politically or morally.

But let us forget for a moment the bitter realities of those years following upon the Italo-Abyssinian conflict. Let us of 31 August 1928 on the Kellogg-Briand Pact when they brought up this question.

Other attempts to help tried to develop a completely new world constitution out of the entirely vague pact by way of logic. They are connected with the name of the American Secretary of State, Stimson, and with the work of the Budapest meeting of the International Law Association in 1934.[32] In order to understand this, it will be found necessary to assume that the Kellogg Pact really did bring about, in a legally conceivable manner, the unambiguous and unconditional renunciation of war. Then, of course, there exists no longer any right to wage wars as and when one likes. War waged in defiance of this prohibition is an offense against the constitution of the community of states. We are immediately faced by the question: Can the legal position of a state which attacks contrary to law be the same as that of a state which is being attacked contrary to law?

If one answers "no," as does for instance the influential French commentator on the League of Nations Covenant, Jean Ray,[33] does not this mean the elimination of the most important fundamental principles of classic international law?

(1) Do the international laws of war — which, after all, spring from the right to wage war freely and from the duel-like character of war and certainly from the equality of the belligerents before the law — apply for the qualification of the acts of the belligerent powers against one another?

(2) Is it possible, or indeed permissible, that neutrality should still exist in such a war?

(3) Can the result of the war, assuming that the aggressor is victorious, be valid under law, especially when compressed into the form of a treaty, or must not the community of states deprive the aggressor of the spoils of his victory by a policy of nonrecognition? Should there not be, or must there not be, joint coercive action by the states against the aggressor?

It must be noted that not even theoretical law has drawn all possible conclusions. The practice of the states, after a few tentative beginnings in isolated points, never came to a definite conclusion in a single case.

With regard to the first point, the validity of the international laws of war during a war, whatever its origin, has never so far been seriously disputed by any state. Any doubts that arose were cleared up in a way which allowed of no misunderstandings. I draw attention to Resolution Number 3 of the League of Nations Assembly of 4 October 1921 and to the report of the Committee of Eleven of the League of Nations for the adaptation of the Covenant to the Pact of Paris.[34]

The aggressor state has the same rights and duties in a war as the attacked nation, that is, those laid down by the traditional international laws of war. The French chief prosecutor appears to wish to deviate from this line, although he does not seem disposed to draw the full conclusions. However, I do not see any tendency to deviate from the present path even in the most recent practice of states.

With regard to the second point:

Attempts have been made to deny the obligation to remain neutral and, in fact, finally to establish for the states not involved the right of non neutrality and even the right to wage war against the aggressor. Some statesmen and scholars have devoted themselves just as passionately to undermining, and even to outlawing, the right to neutrality as other statesmen and scholars have spoken in favor of its undiminished continuance.[35] The clearer it became that the whole system of collective security failed to function in those particular cases which were of decisive importance, namely, where steps would have had to be taken against a great power, the more the idea of neutrality asserted itself with fresh vigor. The complete discredit attaching to the League of Nations and the system of the Kellogg-Briand Pact since the Abyssinian conflict put classical international law back into its old position. In 1935 Switzerland declared her unrestricted neutrality;[36] Belgium, Denmark, Finland, Luxembourg, Norway, Holland, and Sweden followed with their declaration at Copenhagen on 24 July 1938.[37] The failure of the League of Nations was the reason quite openly given.

With reference to the third point:

The idea underlying the policy of nonrecognition is that the states not involved in a conflict should conduct themselves as members of the community of states, that is, they should protect the constitution of the community of states by refusing to recognize the fruits of victory, should the victor have been the aggressor. The situation he has created by force should not even seem to become a legal situation. He will thus be deprived of what he has gained, and one of the main inducements to wage war will thereby be eliminated. Such a policy of nonrecognition is undoubtedly not enough to guarantee by itself a system of collective security, but it is an indispensable part of such an order. There can be no dispute about this. The Brazilian representative, Senhor Braga, gained merit by proposing, at the second League Assembly in 1921, that such a policy be followed by the members of the League of Nations under the name of a "universal legal blockade" *(blocus juridique universel).*[38]

The Finnish representative, M. Procope, interpreted Article 10 of the Covenant in this sense in 1930 before the League Assembly.[39] The notes by the American Secretary of State, Stimson, of 7 January 1932 to China and Japan[40] made this idea echo throughout the world. Their contents are commonly referred to as the Stimson Doctrine. The League of Nations accepted the Doctrine as a resolution of the Assembly on 11 March 1932.[41] The concept was later the focal point of the Pact of Rio de Janeiro of 10 October 1933 and of the Budapest Articles of 10 September 1934.

The conflict between Italy and Abyssinia in 1935-36 became the great test case,[42] which decided the fate of the system of collective security. The League of Nations declared a member, which was a great power, to be the aggressor and decreed economic sanctions but then shrank from coercive military measures and finally, after Italy's victory, struggled painfully in debates on procedure, especially at the 18th Assembly of the League, to find an answer to the question as to how the League, without openly betraying its constitution, could cross the attacked member, the minor power of Abyssinia, off the list of existing states and recognize it as part of the Italian Empire. The United States, too, did not enforce the Stimson Doctrine but remained strictly neutral.[43, 44]

It is necessary to realize all this; and also to know that the British Government, on 20 February 1935, politely but firmly refused, through Lord Chancellor Viscount Sankey,[45] to accept the logical explications and paid tribute to the old truth: "It is not logic but history that creates law."[46] On a later occasion, when Secretary of State Cordell Hull had explained the principle of American policy to all powers on 16 July 1937,[47] the Portuguese Government issued a warning against "the abstract and generalizing tendency of jurists"; it warned against attempts to "find a single formula" and against not studying historic facts sufficiently.[48]

We therefore come to the conclusion that in the actual relations between states there existed—quite a number of years prior to 1939—no effective general ruling of international law regarding prohibited war. No such general ruling existed so far as the leading statesmen and the peoples were aware.

This is, in fact, the ultimate reason why the system of specific rulings on international law was followed to an ever-increasing extent. Two states would thus conclude treaties, in full knowledge of their particular historical conditions and with a view to guarantee peace between each other.

Now, during the second World War the United States Government decided to help Great Britain. Great Britain was able to acquire destroyers, and it later received the assistance of Lend-Lease. The American public recognized this act of assistance as being essentially no longer neutral; it was regretted by some, welcomed by others, sometimes attacked and sometimes defended. The supporters of the measures before the American public, above all Stimson and Cordell Hull, this problem, which overshadowed all others, in Stresemann's note to the American Ambassador, dated 27 April 1928, when unconditionally agreeing to Kellogg's proposal.[29]

Later, the problem of "collective revision" was never seriously tackled. This is not surprising, if only because the very character of such a procedure would presuppose renunciation of their sovereignty by the states. And can such a renunciation be considered in the times we live in? In Philip Brown's melancholic opinion — "less than ever."[30] For that reason a real forward step in the question as to how war could legally be outlawed was impracticable.

In spite of these intricate complications the Government of the United States and the League of Nations did a great deal to comply with the urgent demands of the nations. They subsequently tried to give the pact a precise content, and "teeth." The doctrine of international law provided suggestions for this and checked it. Although it remained completely unsuccessful, we shall have to trace this process briefly, because the seed for the ideas contained in the Indictment are to be found here, insofar as its line of argument is not a political or ethical but a legal one.

In its ban on aggression, the Paris Pact unquestionably starts from the political concept of aggression. But that is quite indefinite. Shotwell and Brierly, among others, tried to assist immediately by deducing a legal concept of aggression from the second article of the treaty, which establishes the obligation to follow a procedure of peaceful settlement.[31] We can leave open the question whether it is permissible to apply this interpretation to the treaty. In practice nothing is gained by doing so; one kind of difficulty is simply put in the place of another. There are no fewer obscurities. Measures for peaceful settlement presuppose good will on both sides; what if that is lacking on one side or the other? And what still constitutes a measure of peaceful settlement, and what no longer does? The Russian Government were quite right in their note suppose for a moment that a general and unambiguous pact had existed, accepted and applied by the contracting parties in fundamental and factual agreement. Would the liability of individuals to punishment for the breach of such a treaty be founded in international law?

No—not even the liability of the state to punishment, let alone that of individuals.

The breach of such a treaty would not be any different, under existing international law, from any other violation of international law. The state violating a treaty would be committing an offense against international law, but not a punishable act.[50] Attempts were occasionally made to deduce from the words *délit* (offense), *crime international* (international crime), and *condamnation de la guerre* (condemnation of war) the existence of an international criminal law dealing with our case. Such conclusions are based on wrong premises.[51] Every lawyer knows that any unlawful behavior can be called a *délit (delictum),* not only punishable behavior. And the word *crime* is used even entirely outside the legal sphere. And this is precisely the case here. When in 1927, on Poland's application, the League of Nations Assembly declared war to be a *crime international,* the Polish representative expressly stated that the declaration was not actually a legal instrument but an act of moral and educational importance.[52] The endeavor to organize a universal world system of collective security on a legal basis failed. But this does not mean that the numerous bilateral treaties whose purpose it is to preclude wars of aggression between the two partners became inapplicable. One will have to examine whether the parties to the treaty may have made the existence or continued existence of a general machinery of collective security the prerequisite for the validity of the treaty.

For unilateral assurances of nonaggression the same holds good as for bilateral treaties.

Many bilateral nonaggression pacts were concluded and several unilateral assurances were given. In some cases a political, in others a legal concept of aggression, or even a number of such legal concepts may determine right and wrong.

The Reich also concluded a series of such pacts. They have been cited by the Prosecution in argument. One must examine whether all these treaties were still in force at the critical moment, and this examination will be left to the individual defendant's counsel. But if the Reich did attack, in some specific case, in breach of a nonaggression pact which was still valid, it committed an offense in international law and is responsible therefor according to the rules of international law regarding such offenses.

But only the Reich—not the individual, even if he were the head of the State. This is beyond all doubt, according to existing international law. It is unnecessary even to speak about this. For up to the most recent times not even the possibility was mentioned, either in the Manchurian, or in the Italo-Abyssinian, or in the Russo-Finnish conflict, of instituting criminal proceedings against those people who were responsible, on the Japanese, Italian, or Russian side, for planning, preparing, launching, and conducting the war, or who simply participated in these acts in any way. And it was certainly not because matters had, paradoxically enough, not been thought out to the end, that they were not prosecuted. They were not prosecuted because this cannot take place as long as the sovereignty of states is the organizational basic principle of interstate order.

THE PRESIDENT: I think this would be a convenient time to break off.

(A recess was taken.)

DR. JAHRREISS: One thing or another[53]—should things reach the point where, according to general world law, the men who participated in the planning, preparation, launching, and conduct of a war forbidden by international law could be brought before an international criminal court, the decisions regarding the state's final problems of existence would be subject to super-state control. One might, of course, still term such states sovereign; but they would no longer be sovereign. In his paper, written late in 1943, which I have already mentioned several times and which was prepared after the Moscow conference of 1 November 1943, Kelsen again and again repeats that in questions of breach of the peace, the liability of individuals to punishment does not exist according to the general international law at present valid and that it cannot exist because of the concept of sovereignty.[54]

For Europeans, at any rate, the state has during the last four centuries, especially following the pronounced advance made by the idea of the national state, achieved the dignity of a super-person.

Of course, acts of state are acts of men. Yet they are in fact acts of state, that is, acts of the state carried out by its organs and not the private acts of Mr. Smith or Mr. Müller.

What the prosecution is doing when, in the name of the world community as a legal entity, it desires to have individuals legally sentenced for their decisions regarding war and peace, is, when facing the issue from the angle of European history, to look upon the state as one would look upon a private individual; indeed, more than that: What it is doing is destroying the spirit of the state. Such an indictment, the moral justification of which is not my concern—such an indictment is, as we have already shown, incompatible with the very nature of sovereignty and with the feeling of the majority of Europeans. It seems, indeed, as though not only Europeans feel that way. In 1919, in Paris, it was the American delegates at the War Guilt Investigation Committee who opposed most strongly any legal sentence on the Kaiser for the very reason of the incompatibility of such a procedure with the sovereignty of the State.[55] And it is impossible to underline the idea of sovereignty more strongly than Kellogg did 8 years later during the negotiations in connection with the Pact of Paris, when he declared, as I have already said, "Every state is the sole judge of its behavior with regard to questions affecting its very existence."

There are epochs which idolize the sovereignty of the state; others deprecate it. Certain epochs have done both at the same time—ours does so. Perhaps we are living in a period of transition. Perhaps a transformation of values is taking place. Perhaps world community will become the supreme political value for the peoples in place of their own particular states, which, at any rate, held this position hitherto. Perhaps we shall reach a point where the unleashing of a war deserving moral and also legal condemnation will, for the general legal conscience, constitute high treason against the world community. Perhaps we shall reach a point where it will be permissible, or even compulsory, to betray a government starting such a war to foreign countries without this being termed high treason toward one's own. At the moment there is in no nation a majority, let alone unanimity, in support of this conclusion.

The punishment of individuals by the legal community of nations for breach of the peace between states can thus be ordered only provided the fundamental principles of international law as at present valid and the scale of values as for centuries they have been firmly rooted in the feeling of the European nations are abandoned—that scale of values according to which the state, one's own sovereign state, forms the indispensable foundation for free personality.

The Prosecution breaks up in its own mind the German State at a time when it stood upright in its full strength and acted through its organs. It must do so if it desires to prosecute individual persons for a breach of the peace between states. It must turn the defendants into private individuals. Then again the defendants—as it were, on the private level—are strung together into a conspiracy by legal concepts rooted in Anglo-Saxon law and alien to us. They are placed on a pedestal provided by the many millions of members of organizations and groups which are designated as criminal, thereby once more allowing them to appear as an "ultra-individual" value.

Insofar as the Charter supports all this by its regulations, it is laying down fundamentally new law, if—concurring with the British chief prosecutor—one measures against existing international law. That which, originating in Europe, has finally spread to the whole world and is called international law is, in essence, a law of the co-ordination of sovereign states. Measuring the regulations of the Charter against this law, we shall have to say: The regulations of the Charter deny the basis of this law; they anticipate the law of a world state. They are revolutionary. Perhaps, in the hopes and yearnings of the nations, the future is theirs.

A lawyer, and only as such may I speak here, will merely have to establish that they are new—revolutionarily new. The laws regarding war and peace between states provided no room for them and could not do so. Thus they are criminal laws with retroactive force.

Now the French chief prosecutor—if I understand correctly—recognized the sovereignty of states in his profoundly moving speech and quite rightly saw that an unbridgeable gulf exists between the Charter and existing international law where it desires to see individuals punished as criminals for breach of international peace. He therefore transposes the Trial from the plane of international law to that of constitutional law. It might have happened that a German State would have settled accounts after the war with those people who were responsible for launching the war. Since the whole life of the German people is paralyzed today, those foreign powers, who jointly on the basis of treaties have territorial power in Germany, are undertaking this settlement of accounts. The Charter has laid down the rules which are to guide the Court in its investigation and verdict.

We can leave the question open as to whether this concept is legally right or not. Even if it is right, our question is not modified thereby. When looking at the problem from this point of view, no differently from that of international law, we must know how far the Charter creates penal law with

retroactive force. But we must now measure the regulations of
the Charter not only against the international law which was
valid for Germany and was recast into national law, as we say,
but also against that national criminal law which was binding
on the defendants at the time of the deed. It is, after all, quite
possible for a state, a member of the community of states,
to be more cosmopolitan in its criminal law than actual international law. Some rule of the Charter, although new with
regard to existing international law, may correspond to an
already existing national law, so that it would not constitute
criminal law with retroactive force. So how was the breach
of peace between states—particularly the breach of nonaggression pacts—treated in that national criminal law to which the
defendants were subject at the time of the preparation and
launching of the war?

It is possible that in some state those people might be
threatened with punishment who prepared or launched or
waged a war in opposition to the international obligations of
that state.[56] That would, it is true, be completely impractical,
for the result of a war determines the internal settlement of
accounts. No criminal court will threaten a victorious government, whereas, in case of defeat, the defeat itself provides the
measure for such settlement. In any case the regulations of
the Charter regarding punishment for breach of the peace
between states are novel for the national criminal law to which
the defendants were subject at the time of the deed. If one is
not prepared to understand the phrase *nulla poena sine lege
previa* as it is understood on the European continent, that is,
as meaning that law in the sense of *lex* is a rule laid down by
the state, a state law, but holds the opinion which—as far as I
can see—is peculiar to English legal thinkers, that law in the
sense of *lex* can also be a deeply rooted rule of ethics or
morality, then we still have one question left: As things happened to be, did the defendants—formerly ministers, military
leaders, directors of economy, heads of higher authorities—at
the time of the deed feel, or could they even have felt that a

behavior which is now made punishable by a retroactive law was originally in violation of their duty? The answer to this question cannot be given without insight into the nature of the constitution of the German Reich at the moment of the deed.

The German Reich was incorporated into the community of states in the form and with the constitution which it happened to have at any given moment. Such is the case with every member of the community of states. The United States and the British Empire, the Union of Soviet Socialist Republics and the French Republic, Brazil and Switzerland, stand in the framework of the family of nations with such a constitution as they happen to have at the time.

The Prosecution, with full justification, has tried to convey a picture of this concrete legal structure of the Reich. Without trying to obtain such a picture, no one in this Trial will be able to arrive at a decision regarding right and wrong. In addition it seems to me that many ethical questions which have been raised here require such an endeavor to be made. However, I am afraid that with the picture presented by the Prosecution one will not come as close to the truth as is possible, notwithstanding the complex nature of the subject.

The Prosecution is based upon the conception of a conspiracy to conquer the world on the part of a few dozen criminals. The German State, if one looks upon things in this way, becomes a mere shadow or tool. But this State had long been in existence; no one could set aside the enormous weight of its history. A number of facts in its history, domestic and especially foreign, accounted for Hitler's rise to power or facilitated it for him, while there were other things in this history that guided, urged, limited, or restrained Hitler in his choice of aims and means, and helped to decide the success or failure of his measures and undertakings.

The Prosecution was certainly right in laying great stress on the so-called Führer Principle. This Führer Principle has, in fact, for the eyes and even more for the ears of the German people and of the world in general, been the organizational guiding principle in the development of the Reich constitution after 1933.

It has never been unambiguous, and it considerably changed in character during the course of the years. In human life leading and dominating present inherent contradictions. There exists one, as it were, soulless, mechanical way of directing mankind, which is to dominate, to rule by issuing commands; and there is another one, which is to precede by setting an example and being followed voluntarily, which is to lead or whatever one wishes to call it. This differentiation between two fundamentally different methods of directing men is often already complicated by the words used; in the German language, for instance this is so because "leading" is sometimes substituted for unconscious domination, while domination is occasionally called leading. The differentiation is rendered even more difficult by the fact that leading may alternate with domination in relations between the same persons or by the fact that methods which are actually applicable to leading are used in dominating and vice versa. Every state has been, is, and will be, faced by the question of how it is to link up both these methods, so that they may complement, promote, and keep a check on each other. Both methods appear continually and everywhere. There has never yet been a truly dominating ruler who was not also a leader, although minor rulers are also subject to this law. And the Hitler regime did bring about—at least to begin with—a synthesis of both methods which had at least the appearance of being tremendously efficient.

To this synthesis has been attributed—perhaps not unjustly —much of what the world registered with wonder, sometimes approvingly, but more often disapprovingly, as the result of an unheard-of mobilization, concentration, and increase in the energies of a nation.

This remarkable synthesis of leading and dominating found its maximum expression in the person of Hitler himself, in his acts of leadership, for instance, in his speeches, and in his commands. Hitler's acts of leadership and commanding became the motive power of the German political life of that time. Above all, this phenomenon must be taken into correct account. It is of absolutely decisive importance in judging the enormous mass of facts which has been produced here. With all due caution, which is natural to men accustomed to think along scientific lines and imbues them with an almost unconquerable mistrust of any attempt to comprehend and evaluate events which have happened so recently, one is perhaps entitled to vouchsafe this assertion: In the course of the years Hitler accorded the act of command an increasingly favored place to the detriment of acts of leadership and finally brought it so much to the fore that commands, not the act of leadership, became the all-decisive factor. Hitler, the man of the people, became more and more the dictator. The speeches in which he repeated himself *ad nauseam*, even for his most willing followers, and shrieked out, to the irritation even of the most faithful disciples, became rarer, while the legislative machine worked faster and faster. A later age will perhaps realize to what extent the great change in the attitude of the German people toward Hitler, which was beginning to show even before the war, was the cause or effect of this modification.

Whereas on a superficial question, that is, the question as to how he wished to be designated, Hitler urged not to be called "Führer and Reich Chancellor" any longer, but only "Führer," the way in which the State was being governed was taking the exactly opposite path; leadership disappeared more and more, and there remained naked domination. The Führer's orders became the central element of the German state edifice.

In the public hierarchy, this development was attended by an increase rather than a decrease in Hitler's power. The great majority of German civil servants and officers had seen nothing behind the organized leadership but a machinery of domination invested with a new label and, if possible, an even more bureaucratic nature functioning side by side with the inherited state machinery. When Hitler's orders became the

Alpha and Omega, they telt themselves, so to speak, returned to the old familiar path. The queer and puzzling apparition had gone.

They were back in their world of subordination. Nevertheless, this development had given the Führer's orders a special aura of sanctity for them too; there was no contradicting the Führer's orders. One could perhaps raise objections; but if the Führer abided by his order, the matter was decided. His orders were sometimes quite different from the orders of any official within the hierarchy under him.

Here we have the fundamental question in this Trial: What position did Hitler's orders occupy in the general order of Germany? Did they belong to the type of orders which were disallowed by the Charter of this Court as grounds for the exclusion of punishment?

It was perhaps harder for a lawyer who grew up in the habits of the state founded on law than for other people to witness the slow and then even more rapid disintegration of that foundation of law supporting the state; he never came to feel at home in the new order and always remained half outside. Yet for that very reason he probably knows better than anyone else the peculiarities of this new order, and he may attempt to make them comprehensible.

State orders, whether they lay down law or decide individual cases, can always be measured not only against the existing written and unwritten law of the state concerned but also against the rules of international law, morality, and religion. Someone, even if only the conscience of the person giving the orders, will always ask whether the person giving the order did not perhaps order something which he had no right to order or whether he may not have formed and published his order by an inadmissible procedure. Now an unavoidable problem for all domination lies in this: Should or can it grant the members of its hierarchy, its civil servants and officers, the right—or even impose on them the duty—to examine at any time any order which demands obedience from them, to determine whether it is lawful and to decide accordingly whether to obey or refuse?

No form of rule which has appeared in history so far has given an affirmative answer to this question. Only certain members of the hierarchy were ever granted this right, and they were not granted it without limits. Such was the case, for instance, under the extremely democratic constitution of the German Reich during the Weimar Republic, and it is again the case today under the occupation rule of the four great powers over Germany.

Insofar as no such right of examination is granted to members of the hierarchy, orders are binding upon them. All constitutional law, including that of modern states, provides for acts of state which must be respected by the authorities, even when defective. Certain acts constituting rules, certain decisions on individual cases which have acquired legal force, are held to be valid even when the person giving the order has exceeded his competency or made a mistake in form.

If only because the process of referring to a still superior order finally comes to an end, there must under every government exist orders that are binding on the members of the hierarchy under all circumstances, and therefore represent law to the officials concerned, even though outsiders may find that they are defective as regards content or form when measured against the previous laws of the state concerned or against rules applying outside the state. For instance, in direct democracies, an order given as the result of a plebiscite of the nation is a fully valid rule or an absolutely binding decree. Rousseau knew how much the *volonté de tous* can be in contradiction to what is right, but he did not fail to appreciate that orders by *volonté de tous* are binding.

In indirect democracies the resolutions of a congress, a national assembly, or a parliament may have the same force.

In the partly direct, partly indirect democracy of the Weimar Constitution of the German Reich the laws resolved by a majority of the Reichstag large enough to modify the constitution and duly promulgated under all circumstances were binding upon all functions, including the independent courts of law, even though the legislator—willingly or unwillingly—might have violated rules not imposed by the state but by the Church or by the community of states. In the latter case the Reich would have been guilty of an international offense, since it would have failed to see to it that its legislation was in accordance with international law. It would, therefore, have been responsible under the international regulations regarding reparation for international offenses. But until the law concerned had been eliminated in accordance with the rules of German constitutional law, all officials of the hierarchy would have had to obey it. No functionary would have had the right, let alone the duty, to examine its legally binding nature with the aim of obeying or refusing to obey it, depending on the result of this examination.

Things are no different in any other state in the world. It never has been and never can be different. Every state has had the experience of seeing its ultimate orders, its supreme orders, which must be binding on the hierarchy if the authority of the state is to subsist at all, on occasion coming into conflict with rules not imposed by the state—to divine law, to natural law, and to the laws of reason. Good governments take pains to avoid such conflicts. To the great sorrow—indeed, to the despair—of many Germans, Hitler frequently brought about such conflicts. If only for this reason, his way of governing was not a good one, even though it was for several years successful in some spheres.

One thing however must be said straight away: these conflicts never affected the entire nation or the entire hierarchy—at least not immediately—but always merely groups of the nation or individual offices of the hierarchy. It was only some of the people concerned who were fundamentally affected, the bulk being only superficially involved—not to mention those conflicts that remained unknown to the overwhelming majority of the people and of the hierarchy, those orders, therefore, by which Hitler not only showed himself to be inhuman in individual instances but simply put himself outside the pale of what is human. Here is a purely academic question: Would Hitler's power have taken such deep root, would it have maintained itself, if these inhumanities had become known to wider sections of the people and of the hierarchy? There can be no answer: They did not.

Now in a state in which the entire power to make final decisions is concentrated in the hands of a single individual, the orders of this one man are absolutely binding on the members of the hierarchy. This individual is their sovereign, their *legibus solutus*, as was first formulated—as far as I can see—by French political science with as much logic as eloquence.

After all, the world is not faced by such a phenomenon for the first time. In former times it may even have appeared to be normal. In the modern world, a world of constitutions based on the separation of powers under the supervision of the people, absolute monocracy does not seem to be proper in principle. And though this may not yet be the case today, one day the world will know that the vast majority of intelligent Germans did not think any differently on this matter from the majority of intelligent people of other nations in and outside Europe.

Such absolutely monocratic constitutions can nevertheless come about as the result of events which no individual can grasp in their entirety, much less control at will.

This is what happened in Germany from the beginning of 1933 onward. This is what happened gradually, stage by stage, to the parliamentary Weimar Republic, which under Hindenburg was changed into a presidential republic, in a process which partly furthered the developments by acts of state which stressed legal forms and which can be read in state documents, but partly simply formed the rules by accepted custom. The Reich law of 24 March 1933, by which the institution of Reich Government Laws was created, whereby the separation of powers in the sense in which it had been customary was, in practice, eliminated, was, according to the transcript of the

Reichstag session, passed with a majority sufficient for altering the constitution. Doubts about the legality of the law have nevertheless been raised on the grounds that a section of the deputies elected had been prevented from attending the session by the police, while another section of the deputies who were present had been intimidated, so that only an apparent majority sufficient for altering the constitution had passed the law. It has even been said that no Reichstag, not even if everybody had been present and all of them had voted, could have abolished the fundamental constitutional principle of the separation of powers, since no constitution could legalize its suicide. We need not go into this. The institution of government laws became so firmly rooted as a result of undisputed practice that only a formal jurisprudence entirely cut off from the realities of life could have attempted to play off paragraphs against life and to ignore the constitutional change which had taken place. And for the same reason one's arguments are faulty if one chooses to ignore how the institution of government laws, that is, cabinet law, was later changed by custom into one of several forms in which the Führer legislated. At the base of every state order, as of any order whatsoever, there lie habit and custom. From the time when Hitler became head of the State, practice quickly resulted in Hitler heading both the hierarchy and the whole people as the undisputed and indisputable possessor of all competency. The result of the development was, at any rate, that Hitler became the supreme legislator as well as the supreme author of individual orders.

He gained this position to some extent under the impression of the surprising successes—or what were considered successes —in Germany and abroad, especially during the course of the past war. Perhaps the German people, although with great differences between North and South, West and East, particularly easily falls a prey to actual power, particularly easily obeys by orders, particularly well conforms to the idea of a superior. Thus the whole process may have been rendered easier.

Finally, the only thing that was not quite clear was Hitler's relationship to the judiciary. For, even in Hitler Germany, it was not possible to exterminate the idea that it was essential to allow justice to be exercised by independent courts, at least in matters which concern the bulk of the people in their everyday life. Up to the top group of Party officials—this was shown by some of the speeches by the Reich Leader of jurists, the Defendant Dr. Frank, as quoted here—there showed resistance, which, it is true, was not very effective, when justice in civil and ordinary criminal cases was equally to be subjected to the *sic volo sic jubeo* of one man. But apart from the judiciary, which in the end also was beginning to succumb, absolute monocracy was complete. The Reichstag's pompous declaration about Hitler's legal position, dated 26 April 1942,[56a] was actually only the statement of what had become a fact long before. The Führer's orders constituted law already a considerable time before this second World War.

In this state order the German Reich was treated as a partner by the other states, throughout the whole field of politics. In this connection I do not wish to stress the form—so impressive to the German people and so fatal to all opposition—which this treatment took in 1936 at the Olympic Games, a show which Hitler could not order the delegations of foreign nations to attend, as he ordered Germans to the Nuremberg Party Rally with its state displays. Rather would I wish to point out that the governments of the greatest nations in the world considered the word of this "all-powerful" man to be the final decision, incontestably valid for every German, and based their decisions on major questions on the very fact that Hitler's order was incontestable. To mention only the most striking cases, this fact was relied upon when the British Prime Minister, Mr. Neville Chamberlain, after the Munich Conference, displayed the famous peace paper when he landed at Croydon. This fact was pointed to when people went to war against the Reich as the barbaric despotism of this one man.

No political system has yet pleased all people who live under it or who feel its effects abroad. The German political system in the Hitler era displeased a particularly large and ever-increasing number of people at home and abroad. But that does not in any way alter the fact that it existed. Its existence was in part due to the recognition from abroad and to its effectiveness, which caused a British Prime Minister to make the now world-famous statement at a critical period, that democracies need two years longer than totalitarian governments to attain a certain goal. Only one who has lived in the outer cold and as though outcast among his own people amidst blindly believing masses, who idolized this man as infallible, can tell how firmly Hitler's power was anchored in the nameless and numberless following who held him capable of doing only what was good and right. They did not know him personally; he was for them what propaganda made of him, and this he was so uncompromisingly that everybody who saw him from close range and summed him up differently clearly realized that opposition was utterly pointless and, in the eyes of other people, did not even represent martyrdom.

Would it therefore not be a self-contradictory process if both the following assertions were to be applied at the same time in the rules governing this Trial? First, the Reich was the expression of despotism of this one man and for that very reason a danger to the world. Secondly, every functionary had the right —in fact the duty—to examine the orders of this man and to obey or not obey them, according to the result of this examination.

The functionaries had neither the right nor the duty to examine the orders of the monocrat to determine their legality. For them these orders could never be illegal at all, with a single exception which will be discussed later—an exception which, when carefully examined, will be seen to be only an apparent one—namely, with the exception of those cases in which the monocrat placed himself, according to the indisputable axioms of our times, outside every human order and in which a genuine question of right or wrong did not arise, so that no genuine examination was called for, either.

Hitler's will was the final authority for their considerations on what to do and what not to do. The Führer's order cut off every discussion. Thus a person who as a functionary of the hierarchy invokes an order by the Führer is not trying to claim exemption from punishment for an illegal action but opposes the assertion that his conduct was illegal; for it is his contention that the order with which he complied was legally unassailable.

Only a person with full comprehension of this can have a conception of the hard inner struggles which so many German officials had to fight out in these years in the face of many a decree or resolution of Hitler's. For them such cases were not a question or a conflict between right and wrong; disputes about legality sank into insignificance. For them the problem was one of legitimacy; as time went on, human and divine law opposed each other ever more strongly and frequently.

Whatever the Charter means by the orders which it rejects as grounds for exemption from punishment, can this be meant to apply to the Führer's orders? Can they come within the meaning of this rule? Must one not accept this order for what it was according to the interior German constitution as it had grown, a constitution explicitly or implicitly recognized by the community of states? Many Germans disapproved of Hitler's position of power from the very beginning; and to many Germans, who welcomed it at first because they yearned for clear and quick decisions, it later became repugnant. But that in no way affects the following: Must not those people who did their duty in the hierarchy, willingly or unwillingly, in accordance with the constitution, feel that an injustice is being done to them if they were sentenced because of a deed or an omission which was ordered by the Führer?

A community of states might refuse to accept or tolerate as members such states as have a despotic constitution. Yet up to now this has never been the case. If it is to be different in the future, the nondespotic powers must take the necessary steps to prevent any member of the family of states turning into a despotic power and to prevent any despotic power from entering the family circle from outside. Today people are realizing more and more clearly that this is the crux of our question. The circumstances must be very special ones if a modern people is to let itself be governed despotically, even when as well-disciplined as the German people. But wherever such circumstances do exist, no domestic countermeasures are of avail. In that eventuality only the outside world can help. If, instead, the outside world prefers to recognize this constitution, it is impossible to see where successful domestic resistance can spring from. In pointing to these special circumstances and to the recognition by the outside world, we are drawing attention to facts for the existence of which, to take our case, no German was responsible but which cannot be ignored when the question is asked how all this was possible.

Attention must also be drawn to certain further facts without knowledge of which one cannot fully grasp the fact that Hitler's absolute monocracy was able to establish such a terribly firm hold. Hitler combined in his person all the powers of issuing legislative and administrative orders of a supreme character, orders which could not be questioned and were absolutely valid; but immediately below him the power of the state was divided up into a vast mass of spheres of competence. The dividing lines between these spheres, however, were not always sharply drawn. In a modern state, particularly in major states of our technical era, this cannot be avoided. The tendency to exaggerate questions of competency is certainly no less marked in Germany than in any other country. This certainly facilitated the erection of barriers between the departments. Every department was jealously watching to see that no other trespassed into its field. Everywhere it was prepared for tendencies of other departments toward expansion. Considering the great mass of tasks which the so-called "totalitarian" state had heaped upon itself, cases where two or three departments were competent for the same matter could not be avoided. Conflicts between departments were inevitable. If a conspiracy existed, as the Indictment assumes, the conspirators were remarkably incompetent organizers. Instead of co-operating and going through thick and thin together, they fought one another. Instead of a conspiracy we would seem to have had more of a "dispiracy." The history of the jealousy and mistrust among the powerful figures under Hitler has still to be written. Now let us remember that in the relations between all departments and within each department, people surrounded themselves with ever-increasing secrecy; between departments and within each department, between ranks and within the various ranks, more and more matters were classed as "secret." Never before has there been so much "public life," that is, nonprivate life in Germany as under Hitler; and also never before was public life so screened off from the people, particularly from the individual members of the hierarchy themselves, as under Hitler.

The single supreme will became, quite simply, technically indispensable. It became the mechanical connecting link for the whole. A functionary who met with objections or even resistance to one of his orders on the part of other functionaries only needed to refer to an order by the Führer to get his way. For this reason many, very many, among those Germans who felt Hitler's regime to be intolerable, who indeed hated him like the devil, looked ahead only with the greatest anxiety to the time when this man would disappear from the scene. For what would happen when this connecting link disappeared? It was a vicious circle.

I again stress the fact that an order by the Führer was binding—and indeed legally binding—on the person to whom it was given, even if the directive was contrary to international law or to other traditional values.

But was there really no limit? During the first period, at any rate, that is, just at the time when the foundations of power were being laid, at the time when the monocratic constitution was being developed step by step, Hitler's followers among the people saw in their Führer a man close to the people, an unselfish, almost superhumanly intuitive and clear-thinking

pilot and believed only the best of him; they had only one
worry: Was he also choosing the right men for his assistants,
and was he always aware of what they were doing? The tremendous power, the unlimited authority were vested in this
Hitler. As in every state, this might include harsh orders. But
it was never intended as giving full power to be inhuman. Here
lies the boundary line; but this line has at no time and nowhere
been quite clearly drawn. Today the German people are
utterly torn in their opinions, feelings, and intentions; but they
are probably in agreement on one thing, with very few exceptions: As accusers, they would not wish to draw this line with
less severity than other people do toward their leaders. Beyond
that line, Hitler's order constituted no legal justification.

It must not be forgotten, however, that this line is not only
vague by nature but also follows a different course in peace
than in wartime, when so many values are changed and when
men of all nations, especially in our days, take pride in deeds
which would horrify them at any other time. And the decision
to wage war does not in itself overstep that line, in spite of its
tremendous consequences—not with any nation in the world.

Hitler himself, at any rate, did not recognize this boundary
line of inhumanity, of nonhumanity, as a limit to obedience in
his relations with his subordinates; and here again opposition
would have been considered a crime worthy of death in the
eyes and judgment of this man, invested as he was with limit-
less power and controlling an irresistible machine. What should
a man who received an order exceeding the line have done?
What a terrible situation! The reply given in Greek tragedy,
the reply by Antigone in such a conflict cannot be imposed. It
would show scant knowledge of the world to expect it, let
alone demand it, as a mass phenomenon.

Before we come to the specific question of who in the Reich
possessed the power of deciding on war and peace, one more
word remains to be said about the forms which Hitler's orders
assumed.

Hitler's orders are solely the decisions of this one man,

whether they were given orally or in writing and, in the latter case, whether they were clothed in more or less ceremony. There are some orders by Hitler which can be recognized as such immediately. They are called "Erlass" (decree), such as the decree concerning the institution of the Protectorate of Bohemia and Moravia of 16 March 1939; or "Verordnung" (order), like the order for the execution of the Four Year Plan of 19 October 1936; or "Weisung" (directive), like the strategic decisions so often cited during this Trial; or simply "Beschluss" (decision) or "Anordnung" (instructions). Often they are signed in Hitler's name only; sometimes we find the signatures of one or more of the highest civil or military functionaries as well. But it would be fundamentally wrong to assume that this was a case of countersignature as understood in the modern democratic constitutional law of nations ruled constitutionally or by a parliament—of a countersignature which makes the signatory responsible to a parliament or to a state court of law. Hitler's orders were his own orders and only his own orders. He was much too fanatical a champion of the one-man doctrine, that is, of the principle that every decision must be made by one and only one man even to consider anything else, especially in the case of his own decisions. We will leave his high opinion of himself entirely aside in this connection. Whatever the more or less decorative significance of such countersigning may have been, there was never any doubt that the Führer's orders represented nothing but his own decision.

Special attention must be drawn to those laws which appeared as Reich Cabinet Laws or Reichstag Laws. Hitler's signing of a law of the Reich Cabinet represented the formal certification of a Cabinet decision. In actual fact, however, a stage was reached where the Reich Cabinet Laws were also merely decisions by Hitler, who had previously given some of his ministers the opportunity to state the opinion of their departments. And when Hitler signed a law which, according to its preamble, had been decreed by the Reichstag, this was again only a case of a formal certification. In reality, however, it was a decision by Hitler. From November 1933 onward, at the latest, the German Reichstag was no longer a parliament but merely an assembly for the acclamation of Hitler's declarations or decisions. These scenes of legislation appeared to many people at home and abroad to amount almost to an attempt to make democratic forms of legislation ridiculous by caricaturing them; nobody, either at home or abroad, regarded them as proceedings during which an assembly of several hundred men arrived at a decision after consideration, speeches, and counterspeeches.

There exist, however, also orders by Hitler which are not signed by him but which can immediately be recognized as his orders. They are drawn up by a Reich Minister or some other high functionary, who states in the introduction "The Führer has ordered" or "the Führer has decreed." This is not an order by the signatory, but a report by the signatory on an order given orally by Hitler. The orders by Hitler as Supreme Commander of the Armed Forces were thus often clothed in the form of such a report.

Finally there are orders by Hitler which can only be recognized as such by a member of the public if he possesses knowledge of the constitutional position. When the High Command of the Armed Forces (OKW) issues an order, it is always an order by Hitler; Hitler himself, together with his working staff, was the OKW. The power to issue OKW orders rested solely with Hitler.

By my explanations regarding the constitution of the Hitler Reich, I have already—as it were by implication—dealt with the question as to who was responsible for the ultimate decisions, for this state's decisions regarding fundamental questions of existence, especially for the decision about war and peace. Kelsen said—in his great treatise of the year 1943,[57] which I have already mentioned above—"probably the Führer alone." We shall have to say: quite definitely alone.

Under the Weimar Constitution the sole body responsible was the Reich legislature, for Article 45 demands a Reich Law for a declaration of war and for the conclusion of peace. And a Reich Law could be passed only by the Reichstag or by a vote of the German people. Neither the Reich President, that is, the head of the State, nor the Reich Cabinet had the power. They might, at most, have created such circumstances by acts lying within their jurisdiction—possibly the Reich President as Commander-in-Chief of the Armed Forces—so as to give the Reich legislature no option in its decisions; a problem which, as far as I know, became a tangible one in the United States with regard to the relationship of the President to Congress and was therefore seriously discussed, while it was never a tangible one for the Germany of the Weimar Constitution. If, however, the Reich legislature had by means of a law taken the decision to wage war, the Reich President and the whole State hierarchy, particularly the Armed Forces, would have been bound by this decision with no right of examination, let alone of objection, even if all the experts on international law in the world had regarded the law as contrary to international law. The Weimar democracy could not have tolerated, any more than any other nation, a state of affairs in which military leaders as such could examine the decision to wage war taken by the political leaders, in the sense that they could refuse obedience if they saw fit. The military means of power must remain at the disposal of the political leaders of a state. Otherwise they are not means of power at all. That has always been so. And it will have to be so all the more if the duty to give assistance against aggression is really to apply among the nations.

I have already shown how, in the course of a gradual transformation which laid particular emphasis on legal forms, Hitler replaced all the highest authorities of the Weimar period and combined all the highest competencies in his own person. His orders were law.

The circumstances in a state can be such that the man who is legally the only one competent for the decision on war and peace, may have, in practice, no—or not the sole—authority.

If, however, both the sole legal competence and the sole authority in actual practice have ever been coincidental in any state, then such was the case in Hitler Germany. And if, in any question, Hitler did ever go as far as to accept the advice of a third party, then that was certainly not the case in the question of war or peace. He was the arbiter of war and peace between the Reich and other nations—he alone.

I conclude: Sentences against individuals for breach of the peace beween states would be something completely new under the aspect of law, something revolutionarily new. It makes no difference whether we view the matter from the point of view of the British or the French chief prosecutors.

Sentences against individuals for breach of the peace between states presuppose other laws than those in force when the actions laid before this Tribunal took place.

The legal question of guilt—and I am here only concerned with that—is thus posed in its full complexity, for not one of the defendants could have held even one of the two views of the legal constitution, on which the chief prosecutors base their arguments.

The Nuremberg Trial Against the Major War Criminals and International Law

DR. HANS EHARD

"THE trial which is now about to begin is unique in the history of the jurisprudence of the world and it is of supreme importance to millions of people all over the globe."[1]

Thus spoke the President of the International Military Tribunal in Nuremberg, Lord Justice Lawrence, upon the occasion of the institution of the so-called Trial Against the Major War Criminals on November 20, 1945. If his statement is correct, then the German people undoubtedly rank in first place among these millions. This also was the opinion of the chief prosecutor which recurred several times in his statements. Thus the French representative, M. François de Menthon, exclaimed:

This work of justice is equally indispensable for the future of the German people.... The initial condemnation of Nazi Germany by your High Tribunal will be a first lesson for these people and will

Read by Dr. Ehard, Minister-President of Bavaria, at the Meeting of Lawyers in Munich on June 2, 1948 and originally published in Süddeutsche Juristen-Zeitung *(July, 1948), Vol. III, No. 7, cols. 353-68. Translated into English by E. C. Jann, Research Assistant, Foreign Law Section, Law Library of Congress and republished in* American Journal of International Law XLIII *(April, 1949), 223-45. Reprinted by permission of Dr. Ehard, the editors of the* American Journal of International Law, *and Mr. Jann.*

constitute the best starting point ... of re-education which must be its great concern during the coming years. . . .[2]

Your judgment ... can serve as a foundation for the moral uplift of the German people, first stage in its integration into the community of free countries. . . .[3]

During the proceedings the German people have become only insufficiently aware of the importance of the trial such as it has been described in the quoted phrases by outstanding men of other nations. It was still too stunned from the collapse, too deeply mired in its increasing distress, too much under the spell of the power of the war propaganda, of distrust and of disappointments, too little familiar with the horrible crimes of the deposed leaders, too unfamiliar with the entire proceedings. Furthermore, the type of coverage given in the press and on the radio was not suited to create understanding and interest.

The passage of time has had a clarifying and calming effect in this respect. We have gained sufficient mental and psychological distance from the trial and the judgment to view them quietly. We now also have at our disposal the essential material required for this objective examination, namely, in the form of the official publication of the records which contains the text of the indictment and of the judgment as well as the transcript of the proceedings and the most important documentary evidence, and which, as is stated in a prefatory remark, is "published in accordance with the direction of the International Military Tribunal, under the jurisdiction of the Allied Control Authority for Germany."

The German people may no longer remain passive before this tremendous amount of material. A judgment which an international military tribunal has rendered on German territory, against Germans, should not leave any German unconcerned. Proceedings in which the law of nations is invoked for the first time in such a magnificent form against the abuse of power should find the lively attention of the German people even if Germany had not been directly involved. In my opinion it is now the duty and the gratifying task of German legal science and politics to investigate the voluminous material of the trial and to make use of it. This task must, if it is to have permanent value, be performed without any preconceived ideas, in the spirit of law and of justice, which cannot be the task of a single people or of individual power groups, but must be the concern of the entire human race.

My office, profession and inclination move me to the present attempt to deliver a contribution to the solution of this comprehensive task by surveying with you the trial and the judgment in the light of the law in force in the entire civilized world, in the light of the law of nations. I primarily select, from the wealth of problems, the question which is highly important to the development of law, namely whether and to what extent new law was applied in Nuremberg. The short time available to me compels me to limit myself to essential points of view. But a group of experts such as the present requires no detailed interpretation of all concepts.

As source material I shall primarily use the volumes of the official record in the German language published up to now. The defense pleadings have not been published yet. Therefore, I shall be able to refer to the arguments of the defense, which undoubtedly are notable, only to the extent that they are quoted in the judgment. My quotations are based upon the official translation, although it does not always seem to have been successful.

In order to prevent any misunderstanding I would like to make this one point clear at the outset of my statements:

Offenses were tried in Nuremberg which the entire German population feels merit the death penalty. These crimes would also have found their retribution by applying the penal codes in force in most nations, including Germany. It is also the conviction of the German people that the society of nations, if it wishes to survive in the age of the most terrible tools of destruction, may and must arm and secure itself against such crimes also with the weapons of law. In our evaluation of the

Nuremberg trial we should not be misled by the unworthy
wish for a milder judgment of the crime, but only by the desire
for an ever-increased perfection of the law and the longing
for the final and universal victory of law over might.

In my paper I first want to explain the formal basis of the
trial, and its course, then I wish to discuss the legal problems
and, finally, draw the conclusions.

The basis in international law of the trial is the agreement
between England, the United States, France, and the Soviet
Union signed on August 8, 1945, which is entitled: "Agreement for the Prosecution and Punishment of the Major War
Criminals of the European Axis."* The treaty makes provision
for an international military tribunal to be constituted from
among the members of the four Powers. A so-called charter
attached to the treaty as an integral part regulates in seven
paragraphs the constitution of the court, its jurisdiction and the
general principles, the composition and the competence of the
prosecution, the rights of the accused; the rights of the court,
and the trial procedure, judgment and punishment, and finally
the question of costs.

The following provisions of the Charter may be stressed:

The Tribunal may not be challenged either by the prosecution or by the defendants, or their counsel.[4]

The Tribunal is competent to try all persons "who, acting
in the interest of the European axis countries, whether as individuals or as members of organizations" committed any of
the crimes enumerated in the Charter.[5] These crimes are:

(a) Crimes against peace,

(b) War crimes,

(c) Crimes against humanity.[6]

Leaders, organizers, instigators, and accomplices participating in the formulation or execution of a common plan or

*For text of Agreement and Charter of the International Military Tribunal,
see Department of State, Executive Agreement Series, No. 472 (Publication
2461); also *American Journal of International Law*, Supp., XXXIX (1945),
257 ff.

conspiracy to commit any of the crimes are responsible for all actions performed by any person in execution of such plan.[7] "The official position of defendants whether as Heads of State or responsible officials in Government departments, shall not be considered as freeing them from responsibility or mitigating punishment."[8] "The fact that the defendant acted pursuant to order of his government or of a superior shall not free him from responsibility, but may be considered in mitigation of punishment. . . ."[9] Article 9 provides the possibility of declaring a group or organization criminal with certain consequences for all members.

In its formal aspect, the Agreement represents so-called particular international law, which originates from an agreement, and, at first hand, is only binding upon the signatories, in contradistinction to universal international law which is based upon customary law and is binding upon the entire community of nations.

The Charter, in its contents, is substantive criminal law and procedural criminal law at the same time. It defines the punishable acts and provides the limits of punishment as is usual in a criminal code. It also contains the provisions regarding the composition of the tribunal and the rules of procedure such as we find them in a judiciary act and in a code of criminal procedure. The Charter represents, particularly in regard to procedural law, a compromise between Anglo-Saxon and continental legal doctrine.

On the basis of the Charter the joint prosecution staff of six signatories brought the indictment against 24 German nationals and six groups or organizations. The following accusations were brought therein in accordance with the definitions of crimes contained in the Charter:

Count 1: The common plan or conspiracy. I quote:

All the defendants, with divers other persons, during a period of years preceding 8 May 1945, participated as leaders, organizers, instigators, or accomplices in the formulation or execution of a common plan or conspiracy to commit, or which involved the commission of, Crimes against Peace, War Crimes, and Crimes against Humanity, as defined in the Charter of this Tribunal, and in accordance with the provisions of the Charter, are individually responsible for their own acts and for all acts committed by any persons in the execution of such plan or conspiracy.[10]

I may at this point briefly enter upon the concept of conspiracy which has been much discussed at the trial against the major war criminals and at later trials. The concept is not one familiar to continental law. It has developed in Anglo-Saxon customary law. With the aid of this concept members and leaders of bands of criminals may be made responsible for all crimes of the band, even if they cannot be shown to have participated actively in each individual crime. By means of the introduction of the Anglo-Saxon concept into the Charter the legal tool was provided to make every leading National Socialist responsible for all crimes of the regime.

The Charter went even further still by introducing a concept of the common plan which hitherto was unknown either in the Anglo-Saxon or in any other law, a "common plan" for the commission of crimes because the existing legal concepts obviously did not appear adequate to its authors for the punishment of the group of persons accused of such horrible crimes. This procedure is, as I want to note briefly, not unobjectionable, particularly since it does not provide any clear limit and is too little adapted to political reality. Since I will not enter upon this problem any further today I wish to state in advance that the judgment did not follow the indictment without reservation on this point.

Count 2: Crimes against Peace: "All the defendants . . . participated in the planning, preparation, initiation, and waging of wars of aggression, which were also wars in violation of international treaties, agreements, and assurances."[11]

In Exhibit C annexed to the indictment there are enumerated 26 international treaties, the violation of which is attributed to the defendants, among them several Hague conventions, the Treaty of Versailles, the Treaty of Locarno, the Pact of Paris of 1928 outlawing war, non-aggression treaties, *e.g.*, the Non-Aggression Treaty between Germany and the Soviet Union dated August 23, 1939, and others.

Count 3: War Crimes: "All the defendants committed War Crimes between 1 September 1939 and 8 May 1945, in Germany and in all . . . countries and territories occupied . . . and on the High Seas."[12]

The following are listed as war crimes: murder and ill-treatment of the civilian population, deportation for slave labor, murder and ill-treatment of prisoners of war, murder of hostages, plundering of public and private property, compulsory recruiting of civilian laborers and others. I give a few quotations from the indictment:

1. They degraded the standard of life of the people of occupied countries and caused starvation, by stripping occupied countries of foodstuffs for removal to Germany.[13]

In connection with this, a French assistant prosecutor in the main proceedings stated the following:

. . . but there is one thing which can never be repaired—the results of privations upon the physical state of the population.

In the occupied countries, in France particularly, many persons died solely because of undernourishment and because of lack of heat. It was estimated that people require from 3,000 to 3,500 calories a day and heavy laborers about 4,000. From the beginning of the rationing in September 1940 only 1,800 calories per day per person were distributed. Successively the ration decreased to 1,700 calories in 1942, then to 1,500, and finally fell to 1,220 and 900 calories a day for adults and to 1,380 and 1,300 for heavy laborers; old persons were given only 850 calories a day. . . .

Incurable sicknesses such as tuberculosis developed and will continue to extend their ravages for many years. The growth of children and adolescents is seriously impaired. The future of the race is a cause for the greatest concern. . . .[14]

In the indictment it is further stated:

2. They seized raw materials and industrial machinery in all of the occupied countries, removed them to Germany and used them

in the interest of the German war effort and the German economy.

3. In all the occupied countries, in varying degrees, they confiscated businesses, plants, and other property.[15]

5. They established comprehensive controls over the economies of all the occupied countries. . . .

6. . . . They imposed occupation levies, exacted financial contributions, and issued occupation currency, far in excess of occupation costs. . . .

8. . . . they destroyed industrial cities, cultural monuments, scientific institutions, and property of all types in the occupied territories to eliminate the possibility of competition with Germany.[16]

Another quotation: "Civilians of occupied countries were subjected systematically to 'protective arrests' whereby they were arrested and imprisoned without any trial and any of the ordinary protections of the law, and they were imprisoned under the most unhealthy and inhumane conditions."[17]

In regard to the treatment of the prisoners of war, it is stated, among other things: "The defendants murdered and ill-treated prisoners of war by denying them adequate food, shelter, clothing and medical care and attention; by forcing them to labor in inhumane conditions; by torturing them and subjecting them to inhuman indignities and by killing them."[18]

I quote here also a passage from the judgment. A letter by Admiral Canaris dated September 15, 1941, is mentioned there in which it is stated:

. . . the principles of general international law on the treatment of prisoners of war . . . since the 18th century . . . have gradually been established along the lines that war captivity is neither revenge nor punishment, but solely protective custody, the only purpose of which is to prevent the prisoners of war from further participation in the war. . . .[19]

The judgment holds expressly that these statements have represented the legal situation correctly and that any treatment of prisoners of war which is contrary to these principles, does not correspond to international law.

Count 4 reads: Crimes against Humanity:

All the defendants committed Crimes against Humanity during a period of years preceding 8 May 1945 in Germany and in all those countries and territories occupied by the German armed forces since 1 September 1939 and in Austria and Czechoslovakia and in Italy and on the High Seas.[20]

Particularly the following are enumerated: murder, extermination, enslavement, deportation, and other inhuman acts against the civilian population before and during the war, persecution for political, racial, and religious reasons.

The indictment was based upon an abundance of exact facts on each count. The main trial was instituted on November 20, 1945. The judgment is dated October 1, 1946.

From a technical point of view the trial was an important accomplishment. German, English, French and Russian were admitted as languages in which the proceedings could take place. Each word that was spoken in one of these languages could be heard over the ear-phones, translated into one of the other three languages. A tremendous amount of documentary proof was submitted, explained and worked over. Within the framework set by the Charter all participants were obviously endeavoring to be objective. Occasional deviations from this rule were stopped immediately by the President.

The German defense saw itself faced with a difficult task, since in all technical questions it was dependent upon the court or the prosecution because it did not become cognizant of the tremendous amount of incriminating material of the prosecution until during the course of the trial, and had to find its way in a trial procedure which deviates substantially from the German criminal procedure. The performance of the defense should receive particularly high credit under the circumstances.

In very extensive speeches by the prosecution the prosecutors endeavored, particularly the American chief prosecutor, Justice Jackson, to do justice also to the German people. Justice Jackson says, among other things: "We would also make clear that we have no purpose to incriminate the whole German people."[21] In another place: "The democratic elements . . . got inadequate support from the democratic forces of the rest of the world, including my country."[22] Furthermore, he says: "The German, no less than the non-German world, has accounts to settle with these defendants."[23]

The crushing documentary evidence which the prosecution submitted during the oral hearings for the most part was taken from captured German archives. Its authenticity could not be contested. The indictment, the protocols of the proceedings and the judgment described the fateful course of National Socialism in Germany and in the world as objectively and impressively as hardly any German description could have done. We experience once again the entire development: the road to power, the strengthening of power by deception, compulsion, cunning and terror, the battle against the working class, against the Church, the persecutions of the Jews, and the war with its horrors. Much is uncovered before our eyes which was unknown to the German people. The blush of shame must rise in the face of every German if he hears the incontrovertible proof thereof and sees how cowardly cruelty, currish fealty, insane obsession debased honor and humanity and forfeited the German reputation. One would like to tell every German to read these documents, particularly those people who forget too soon and would like to avert their eyes from the horrors of the near past. Then they would understand more readily that the tragic today had to develop from the criminal yesterday.

After this short résumé permit me to pass on to the legal problems which we are to discuss today.

1. The criminal law which was to be applied is the Charter. It dates from August 8, 1945. However, the indictment is directed against acts which were committed before May 8, 1945, *i.e.*, long before the promulgation of the Charter. Furthermore, the Charter declares that, among other things, certain acts which heretofore had merely been judged as political or military conduct, but never had been subjected to an appraisal

from the viewpoint of international criminal law, were declared by the Charter to be crimes. Thus, particularly in Article 6(a):

Planning, preparation, initiation or waging of a war of aggression, or a war in violation of international treaties, agreements, or assurances, or participation in a common plan or conspiracy for the accomplishment of any of the foregoing.

In addition, the Charter makes responsible a group of persons such as has heretofore never been subjected to criminal jurisdiction under international law. According to the weight of doctrine, international law has only to do with nations, not with individual persons. In cases of acts of a predominantly political character, also of the so-called political crimes, only the state as such, and not the offender personally, is responsible according to this view.

Therefore, the question comes up whether the principle almost generally recognized in the criminal law of civilized nations is not violated by the Charter and the proceedings, namely, that an act shall only be punished if at the time of its commission it was under penal sanction. It is the principle which excludes the retroactive force of penal laws and which is usually expressed by the Latin formula: *nulla poena sine lege* or *nullum crimen sine lege.* Many representatives of international law doubt whether this principle is applicable to international law at all, namely, because it would presuppose a stage in the legal organization which has not yet been attained in international law. But I need hardly enter upon this objection, since neither the prosecution nor the judgment have in principle denied that this principle also applies in international law. Moreover, the same view was expressed by the Court of International Justice at The Hague in an advisory opinion concerning the admissibility of the introduction of analogy in the criminal law of Danzig, which the Court delivered in 1934 upon the request of the Council of the League of Nations. Against the votes of the Italian and the Japanese judges, it is stated there that the maxim *nulla poena sine lege praevia* must also apply in international law.

2. The Charter has been promulgated by the victors and is directed exclusively against the vanquished. The party on the one hand is, as has been stated in the joint defense, "all in one: creator of the statute of the Tribunal and of the rules of law, prosecutor and judge."[24] The question arises whether these facts do not run counter to the generally recognized principles of modern penal jurisprudence and to the requirements of an international court.

The prosecutors and the court could simply have avoided any discussion of these questions by referring to the Charter as the sole authoritative source of law. It is to the credit of the court as well as of the prosecution that, in putting full emphasis upon the authoritative importance of the Charter, they did not avoid these fundamental legal questions, but tried to meet the above-mentioned objections in their statements, which in part are masterpieces of forensic oratory, full of great perspicacity and considerable dialectic adroitness, although they did not at all agree with one another on every detail and every argument.

The chief prosecutors themselves stress the novelty of the procedure. They admit that for the first time in history such an international criminal court is in session and that for the first time the men responsible for the war of aggression and its consequences are being taken personally to account. However, they nevertheless represent the viewpoint that the principle *"nulla poena sine lege"* has not been violated; that the legal norms applied are not fundamentally new but correspond to the general conviction of what is right. International law originates—so they state—not only from agreements between nations, not only as enacted law, but also from gradual observance, from customary law; that this customary law, which already before was in force, was, so to speak, codified in the Charter; that not the penal law as such, but only its formulation is new. Thus, for instance, the chief American prosecutor states:

It is an outgrowth of treaties and agreements between nations and of accepted customs. Yet every custom has its origin in some single act. . . . Unless we are prepared to abandon every principle of growth for international law, we cannot deny that our own day has the right to institute customs and to conclude agreements that will themselves become sources of a newer and strengthened international law.[25]

Now, the indictment for planning and waging aggressive war is the salient part of the trial, as has been stressed again and again. If, however, aggressive war were not punishable, there would not be any basis for the punishment of crimes against peace, in other words, of the so-called political crimes which were so strongly emphasized. The chief prosecutors therefore have built up the thesis with a considerable array of oratory and historical material, that the war of aggression, defined as a crime in the Charter, was considered a crime under international law not later than after the Paris Pact of 1928 to Outlaw War, the so-called Briand-Kellogg Pact.

Now, if war of aggression is a crime—thus they argue, perhaps in a theoretically somewhat top-heavy argument—the aggressor automatically loses all rights which a party waging war has in a justified war. War of aggression therefore is nothing other than a murderous and predatory enterprise. The English chief prosecutor says:

What statesman . . . could doubt, from 1928 onwards, that aggressive war . . . was unlawful and outlawed?[26]

It is, indeed, not necessary to doubt that some aspects of the Charter bear upon them the imprint of significant and salutary novelty. But it is our submission and our conviction, which we affirm before this Tribunal and the world, that fundamentally the provision of the Charter which constitutes wars . . . a crime, is not in any way an innovation. This provision of the Charter does no more than constitute a competent jurisdiction. . . .[27]

It fills a gap in international criminal procedure.[28]

According to the statements of the prosecutors, the personal liability on the part of the men responsible for the war also for political acts committed in the name of the state is a logical conclusion and a requirement of justice. The state is only an idea. Acts, crimes are always committed by human beings only. Justice Jackson says:

The very minimum legal consequence of the treaties making aggressive wars illegal is to strip those who incite or wage them of every defense the law ever gave, and to leave war-makers subject to judgment by the usually accepted principles of the law of crimes.[29]

This principle of personal liability is a necessary as well as logical one if international law is to render real help to the maintenance of peace.[30]

Those in lower ranks were protected against liability by the orders of their superiors. The superiors were protected because their orders were called acts of state.... Modern civilization puts unlimited weapons of destruction in the hands of men. It cannot tolerate so vast an area of legal irresponsibility.[31]

But the ultimate step in avoiding periodic wars ... is to make statesmen responsible to law. And let me make clear that while this law is first applied against German aggressors, the law includes, and if it is to serve a useful purpose it must condemn aggression by any other nations, including those which sit here now in judgment.[32]

Thus far Justice Jackson. The English prosecutor exclaims:

... the great powers responsible for this Charter ... draw the inescapable conclusion from the renunciation, the prohibition, the condemnation of war ... and they refuse to reduce justice to impotence by subscribing to the outworn doctrines that a sovereign state can commit no crime and that no crime can be committed on behalf of the sovereign state by individuals acting in its behalf....[33]

The objection that the Charter represents the law of the victor is discussed by the American representative in the words:

Unfortunately, the nature of these crimes is such that both prosecution and judgment must be by victor nations over vanquished foes. The worldwide scope of the aggressions carried out by these men has left but few real neutrals. Either the victors must judge the vanquished or we must leave the defeated to judge themselves.[34]

The French chief prosecutor, in a well-founded legal construction, justifies the law of the Charter somewhat differently from Anglo-Saxon representatives. He states that the jurisdiction of the court rests upon the recognition in international law of the territorial principle in force in the sovereign states. According to this principle every nation may punish the crimes which are committed on its territory. Since the crimes of the defendants apply to several national territories, the creation of a joint court seemed advisable.[35] If responsibility under international law is recognized, it usually does not concern the individual but the national community as such. In such case, it is the duty of the state to deal with, either politically or as a crime, the conduct of the men who were the perpetrators of a violation of international law. At the present time, however, there is no German state. The highest authority in Germany is exercised by the four occupying Powers. Therefore, they have the right to have the guilt of German nationals tried before the court.[36] According to this French thesis, therefore, the court would act as the curator of German sovereignty.

The chief prosecutor of the Soviet Union, General Rudenko, does not recognize, in contradistinction to the other chief prosecutors, the customary law as part of the law of nations, but rather considers the agreements between states as the only source of establishing law and as the sole legally binding act. He says: "The Charter . . . of the International Military Tribunal is to be considered an unquestionable and sufficient legislative act, defining and determining the basis and the procedure for the trial and punishment of major war criminals."[37] The references to the principle *nullum crimen sine lege*, he states further, "are not applicable because of the following fundamental, decisive fact: The Charter of the Tribunal is in force and in operation and all its provisions possess absolute and binding force."

These statements perhaps simplify the problem too much.

The judgment substantially follows the fundamental statements of the chief prosecutors. It emphasizes that the law of the Charter is binding for the court. According to the statement of the judgment, the Charter has been enacted on the basis of the indubitable right of the occupying Powers to enact laws for the occupied territories. The Charter does not represent an arbitrary exercise of power on the part of the victorious nations, but the expression of international law as it existed at the time of its creation.[38]

With regard to the retroactive force of the Charter the judgment states the following:

In the first place, it is to be observed that the maxim *nullum crimen sine lege* is not a limitation of sovereignty, but is in general a principle of justice. To assert that it is unjust to punish those who in defiance of treaties and assurances have attacked neighboring states without warning is obviously untrue, for in such circumstances the attacker must know that he is doing wrong, and so far from it being unjust to punish him, it would be unjust if his wrong were allowed to go unpunished.[39]

If I understand these sentences correctly, they state that the sovereign state may enact binding law for its courts without regard to the principle *"nullum crimen sine lege,"* provided that higher justice requires it.

The judgment then states that war of aggression has been outlawed by the Briand-Kellogg Pact of 1928 as a crime. I quote:

In the opinion of the Tribunal, the solemn renunciation of war as an instrument of national policy necessarily involves the proposition that such a war is illegal in international law; and that those who plan and wage such a war, with its inevitable and terrible consequences, are committing a crime in so doing.[40]

The judgment argues that the Pact does not expressly state that such wars are crimes and does not appoint any courts for the trial of the aggressor. In interpreting the Pact, however,

it must be remembered that international law is not the product of an international legislature, and that such international agreements as the Pact of Paris have to deal with general principles of law, and not with administrative matters of procedure. The law of war is to be found not only in treaties, but in the customs and practices of states which gradually obtained universal recognition, and from the general principles of justice applied by jurists and practised by military courts. This law is not static, but by continual adaptation follows the needs of a changing world.[41]

The responsibility of individuals under international law is affirmed by the court. In its opinion international law imposes duties and liabilities upon individuals as well as upon states. In this connection it is stated in the judgment: "only by punishing individuals who commit such crimes can the provisions of international law be enforced."[42]

These, in a short summary, are the essential arguments of the indictment and of the judgment in regard to the questions which we are discussing here. In a critical survey I need not enter upon certain arguments which are more of rhetorical than legal importance. I give as an example only the contention made several times that the defendants may not make reference to the principle which excludes the retroactive force of a law because they themselves have disregarded all laws. Here it could be said that it is immaterial whether the defendant considers himself above the law and the statute. Even the criminal enjoys the protection of the law, although he does not in his own mind recognize the binding force of the legal order.

I shall now direct my attention to the more important question whether and to what extent new law has been applied in this trial and the principle *"nulla poena sine lege"* has been violated.

Let us once again establish the meaning of this sentence first. We know that it is the purpose of all law to regulate the relations of men among themselves. The law tells everyone what he may do and what he may not do. Whoever commits an act must know what legal consequences it will entail. That is only possible if the rules of conduct are already fixed in advance. The more serious the legal consequences are, the more it is necessary that they be capable of being anticipated clearly and unequivocally. That is particularly true if the community claims the right to punish, which by its very nature is a painful interference with the legal sphere of the individual. The legal norm upon which a right to punish is based must declare certain conduct not only as unlawful, but must make it appear as punishable conduct, as a crime, and it must finally make provision for the execution of the right to punish. The legal norm which prohibits or outlaws the act must be accompanied by the penal sanction which is capable of execution in practice. It therefore does not suffice if the act is condemned from the moral point of view and is felt to be worthy of punishment; rather, it must also be branded as punishable. If, in the course of development, a legal norm evolves which makes punishable an act heretofore not punishable, then this norm, if it really is to be considered law, may only apply to the future. For, up to that time, the act was not contrary to law—and the legislator cannot change the past. This is the idea upon which the maxim *nulla poena sine lege* is based. In that connection the word *lex* should not only be taken to mean the law in the narrower technical sense, *i.e.*, a rule issued in a definite form by authorities specially empowered, but it must be understood to include every legal norm, whether it be founded upon formal law or upon customary law, *i.e.*, upon legal principles generally believed to be binding. The word *lex* in this connection corresponds to the concept of the English expression, "law," which in German also means *"Gesetz"* as well as *"Recht"* or *"Rechtsnorm."*

If we apply these criteria to the Nuremberg trial, the first question arises: Does the provision of the Charter, which designates the planning or waging of a war of aggression as a punishable crime, correspond to a legal norm laid down by international law or to general legal principles already in existence in 1939?

First, it must be stated that the concept of war of aggression is not defined in the Charter and that no generally binding agreement has been reached in regard to this term in international law. This fact is not unimportant. Whoever starts a war will always be prepared with a more or less credible justification. We need only remember the speeches of Hitler. However, as the American chief prosecutor rightly emphasizes, "no political, military, economic, or other considerations shall serve as an excuse or justification for such actions. . . ."[43] It is true that endeavors were made to clarify the concept. Jackson quotes as an example the "Agreement concerning the Definition of the Concept Aggression" which was signed in London in 1933 by the Soviet Union, the Baltic States, Poland, Rumania, Turkey, Persia and Afghanistan,[44] and he designates it as "one of the most decisive sources of the law of· nations." What now is termed a decisive source of international law at that time was considered merely a diplomatic maneuver on the part of the Soviet Union. Among the states represented in the court neither the United States nor England nor France has joined this or any agreement of similar contents, namely, for the reason that they did not want to have the definition apply to themselves. Incidentally, the agreement did not prevent the Soviet Union from moving into the territory of the contracting parties, of the Baltic States and of Poland, and from occupying Rumanian Bessarabia without worrying about its own definition of aggression and without regard to diplomatic protests.

Let us leave theory aside and assume without further discussion that the wars upon which the court had to decide were in fact wars of aggression in the meaning of Article 6(a) of the Charter. What about the question whether these wars were punishable? One would think that, on such an important question, international law would provide a clear and unequivocal provision. Alas that is not the case. It is true that after a detailed description of the movements to prevent war since the time of the first World War, the indictment and judgment, as I have already stated, arrived at the conclusion that, at the latest, the General Treaty for Renunciation of War of August 27, 1928, which is better known under the name Paris Treaty to Outlaw War, or Kellogg Treaty, establishes punishment for wars of aggression. Article 1 of the treaty states:

The High Contracting Parties solemnly declare in the names of their respective peoples that they condemn recourse to war for the solution of international controversies, and renounce it as an instrument of national policy in their relations with one another.

This contractual renunciation of war as a tool of national politics implies, of course, that such a war is contrary to international law and that any nation which in spite thereof wages such a war commits a breach of contract. To this extent one must agree with the judgment. On the other hand, I do not find in the statements of the indictment and of the judgment any convincing proof for the further conclusion that after the treaty such a war was not only unlawful, but that those who plan such a war and wage it thereby commit a *crime*. In the treaty itself war is not designated as a crime and the renunciation is not reinforced by a sanction. It must be regretted that the treaty is a *lex imperfecta* to this extent, but in my opinion this cannot be disputed. It certainly is not satisfactory from a moral point of view if, subsequent to the treaty, monstrous deeds such as the waging of a war of aggression may be considered unlawful but not as a punishable offense. But such imperfections are not infrequent in the development of law and they are not always avoidable.

It is stated in detail in the trial and in the judgment that international law not only consists of treaties but also develops from usages and customs which gradually have found general recognition, and from legal principles which were worked out by jurists and which then slowly became general legal conviction. Furthermore, legal norms which originally were only contractual law may gradually become universal international law which applies to all nations We fully agree with this view, which is also represented 'ı German science of international law. Therefore, it remains to be examined in the present case whether war of aggression, even though no contractual norm has declared it punishable, perhaps was a punishable crime according to general legal conviction.

In this connection the judgment refers to resolutions which

term war of aggression an international crime, namely, to a Resolution of the League of Nations dated September 24, 1927, and to a Resolution of the Sixth Pan American Conference in Havana dated February 18, 1928, as well as to the so-called Geneva Protocol of 1924. These demonstrations without a doubt show that in the community of nations the desire increased to see wars of aggression declared an international crime. But they in no way prove that this wish has already been realized in international law. On the contrary, it must be stated that none of the participating governments has gone beyond a declaratory or declamatory demonstration and that no government has committed itself to the international law viewpoint that war of aggression is punishable. The Geneva Protocol at that time was recommended for adoption by unanimous resolution of the Members of the League of Nations. But nevertheless it was never ratified and has never achieved validity as international law. This circumstance, in my opinion, speaks not for, but against, the existence of a general legal conviction.

Finally, let us consider the practice of nations, which is also an important source of international law.

If, since 1928, a general legal conviction had existed which regarded war of aggression as a punishable act under international law, it would in all probability have expressed itself in practical politics. There was no lack of suitable or even compelling occasions therefor. Japan started war against China and occupied Manchuria by armed force. Italy engulfed Abyssinia in a war, the Soviet Union conducted war against Finland. However, no official statement has become known in which the United States or the English, French or Soviet government would have designated these wars of aggression as international crimes under reference to the international law in effect, threatened with an international punishment and made the statesmen responsible for it personally liable. It is true that at the end of 1939 the Soviet Union was expelled from the League of Nations because of the war with Finland, but the prosecution and the judgment have not made reference to this resolution, nor to the "sanctions" decided upon in individual cases, as proof of the punishable character of a war of aggression under international law.

Furthermore, the urgent warnings which the various statesmen directed to Hitler upon the eve of the war and which speak a very earnest language, contain no reference to a general legal conviction of this type and no warning with regard to crimes and no threat of punishment. According to my knowledge, the Soviet Union in no way condemned the impending war of aggression against Poland, concerning which it was precisely informed, as a "crime" under international law.

I believe that these facts and considerations must lead to the conclusion that the punishable character of the war of aggression stipulated in the Charter does not correspond to a general legal conviction in force in 1939, but that it is *new* law and that to this extent the principle of *nullum crimen sine lege* has been violated.

We must ask ourselves why the punishable character of the war of aggression has been made the salient feature of the first Nuremberg trial, for the defendants would not have escaped their justified punishment because of their acts, which violate the penal laws of all civilized countries, even if the punishment of war of aggression as an international crime had been dispensed with. The explanation for this procedure probably lies more upon the political than upon the legal plane. A prosecution "in court" of the criminally induced world catastrophe just could not be avoided unless recourse was to be had to considerably more far-reaching methods, methods of punishment more questionable for the development of law which necessarily would have entailed a higher degree of arbitrariness. The emphasis upon war of aggression in the indictment has made it possible for the defendants to introduce primarily political viewpoints for their defense. This in part has had the regrettable consequence that their acts which would clearly have been punishable according to existing law, have to a certain extent been overshadowed by the controversial question whether war of aggression is an international crime which should be tried, if an individual is involved, before a tribunal of the victorious Powers.

But it would be much more regrettable if, in the future, because of the condemnation of war of aggression, the rules of warfare which are of primary importance for the protection of the individual, such as the Hague Rules of Land Warfare, the Geneva Convention on the Treatment of Prisoners of War and others should be neglected or ignored and lose their value. It is doubtful whether humanity will ever succeed in making war impossible, but it is established beyond any doubt that, in view of the present stage of technical progress, a barbaric method of total war would ensue, endangering the entire human race, if all warring parties, aggressors as well as defenders, did not feel themselves bound by these rules of warfare which have become established in the community of nations.

After this short discourse I shall proceed to the question of the personal responsibility of the men who acted in the name of the state. The court rejected the view that persons who perform an official act assume no responsibility of their own under international law but are protected by the doctrine of the sovereignty of the state. In this connection it may be stated that the view at one time generally in vogue, that international law is only the law between nations that does not concern the individual, has not at all been generally relinquished. The allegation advanced several times, that crimes are always committed by individuals, is undoubtedly correct, but it is a truism. It applies to every human act and of itself proves nothing with regard to criminal responsibility in the individual case. I recall the English maxim: "The King can do no wrong." International military tribunals also are made up of human beings, conventions also are entered into by human beings, a charter also is created by human beings, the indictment is brought by individual human beings—and nevertheless the indictment in the trial begins with the words: "The United States of America, the

French Republic, the United Kingdom of Great Britain and Northern Ireland, and the Union of Socialist Soviet Republics hereby indict. . . ."

Finally, the apodictic statement of the judgment that the principle of international law which, under certain circumstances, grants the representatives of the state protection, may not apply to acts which were branded as criminal by the law of nations, would require a more profound justification. In any event, no single case is known in which a statesman would have been subjected to criminal responsibility for any act committed in the name of the state. All representatives of the prosecution emphasize with fervor that the trial of those responsible for official acts is something completely new. Thus we come to the conclusion that, with regard to this question also, new law was applied with retroactive force.

Finally, a word on the procedural aspects of the trial. It is disposed of by the representatives of the prosecution in the otherwise extensive and thorough pleadings in a relatively short manner. It is true that all concede that this court is a novel institution and that no such international criminal proceedings have taken place, not even after the Treaty of Versailles which originally had provided for a trial of the war criminals. The prosecutors say: The Charter "only" fills a gap. The Charter "only" provides a competent jurisdiction. But these are in reality tremendous innovations. A law which fills a gap is new law; a law which creates a jurisdiction not hitherto existing is also new law. It makes a great difference to the offender whether the judiciary act and the trial procedure were already determined at the time of the commission of the offense, or whether it was merely created subsequently, with confinement of its application to his case. It is not without reason that many constitutions and also Article 86 of the Bavarian Constitution declare special courts unlawful.

The observations which we have made, in my opinion, lead to the conclusion that the Charter and the trial have proceeded beyond international law as in force and have applied new law retroactively. I believe it would befit the reputation of the judge and international administration of justice better if we concede this fact than if we stretch the law upon the bed of Procrustes until it seems to serve the requirement of the hour.

The defenders of the Charter apparently have also felt that one cannot subsume satisfactorily the tremendous complex of political, military, and legal problems which faced the court under existing international law by means of legal constructions which depend entirely upon the substantive law in force. After exhausting all legal arguments they finally have made a subsidiary appeal against the restrictive substantive law to higher justice, to which all substantive law is to be subordinated. That is understandable. A number of horrible deeds have been committed. Was humanity to be deprived of the privilege of punishing these deeds and of exacting expiation from the guilty ones? Every feeling of law and order revolts against it. This desire for higher justice must be fulfilled even if one should have to proceed beyond the law as in force at the time of the commission of the deeds.

It probably is no coincidence that the prosecutors developed the noblest eloquence particularly on this point where substantive law no longer offers any conclusive arguments. Indeed, the ultimate and deepest justification of the Charter and the trial would be and would have to be the fulfillment of this ethical requirement. Whoever wishes to free the way to this higher justice would like to exclaim in the words of the British chief prosecutor:

If this be an innovation, it is an innovation long overdue—a desirable and beneficent innovation fully consistent with justice, fully consistent with common sense and with the abiding purposes of the law of nations.[45]

These are memorable words. If we follow them they will lead very far. Justice, sound human reasoning and the eternal aims of the law of nations demand that these norms, old or new, must apply to the strong as well as to the weak if they are to be felt to be law. For all nations are equal before the law of nations. It is contrary to law if one nation invokes legal norms against another nation which it does not consider binding also for itself. It is regrettable that this general recognition [of the binding force] by the nations sitting in judgment has not been made expressly. The Powers could have solemnly declared in the London Agreement that they consider the norms established in the Charter as generally binding for the community of nations. They have not done so. The United Nations in whose interest the four Powers acted, as is stated in the preface to the London Agreement, have stated their "conviction" in a resolution of the General Assembly of December, 1946, with reference to the Nuremberg judgment, that the principles applicable to the criminals of a war of aggression are to be generally valid. However, this resolution, just as the resolutions already mentioned, did not of itself create international law, but it is only a recommendation *de lege ferenda*. A competent court was not constituted.

It is true that the representatives of the prosecution have stated repeatedly that the signatory Powers have subjected themselves to this international law by virtue of the Charter. Thus the American representative states:

We must never forget that the record on which we judge these defendants today is the record on which history will judge us tomorrow. To pass these defendants a poisoned chalice is to put it to our own lips as well.[46]

And in another place:

And let me make clear that while this law is first applied against German aggressors, the law includes, and if it is to serve a useful purpose it must condemn aggression by any other nations, including those which sit here now in judgment.[47]

I am afraid that the light which this brilliant rhetoric sheds on sober reality is too rosy. At any rate the signatory Powers have not bound themselves in any way by contract to have the law of the Charter apply against themselves also.

Now we may perhaps be inclined to assume that the judgment must have binding force as a precedent particularly for the Anglo-Saxon legal mind. However, this hope might also be deceptive. The British chief prosecutor, it is true, stated once: "Insofar as the Charter of this Tribunal introduces new law, its authors have established a precedent for the future—a precedent operative against all, including themselves. . . ."[48] However, the American chief prosecutor expressly stated during the oral argument:

One of the reasons this was a military tribunal, instead of an ordinary court of law, was in order to avoid precedent-creating effect of what is done here on our own law and the precedent control which would exist if this were an ordinary judicial body.[49]

Since Jackson probably is the chief author of the Charter, his words have particular weight. It must be regretted that a judgment whose fundamental importance has been stressed on all sides so loudly was restricted so considerably in its legal effect.

Justice, sound human reasoning and the eternal aims of the law of nations also demand, finally, that the international jurisdiction, to which the lofty norms, may they be old or new, are entrusted for interpretation and application, offer in its constitution and in its composition every attainable guarantee of impartiality. The principles of modern criminal procedure are hardly disputed in this respect. It is the undisputed general sense of justice that the legislator should not also be prosecutor and judge. It is the general sense of justice that the accessory to the crime should not be legislator and judge over the perpetrator. Whoever himself enters into pacts with the aggressor, encourages him in his aggression and has shared the spoils with him, is not justified in sitting in judgment upon him. It is the general sense of justice, and it is a practice of hitherto existing international jurisprudence, that the judicial decision should be made by neutrals and that the opposing parties should be represented.

It is regrettable that in Nuremberg the law was applied only by the victors. The assurance that, in spite thereof, not the law of the victors but only the law of nations was to be applied, would have been more convincing if the sword of law had been put into the hands of neutral Powers. It is true that there were few neutrals in this World War, but nevertheless there were Switzerland, Sweden, Portugal, countries in which persons conversant with international law and wise judges are not scarce.

Finally, the confidence in the jurisprudence of this court and the moral effect of the judgment would undoubtedly have been greater among the German people if German judges also would have been seated and had a voice in this court sitting over Germans.

However, all these statements should not in any way minimize the importance of the trial. It was, after all, our purpose in today's meeting to clarify in our minds the importance of the trial, not by regarding it from the narrow German viewpoint, but by setting it within the appropriate frame of the law of nations which embraces all civilized peoples. Only within this frame are we able to recognize to what extent the Charter and the trial represent and introduce a step forward.

Let us consider the following! During the trial nearly the entire law of nations, particularly the law in regard to the prevention of war and the rules of warfare, was restated by shrewd representatives of the four great victorious Powers. The conventions of The Hague, the law of occupation, the Geneva Convention Relating to Prisoners of War, everything which science has worked out, practice has observed and the governments have expressly and impliedly recognized, including the Charter, were submitted to the court as the law in force, as the expression of the general sense of justice, as the realization of justice, and the court was entreated to apply this law even if there were no precedent in the past for such application because otherwise the community of nations must perish! And the court, established by the four great Powers, manned by outstanding men from the four nations, has confirmed that these norms contain or represent the general sense of justice and are generally binding!

Thus the trial and the judgment solemnly declared priority of law over force. This commitment to a law applying to all cannot be restricted to the individual case, but must morally bind all nations even if they have undertaken no express legal obligation. Nineteen nations have joined the London Agreement and the prosecutors have themselves declared that the law stated by them represents "the wisdom, the sense of justice, and the will of 21 governments, representing an overwhelming majority of all civilized people."[50] This law applies for all times, in all places and for everyone, victor and vanquished. For victory and defeat may never establish a moratorium for law and justice.

Nor let us forget that the future is more important than the past! With this understanding we may salute the Nuremberg trial as a guide-post for the further development of the law of nations. A democratic Germany will further this development with all its strength. We also are of the opinion that it represents a tremendous advance of the law of nations if, in the future, war of aggression is prosecuted as an international crime without regard to the nation or the person, and if the responsible statesmen are personally taken to account. We consider it correct if, in the future, murder, ill-treatment of members of the civilian population of the occupied territories or their deportation for slave labor, or their banishment from their homes, the taking away of their property, plunder of public and private property, persecution for political, racial or religious reasons are punished by international law regardless of the person. We agree with the statement that it must be considered a punishable crime if the population of an occupied territory wastes away because of malnutrition and lack of fuel, if prisoners of war are mistreated and deported for slave labor, contrary to international agreements and the customary rule of international law. Subject to this law, and on the basis of this law, we shall serve peace and reconciliation, when it will again be granted us to cooperate, with our modest contribution, in the development of relations among nations.

Gentlemen: The volumes of the official documents relating to the trial show on the cover a hand which holds the scales of justice over the globe. In the picture the golden scales are resting in serene balance. In the reality of our world, however, they move up and down precipitately, and often it would seem that the scale of injustice descends lower and lower under ever-increasing weight. It would be stupid to gloat about it and to press it even lower by hatred and revenge. No, we only want to cooperate to weight the scale of justice heavily. We will put into the scales of justice, as an expiation for the crimes committed, even though we did not want them or commit them, or even know of them, the punishment of the criminals who came forth from our people, as well as the suffering of our prisoners of war, the homesickness of the mothers and wives, the tears of those driven from their homes. We want to put into these scales the desire for justice and our honest will to cooperate in the reconstruction of the community of nations in order that, at last, law come to power and that also in the world of reality the scales of justice remain in serene balance over the entire human race.

Nuremberg as a Legal Problem

VON OTTO KRANZBÜHLER

IN considering Nuremberg as a legal problem I have first of all to define the limits of this subject with reference to the political problem which is also associated with the word Nuremberg. As interesting as the latter phase of the question may be, and as impressive as every defense counsel of Nuremberg senses it to be, Nuremberg as a tool of Allied foreign policy and of American occupational policy will not be considered in the following discussion. Nor will I consider whether the objective of preventing war seems to be attainable at all by means of criminal law.

Furthermore, I will not include in this subject a confrontation of the various principles which have been worked out by the Nuremberg Tribunals or of the legal maxims of classical international law. The application of this standard would, presumably, from the beginning lead to an unfruitful review of the Nuremberg Jurisdiction. For in spite of all efforts which

Read at the meeting of the German Society for International Law, Hamburg, April, 1950. Translated by Dr. Fredo E. Dannenbring; published by consent of the author.

Von Otto Kranzbühler, a German attorney at law, was defense counsel for Dönitz in the trial of the major war criminals at Nuremberg.

the courts have made to invalidate the objections of ex post facto application of their principles, I feel free in this circle to start without further proof from the premise that Nuremberg constitutes a revolutionary event in the field of international law. With regard to the validity of the law existing prior to Nuremberg, I refer to the article by Mangoldt completed in June, 1945: "The War Crime and Its Prosecution in the Past and Present."[1] Nuremberg is a revolution, and it appears to me to be of little significance to measure a revolution by the standards of the situation which has been overthrown by it or was meant to be overthrown by it. In a revolution one will always have to accept violence and injustice in the existing conditions. Its worth or worthlessness is determined by what it contains for the future. Hence, in my discussion the Nuremberg problem has evolved to a great extent into a problem of public policy.

Before I raise the question whether the decisions of Nuremberg can become precedents of international law, I should like first to define some basic questions, namely: What was the nature of the Nuremberg courts, and what was the nature of the law upon which they relied?

From the very beginning of the International Military Tribunal the public was told again and again that here a tribunal was in session which would speak on behalf of the civilized world. The IMT itself considered its mission more soberly. It stated:

The Signatory Powers [of the London Agreement of August 8, 1945] created this Tribunal, defined the law it was to administer, and made regulations for the proper conduct of the trial. In doing so, they have done together what any one of them might have done singly. . . .[2]

Since none of the four Signatory Powers could have established an international tribunal by itself, the IMT does not claim an international character for itself either. Rather it refers to itself as a military tribunal jointly established by the four belligerent powers.

The subsequent courts, composed of Americans exclusively, never agreed on their legal nature. The Milch Judgment states: "It must be constantly borne in mind that this is an American court of justice, applying the ancient and fundamental concepts of Anglo-Saxon jurisprudence . . ."[3]

A couple of months later the Justice Judgment states: "The jurisdiction of this Tribunal rests on international authority."[4]

The later judgments, as far as they were confronted with this question at all, acknowledged the international character of the Nuremberg Courts; and the same opinion was held by the court of appeals in Washington in the habeas corpus proceedings of the industrialist Flick.[5] In the same proceedings a number of German, French, and American scholars (Kaufmann, Kraus, Gidell, Rousseaux, and Finch) have given advisory opinions with concurring result stating that the so-called subsequent proceedings in Nuremberg were administered by American courts only. It appears to me too that this result cannot be doubted.

The second question, on what law the Nuremberg Tribunals relied, can likewise not be clearly deduced from their judgments. There are numerous examples to be found in which the judgments are based on international law, in the matter of the definition of crimes, as well as the question of culpability and the reasons for exoneration. For example, the Weizsäcker Judgment states: "The defendants here are charged with violation of international law."[6]

Parenthetically I should like to remark: By the Weizsäcker Judgment is always to be understood in the following the first judgment rendered after the trial hearing, not the judgment of the same court which was rendered in America without a trial hearing after several months of new counsels.

The High Command judgment makes the culpability dependent on "a breach of some moral obligation fixed by international law."[7] And the Justice Judgment believes itself to be entitled to enforce international law.[8] The Flick Judgment will not consider any act as criminal unless it was already "criminal under international law"[9] at the time when the act was committed. Almost all courts refer both to international law and to the general principles of criminal law to which they seem to attribute the character of international law.[10] Probably it is only for the reason of human insufficiency that they sometimes applied the principles and the concepts of Anglo-American law instead of the general principles of criminal law.

Although this seems to indicate that the Nuremberg Courts felt they were entitled to administer international law, in the leading decisions on their legal source they ruled the contrary point of view. The IMT replies to the contentions against the principles established in the London Statute which were based on international law:

> The law of the Charter is decisive and binding upon the Tribunal.
> The making of the Charter was the exercise of the sovereign legislative power by the countries to which the German Reich unconditionally surrendered; and the undoubted right of these countries to legislate for the occupied territories has been recognized by the civilized world.[11]

The IMT knowingly applies occupation law. The question of the legality of an occupation law of this kind is cut off by the court itself with the statement that the Statute is binding for the court. Over and above this observation the opinion, according to which the Statute is the expression of existing international law, is of merely declaratory worth. It is applied not on the ground that it is as international law, but as binding occupation law. This is still further emphasized by the language: the Statute is an expression of international law "at the time when the Statute was passed," and not at the time of the act.

This opinion is also expressed with corresponding clarity in the Justice Judgment with respect to Control Council Law No. 10: "It is an exercise of supreme legislative power in and for Germany. It does not purport to establish by legislative act any new crimes of international applicability."[12]

This knowledge seems to me to be very essential to the

importance of the Nuremberg judgments as precedents. We must realize clearly that international law and the general principles of law, however often they are mentioned in the judgments, were actually of only subsidiary importance to the courts. In the first place, the courts felt bound by the occupation law established in the London Statute and Control Council Law No. 10. I am inclined to believe that many judges of Nuremberg have suffered from this narrow route they had to follow in order to reach the aim they were supposed to reach.

This aim, and this time not the political one but the aim of public policy which the Nuremberg judges had in mind, is formulated in the Weizsäcker Judgment in the following manner:

. . . We are here to define a standard of conduct of responsibility, not only for Germans as the vanquished in war, not only with regard to past and present events, but those which in the future can be reasonably and properly applied to men and officials of every state and nation, those of the victors as well as those of the vanquished.[13]

The fact that Judge Powers too has deposed in his important dissenting opinion his " I violently disagree" only emphasizes the well-considered importance of the subject as it was perceived by the majority of the judges. A review of the Nuremberg jurisdiction, therefore, will have to admit a critical examination of the accomplishment of this aim.

In the beginning I indicated that I consider the steps undertaken in Nuremberg toward the accomplishment of this aim to be revolutionary, and therefore do not intend to measure them by the standards of the former law.[14] When I nevertheless quote literally what international law in the Anglo-American conception has held about war crimes before Nuremberg, I do so only in order to obtain a relatively safe starting-point for the later discussion. Oppenheim-Lauterpacht[15] distinguishes the following types of war crimes: (1) violation of recognized rules regarding warfare committed by members of the armed forces; (2) all armed hostilities committed by individuals who are not members of the enemy armed forces; (3) espionage and war treason; and (4) all marauding acts.

If the cases of espionage, war treason, and marauding acts, which are unimportant to the development in Nuremberg, are left out of consideration, there remain only two classical types of war crime: the violation of rules regarding warfare committed by members of the armed forces, and armed hostilities committed by individuals who are not members of the armed forces.

Within these restricted boundaries you will not find anything which could justify the punishment of statesmen and generals because of a policy leading to war, of jurists because of laws worked out by them, or of industrialists because of their pursuing the economic war policy of their government. This narrow basis shows strikingly the magnitude of the step made in Nuremberg.

The logical proposition for all Nuremberg decisions is the thesis of the direct obligation of the individual under international law. Here again I could give you proof by means of citations from Oppenheim and numerous others that this thesis is new. My point here is to give you the precise actual Nuremberg wording and the arguments by which it was arrived at. The IMT states:

That international law imposes duties and liabilities upon individuals as well as upon states has long been recognized. . . . the very essence of the Charter is that individuals have international duties which transcend the national obligations of obedience imposed by the individual State.[16]

The Flick Judgment states: "International law, as such, binds every citizen just as does ordinary municipal law."[17]

As these quotations show, the international obligation of the individual is not restricted in any manner. If an international law maxim can by its nature have any obligatory effectiveness at all for the individual, then it has—according to Nuremberg

—this meaning. The individual is unrestricted and directly subject to international law.

The courts have endeavored to give reasons for this result. The decisive argument is the case *Ex parte Quirin* which was decided in 1942 by the United States Supreme Court, and which is mentioned by the IMT and later frequently quoted again. This case deals with a proceeding against Germans who had landed from submarines in the United States for the purpose of sabotage. After they had been captured they were tried by an American Military Commission, and in order to avoid this proceeding they prayed for a writ of habeas corpus, which is some sort of *Haftprüfung*. The Supreme Court denied a habeas corpus decree on the ground that the acts the defendants were charged with had to be tried by a court-martial, and that Congress had sanctioned this rule of martial law. In the decision in *Ex parte Quirin* is to be found this principle, which became well known through Nuremberg:

From the very beginning of its history this Court has recognized and applied the law of war as including that part of the law of nations which prescribes, for the conduct of war, the status, rights and duties of enemy nations as well as of enemy individuals.[18]

The wording of this decision speaks of the duties of the individual under martial law only, and not—as do the Nuremberg judgments—under international law. Furthermore, the tenor of this judgment shows also that these duties under martial law are restricted to cases in which the acts of an individual could customarily be classified as war crimes. Consequently, the judgment does not examine whether the proscribed acts generally violated martial law. Rather, it states: "We must therefore first inquire whether any of the acts charged is an offense against the law of war cognizable before a military tribunal. . . ."[19]

The Supreme Court thus restricts itself to the statement that in cases where the individual perpetrator would be punishable under customary martial law for the commission of unlawful acts of warfare, he also is directly subject to this law. I have shown by my citation of Oppenheim of the year 1944 which cases were so considered by the Supreme Court: the small number of classical war crimes.

The decisive argument of Nuremberg for the obligation of the individual under international law, therefore, is weak. It seems to me that the attempt to legalize a revolutionary step has proved unsuccessful. This, however, does not affect the worth or worthlessness of this step from the standpoint of public policy. Let us see, therefore, what conclusions the Tribunals have drawn from it.

The first conclusion is the criminal responsibility of the administering authorities for their policy. This is best illustrated by the new crimes against peace and humanity.

The demonstration of evidence for the punishableness of aggressive war based upon the Briand-Kellogg Pact is well known. The admissions into which the courts were misled may be shown by a citation from the Weizsäcker Judgment: "We hold that aggressive wars and invasions have, since time immemorial, been a violation of international law."[20] I need not repeat here the arguments which have been alleged against the correctness of such a thesis.

To me it is important how the courts have handled the provision of aggressive war as provided for in their Statute, and how far they have defined the limits of responsibility for it. In this connection it is not exact when I speak of a provision of aggressive war, because here, as in many other Nuremberg crimes, a precisely defined provision is missing. What characteristics a war must have to be classified as an aggressive war cannot be learned from the Nuremberg judgments.

"The crime denounced by the law"—as the High Command Judgment states—"is the use of war as an instrument of national policy."[21]

If this is supposed to be a definition it would also be applicable to defensive war. The requisite of the "instrument of national policy," however, which was taken from the Briand-

Kellogg Pact, has made it easier for the courts to find the limitations of responsibility for an aggressive war. Contrary to the efforts of the prosecution to draw into the responsibility for the war such categories of persons as were logically no longer to be defined, the courts have fairly unanimously limited this responsibility to the so-called "policy making level." The High Command Judgment formulates this as follows: "It is not a person's rank or status, but his power to shape or influence the policy of his state, which is the relevant issue for determining his criminality under the charge of crimes against peace."[22]

This language is still far away from an exactness desirable in criminal law. By its practical application, however, it has led to a reasonable limitation of the circle of perpetrators. Except for two members of the cabinet, only the two commanders in chief of the Kriegsmarine and Generaloberst Jodl have actually been sentenced by the IMT on the ground of crimes against peace. The verdict against military commanders who were not members of the government because of political decisions presents, as it seems to me, the problem whether the military commanders in chief are provided by international law with an influence on foreign policy which they do not and must not have under constitutional law.

The subsequent American proceedings did not render sentences on the ground of crimes against peace, with the exception of the sentence in the Wilhelmstrassen Proceeding. This proceeding exceeded all limits rec¹ gnized in all the rest of the Nuremberg Tribunals by the ʟnviction of Lammers, Körner, and Keppler.

The criminal liability of the political leadership for a policy leading to aggressive war is perhaps the most important result of the Nuremberg proceedings. While examining this result by standards of public policy we must remember that the Nuremberg Courts are not institutions of the community of nations, but authorities of a victorious occupation power. The question of the responsibility for aggressive war requires the previous proof that an aggressive war had actually been waged.

If this question is to be cognizable, that is subject to a judicial decision, there has to be the possibility of answering it in the negative. But if the victor charges the politicians of the defeated in his own court with waging of aggressive war, then the question of an aggressive war cannot be answered in the negative. After all, the victor carries on a proceeding of this sort because he wants to justify the realization of his war aims against the defeated. It would be absurd to assume that any court established by him would prevent a policy for which his nation has made severe sacrifices during the war by answering the question of aggressive war in the negative. The impossibility of holding the victor to be the aggressor seems to prove that a political fact like the question of aggressive war cannot be cognizable before a national court.

For this thesis I should like to give some further reasons from the Nuremberg judgment on the aggressive character of preventive war. To give first an example from the practice of the Allies, I cite the reasons with which President Roosevelt justified the landing of American troops in North Africa, a territory with which the United States was not at war:

In order to forestall an invasion of Africa by Germany and Italy, which if successful would constitute a direct threat to America across the comparatively narrow sea from western Africa, a powerful American force . . . is today landing on the Mediterranean and Atlantic coasts of the French colonies in Africa.[23]

I ask you to look at the jurisdiction of the IMT in the light of this statement.

The IMT admits the possibility of a lawful preventive war.[24] As a rule, however, it denies it as far as German campaigns are concerned. In my opinion, the reasons given in the cases of Norway and Russia are characteristic of the political necessity of such denial. During the London negotiations in the summer of 1945, the English representative expressed the fear that a discussion of the Norway campaign might bring up the British plans to occupy this country. The judges of the

IMT, two of whom—Nikitchenko and Falco—had participated in the London negotiation, knew of these fears. In spite of this the judgment declared the Norway campaign to be an aggressive war on the ground that it had not been waged "for the purpose of forestalling an imminent Allied landing, but, at the most, that they might prevent an Allied occupation at some future date."[25]

The Russian example is also very educational. The argument especially put forward by Generaloberst Jodl that the masses of troops assembled at the Russian west border presented such an acute threat that the German side was forced to a preventive blow, was done away with by the words: "It is impossible to believe that this view was ever honestly entertained."[26]

These reasons, speaking for themselves, seem to me to affirm that the aggressive character of a war is not cognizable before a court of the victor.

It is a different question whether the crime against peace would be cognizable before a true international court of justice. A decision, however, going against the victor would paralyze all his policy against the defeated. Therefore, one can hardly imagine this decision being rendered by an international court of justice in our present international organization. If this organization should some day be powerful enough to take away the fruits of the war from the victorious state by a judicial decision, then it would also have the power to prevent such war in advance. In such an organization war can be considered only as a rebellion against the community, and therefore must necessarily be subject to the sanction of the community.

I therefore consider the attempt undertaken in Nuremberg to make statesmen responsible for a policy leading to war to be unaccomplishable for legal reasons. On the other hand, it seems to me that the liability of statesmen for the command to commit war and crimes against humanity can be executed under standards of criminal law.

I am going to deal with the simpler subject of war crimes first, and that with reference to the commissar order. General international law prohibits—and the Geneva Convention affirms the prohibition—the act of showing no mercy to members of the enemy forces or of killing them after they have been captured. Soldiers who violated this martial law could, under classical international law, be court-martialed after their capture. I consider the step of holding responsible for crimes of this kind those in particular who have ordered them as fully justified and belonging to the trend of a cautious development of martial law. Since, in spite of all political passion, the question whether such a crime has been committed and ordered is one on which the full realization of the war aims does not depend, it can in my opinion also be cognizable before a national court-martial of the victorious power. In cases like this it may be recognized even in our inadequate international organization that members of the government should not be allowed the defense that they acted as representative of their state.

Here I should like to make two reservations. On the one hand one must notice the double character of a war crime, particularly as to the liability of members of the government. There are some which have been branded as war crimes because they violate the moral public opinion of mankind— for example, the killing of prisoners of war. But there are also others where international law permits a party in war to sentence the captured perpetrators as a means of self-defense against certain acts of war of the enemy. The spy, the saboteur, and the insurgent are examples of this sort of war crime, of which the Hostage Judgment states correctly:

Just as the spy may act lawfully for his country and at the same time be a war criminal to the enemy, so guerrillas may render great service to their country and, in the event of success, become heroes even, still they remain war criminals in the eyes of the enemy and may be treated as such.[27]

It should be taken for granted that members of the government should not be held responsible for commanding such acts as have been added to the category of war crimes for the reason of self-protection only.

Further, I want to point out the danger of extending the concept of war crime in the Nuremberg jurisdiction by holding the members of government responsible for them. Whereas until then only the most severe and somehow violent wrongs were considered as war crimes, the Nuremberg judgments regard every violation of any provision of martial law as a crime. This extends, for example, to measures of national economy. The IMT considers it to be a crime that "the territories occupied by Germany were exploited for the German war effort in the most ruthless way, without consideration of the local economy, and in consequence of a deliberate design and policy."[28]

If by this all political economy in the occupied territories is considered as a war crime then this decision—because of its great importance for the problem of reparations—may easily become a political question, and no national court will have the freedom of an impartial judge to decide it.

In this connection there are still more severe problems regarding the new crime against humanity. As far as this new concept has been created only in order to censure more strongly the cruelest war crimes or those committed on the widest basis, it is without legal particularity. But the crime against humanity excels war crimes when the acts in question are committed in either peace or war against one's own citizens. It is the typical feature of this crime that according to its requisites it is a governmental crime. It cannot at all be committed by an individual without participation of his government. This is, for example, clearly expressed by the Justice Judgment, which excludes every isolated case of atrocity and regards it as a crime against humanity: "Participation in systematic government organized or approved procedures amounting to atrocities . . . and committed against populations or amounting to persecutions on political, racial, or religious grounds."[29]

This means that the acceptance of this crime necessarily includes the liability of the perpetrators, namely the government. Such a crime clearly offers a possibility for intervention by any foreign power in the domestic policy of a defeated country before and during the war, depending only on vastly undefined moral concepts. What justification—we must ask ourselves—does international law provide for such an intervention? The Justice Judgment answers:

The force of circumstance, the grim fact of world-wide interdependence, and the moral pressure of public opinion have resulted in international recognition that certain crimes against humanity committed by Nazi authority against German nationals constituted violations not alone of statute but also of common international law.[30]

I do not consider these reasons to be very convincing from the legal point of view. On the other hand, the appearance of states whose political methods hurt the moral feelings not only of foreign countries but also of their own people presents entirely new problems. The fact that the UNO has declared genocide, the murder of a people, an international crime[31] must certainly be considered as an attempt by the civilized world to recognize certain minimum standards of humanity in the methods of a state in interior policy as an international obligation. Despite the danger of abuse inherent in this concept of a crime against humanity, I still believe that this newly created notion, and with it the international liability of the government for trespassing the limits drawn by it, was necessary, and could not be avoided after the experiences of the immediate past and present.

Here again I want to make the reservation that in the Nuremberg jurisdiction the new concept has been too far expanded, and that future development should restrict it to the most severe mass crimes.

In summary, I reach the following result of the review of the first great Nuremberg problem: the responsibility of state leadership for the ordering of war crimes and crimes against humanity can be decided upon by national courts applying the principles of criminal law. On the other hand, I consider criminal responsibility for a policy leading to war as a question beyond the competence of national courts.[32]

Now I turn to the second great problem: the position of a private citizen in the conflict between international law and the law of his own country. Here I would like to anticipate by saying that the Nuremberg Tribunals, in opposition to some attempts of the prosecution,[33] considered as lawful acts of war committed in an unlawful aggressive war.[34]

Whereas the responsibility of members of the government was the main problem of the first Nuremberg proceedings, the main problem of the subsequent proceedings is presented by the responsibility of private citizens. The principle of the applicability of international law to the individual does not, as yet, affect the decision of those cases in which obligatory international law enters into conflict with obligatory state law. The members of the government who themselves create the law which causes such a conflict may not cite for their justification the state law for which they themselves are responsible. Thus far, the Justice Judgment is right in holding that Hitler may not cite his own decrees.[35] The conflict becomes a problem only in the case of those who do not enact the state law but are subject to it. I should like to throw light upon the step through which the Nuremberg decisions deviate on this point from the hitherto prevailing legal opinions, by giving two citations. Oppenheim says: "And if it happens that a rule of Municipal Law is in indubitable conflict with a rule of the Law of Nations, municipal courts must apply the former."[36]

According to the Anglo-American opinion, discussed in greater detail by Oppenheim, which was also in accordance with the continental European view, in case of conflict the law of the state prevails. On the contrary, the Nuremberg opinion in its High Command Judgment states:

International law . . . may also limit the obligations which individuals owe to their states, and create for them international obligations which are binding upon them to an extent that they must be carried out even if to do so violates a positive law or directive of state.[37]

The practical meaning of this principle can be seen quite clearly by examining the defense possibilities admitted in Nuremberg for the individual citizen who is indicted for an act committed by order or with permission of his government.

It would follow from this point of view that the German law provides no protection. "Hitler's decrees were a protection neither to the Führer himself nor to his subordinates," the Justice Judgment states.[38] And in the judgment of the accused Oberreichsanwalt Lautz appear the words: "If German law were to be a defense, which it is not, many of his acts would be excusable."[39] According to the Krupp Judgment, the defendants may not plead that in their economic measures in the occupied territories they "were authorized and actively supported by certain German governmental and military agencies or persons."[40]

Even the matter of distribution of competence under state law is without interest for the Nuremberg Tribunals. A commanding general in an occupied territory may not plead that he could not give orders to police units according to the German distribution of competence.[41] An official may not claim that he had no authority under state law. The alleged incompetence could, it is said in the Weizsäcker Judgment, "only be quoted for the examination of punishableness under German law but would not be decisive against the charge of a crime under international law."[42]

The nonconsideration of the military order has already been so vastly discussed in public that I need not enter into full particulars. The official British *Manual of Military Law* provides in the wording of 1929—which, however, was changed in 1944—with respect to the intended war criminal proceedings: "Members of the Armed Forces committing such violations of recognized rules of war are not war criminals, and cannot be punished by the enemy insofar as they were ordered to do so by their government or their commanders."[43] To this the Hostage Judgment against the Southeast Generals merely replies: "The fact that the British and American Armies may have adopted it for the regulations of its own armies as a matter of policy does not have the effect of enthroning it as a rule of international law."[44]

In principle an order, in Nuremberg, never constitutes an excuse but rather always an extenuating circumstance. The High Command Judgment, however, grants the soldier "in a subordinate position" "within certain limitations" "the right to assume that the orders of his superiors and the state which he serves . . . are in conformity with international law."[45]

According to the same judgment, however, "high command-ing officers" are excluded from this privilege: "If international law is to have any effectiveness, high commanding officers, when they are directed to violate it by committing murder, must have the courage to act, in definite and unmistakable terms, so as to indicate their repudiation of such an order."[46] The same court of justice recognizes, however, the conflict created by this principle as "the tragedy of the German Wehrmacht."[47]

Likewise the important defense of the individual citizen that he was ignorant of the provisions of international law is, in principle, not allowed. Only, according to the High Com-mand Judgment, the personal act committed must have been "voluntarily done with knowledge of its inherent criminality under international law."[48] According to the same judgment, "Such a [field] commander . . . cannot be held criminally responsible for a mere error in judgment as to disputable legal questions."[49]

In cases where extraordinary doubtful legal questions must

be discussed, as in the Industry Proceedings, the courts as a rule do not consider the error in international law to be a reason which excludes the guilt, but eventually, as the Flick Judgment holds, to be a reason for mitigating punishment.[50]

An accused state might well object to the reproach of having violated international law on the ground that the accusing state has committed the same acts. This defense is, in most cases, not granted to the individual defendant. The only exception is the IMT Judgment against Dönitz, who was not sentenced by the Tribunal on grounds of submarine warfare against a neutral merchant navy—which usually is considered by the court as a violation of international law—because the English and Americans had proceeded in the same manner. This important passage reads:

> In view of . . . an order of the British Admiralty announced on 8 May 1940, according to which all vessels should be sunk at sight in the Skagerrak, and the answers to interrogatories by Admiral Nimitz stating that unrestricted submarine warfare was carried on in the Pacific Ocean by the United States from the first day that Nation entered the war, the sentence of Doenitz is not assessed on the ground of his breaches of the international law of submarine warfare.[51]

Elsewhere the *tu quoque* demurrer is overruled completely. The Weizsäcker Judgment, for example, states: "But if we assume, *arguendo*, that Russia's action was wholly untenable and its guilt as deep as that of the Third Reich, nevertheless this cannot in law avail the defendants . . ."[52] The High Command Judgment, which likewise denies the *tu quoque* demurrer in principle, sustains it at least as a reason for mitigating punishment.[53]

Only two judgments made allowance, to a certain extent, for the real tragedy which followed for the citizen who acted lawfully within the limits of his own law. The Flick Judgment first, followed by the I.G. Farben Judgment, brought up the thought of the state of distress. This thought is already to be found in the IMT Judgment, which raises the question "whether a choice consistent with the moral law was actually possible."

This possibility was therefore not more closely examined in the IMT Judgment; and there was not the same necessity for it as in the subsequent proceedings, because these generally were concerned with the leading men of the state. Consciousness of this necessity was very strongly shown in the Flick Judgment, where it was expressed in these words:

The Reich, through its hordes of enforcement offic ls and secret police, was always "present," ready to go into instant action and to mete out savage and immediate punishment against anyone doing anything that could be construed as obstructing or hindering the carrying out of governmental regulations or decrees. . . . This Tribunal might be reproached for wreaking vengeance rather than administering justice if it were to declare as unavailable to defendants the defense of necessity here urged in their behalf.[54]

With this an outlet is created at least for those acts which are based upon a command of state law. I say purposely "an outlet." For to me the thought of the state of distress does not seem to be a real solution. In the first place, it would be in favor of a citizen in a terroristic police state only, but not for the benefit of a citizen in a constitutional state. Undeniably, however, for the latter as well conflicts between state law and international law can arise. Moreover, the state of distress covers only those acts which are *ordered* by state law and not those which are merely *permitted* by state law.

In my opinion the entire fundamental thesis—that in the event of conflict international law prevails over state law in matters affecting the individual citizen—is unsound and in our present political organization indefensible. This problem cannot be solved by considering that the system of international law necessarily is placed above the system of state law.[55]

The question to me, nevertheless, seems to be to which one of these systems of law the individual owes greater allegiance. If I were to rely on the concept of mankind so frequently conjured in Nuremberg, I would say: In time of war allegiance to one's own country prevails, in principle, over allegiance to the community of nations under international law. To me the problem seems to be whether, and in what cases, this major principle tolerates exceptions. The farther the concept of war crime is expanded to measures which do not quite obviously have the character of a crime, the more difficult it will be to give precedence to an obligation under international law, rather than to the obedience due to one's own state. Already in the first proceeding the pleading of Professor Jahrreiss was concerned with this problem. It has been discussed again and again ever since. This most difficult problem has not been solved in Nuremberg. With obvious concern, the French judge of the IMT, De Vabres, remarks in a later lecture on the provisions of conflicts in the London Statute:

With these provisions the Statute whose rules were binding for the Tribunal has exceeded the provisions of state law in the sense of individualism. It is subject to a reproach, namely, this one: to endanger the discipline which is necessary for the maintenance of states. A provision of this kind should be applied in the future with caution and power of discernment only.[56]

In the entire public political appraisal of the Nuremberg proceedings one fact must be regarded in the right light: the fact that proceedings of this kind have been, and in the near future will be, conducted against members of defeated nations only. This inequality is indeed no decisive objection against such proceedings in general. It is, as Oppenheim rightly stresses, "the unavoidable concomitant of the existing imperfections of international organization and of the institution of war itself."[57]

If this is true, it must also be understood that every perfecting of the prosecution of war crimes permanently enlarges the inequality between the victor and the loser. The idea of law requires that it be dominated by the striving for equality. As long as the application of the recognized legal maxims to the victor also is not secured, the perfection of these legal principles strengthens the imperfection of the law as a whole. The farther the elements of crime and the liability are expanded on the part of the loser only, the more he will be held completely liable for the failure, as the Milch Judgment reveals: "He who elects to participate in a venture which may result in failure must make his election to abandon the enterprise if it is not to his liking or to stay as a participant, and win or lose according to the outcome."[58]

The Nuremberg Judgment

Penal Jurisdiction Over Citizens of Enemy States

DR. KARL-HEINZ LÜDERS

AFTER the conclusion of World War I, 1914-1918, among other things a commission was established during the peace conference in Paris, which was to concern itself with the question of a trial for offenses committed during the war. Chairman of this commission was United States Secretary of State Lansing. The majority of the members of the commission adopted first the standpoint that such offenses could be investigated and tried by an international tribunal; thus one was to proceed according to the laws of humanity and the regulations of international law.

The American delegates pointed to the fact, however, that such an international tribunal did not have a current penal law which it could apply. No regulation of international law and no state treaty—not to mention the principles of humanity—rendered the violations of the customs of war and the law of war an international crime which was to be punished.

But the Americans drew attention to the possibility that

First published in Süddeutsche Juristen-Zeitung, *Nos. 8/9 November/December 1946, pp. 216-18. Translated by Dr. Georg Grimm.*

Dr. Karl-Heinz Lüders *is Regierungs-Direktor in the Ministry of the Interior of the German Federal Republic in Bonn.*

enemy war criminals could be tried by military courts of the individual states according to their military penal laws. At the same time they referred to the only precedent case of this kind until then known: Henri Wirz, the commandant of a prisoner camp of the Confederates in Andersonville, had neglected this camp during the Civil War and thereby caused the death of many prisoners. He was convicted by a military tribunal in Washington of having violated the laws and customs of war and was executed.

After this American suggestion the commission gave up the plan for an international tribunal for the conviction of the war criminals and demanded instead their extradition to the military judicature of the injured enemy power. In this way was created Article 228 of the Treaty of Versailles, which might also be designated with good justification *lex Henri Wirz.*

On the German side the countersuggestion was made that an impartial international tribunal should first investigate the extent to which international law had been violated by the accused; this decision was to be taken as a basis for the penal proceedings which were to be administered by the military courts of the individual victorious states. Wilson and Lansing insisted, however, that since one party to the war could render judgment upon the acts of the other party, the decision under international law need not be exempted, either; in view of the international practice which had developed on this question the fact that prosecutor and judge were represented by the same party did not stand against it. The Allies, as is well known, later gave in under the influence of Lloyd George; they even declared themselves willing to admit and await the trial of the accused under German law by the *Reichsgericht.*[1]

It is appropriate to remember these occurrences if one wishes to comment today on the trial of German war criminals before the courts of the victorious states. These numerous proceedings in this country are, as is well known, first of all subject to the reproach that the victorious nation was sending both prosecutor and judge. During the Nuremberg Trials, some declared that the judges of the International Tribunal, as citizens of the victorious states, were not in a position to judge the German problem objectively, free from national resentment and without any passion. Some German lawyers assert that for victors to try the defeated is in contradiction to international law.

The punishment of so-called war criminals undoubtedly constitutes a problem of international law of the first order which has for a long time been contended not only in our country but also in other countries. In spite of this dispute, certain opinions which have become authoritative for the practice of law have successfully asserted themselves in the individual countries. But regrettably there existed from the beginning a contrast between the prevailing German opinion and the legal application of most other nations. This contrast was overcome, it is true—as I shall demonstrate—even during World War 1, inasmuch as for public reasons we adopted the practice of the others. The two opinions did not, however, approach each other.

To me three counts seem to be typical of the opinion which prevailed—particularly before World War I—in Germany:

1.§158 of the old military penal code (*Militärstrafgesetzbuch*) of 1872 stated: The regulations of this law are to be applied to punishable acts of a prisoner of war according to his rank.

The wording of the regulation leaves the important question open: Is the German judicature competent for the trial of crimes which the foreign soldier had committed before he was taken prisoner? Until World War I the almost unanimous German opinion, as represented by the *Reichsmilitärgericht* (Reich Military Tribunal) and the ordinary penal courts, was: No.[2] Only the soldier's native state possesses penal jurisdiction over those crimes which he committed before he was taken prisoner, even if those crimes were directed against the enemy state or its citizens.[3] Their trial should therefore be reserved to the national courts; the enemy state had no right to punish even when it apprehended the culprit by taking him prisoner.

2. §91 of the *Reichsstrafgesetzbuch* (Reich Penal Code) in the wording current during World War I read as follows: Aliens are to be prosecuted for the acts specified in §§87 (high treason), 89 (support of the enemy), 90 (war treason) according to the customs of war.

This regulation was of great significance for the military jurisdiction in the field. Under "customs of war" were understood the unwritten rules of the law of war, including the so-called commandments of war necessity, which belonged to international law.[4] On account of these customs of war francs-tireurs and spies, for instance, were shot. But—and this is important— according to the opinion[5] at that time, it was not sentences in the legal meaning which were concerned in this, but security and defense measures for the execution of the war purpose. Consequently prior judicial proceedings for the pronouncing of such a measure of punishment were not deemed necessary, although such a procedure was not in contradiction to the customs of war, as it was viewed from the German side.

3. Finally, independent crimes were not recognized by the Germans in international law. A delict in international law cannot be committed by individual persons—and the defense counsels of Nuremberg also asseverated this again and again—but only by states. In proof of this Article 3, paragraph 2 of the Hague Convention of 1907 was referred to, which says: "The State is responsible for all acts in violation of international law committed by persons under its sovereignty." This regulation was at that time taken into the Hague Convention at the request of Germany. Certainly, it cannot be proved thereby that the other Signatories of the Hague Convention adopted the German opinion. For this regulation merely states something on the liability of the state for its citizens under civil laws, but does not touch in detail the question of the penal responsibility of those who violate international law.

In the view of this opinion which prevailed in Germany, the *Reichsgericht* was faced with a difficult decision in the war crimes trials, which had been forced upon it in 1920. But the

Reichsgericht proved itself resourceful without leaving the former standpoint. For it did not make the inevitable investigation of each case under international law in connection with the penal facts but in connection with the eventual justification of the factual acts. The *Reichsgericht* therefore did not recognize any independent facts of war crimes, but it applied the penal facts of the *Reichsstrafgesetzbuch* (e.g., murder or manslaughter according to §§211 or 212) but then always adjudged a cause of justification when the war measures in question had been executed in accordance with the rules of international law.

England's thoughts on these three points were different even before World War I. There, too, we of course find deviating opinions of individual jurists, but the English jurisdiction ever since has started out from these facts: (a) that there exist certain war crimes based on international law; (b) that British war tribunals thus far have also martial jurisdiction over citizens of enemy states; and (c) that measures against these enemy persons are to be regarded as penal acts of justice and therefore always require a court judgment.

1. In Oppenheim's English textbook on *International Law*, which thus far is relative to the matter since Oppenheim was the councilor of the British Admiralty during World War I,[6] four kinds of crimes of war are distinguished: (a) crimes of citizens of the belligerent power against the inimical power; (b) crimes of noncombatants against the inimical power; (c) espionage and war treason; and (d) delicts of plundering.

Today these crimes of war are to be supplemented by the most typical and most important war crime, the crime against the peace, as it has been tried in Nuremberg. While there can be doubt here and there about the war crimes specified under (a) and (b), whether the legal foundation was really international law and not eventually the national law corresponding with international law, the crime against the peace undoubtedly rests directly upon international law.

As has been stated earlier in connection with the preliminary negotiations to the Treaty of Versailles, the United States did not originally share the English standpoint of a directly applicable international law. Characteristic of its view is the statement of the Supreme Court of the United States, in the penal proceedings *U.S.* v. *Hudson,* to the question whether directly applicable penal norms were to be taken from international law: "The legislative authority of the Union must first make an act a crime, affix a punishment to it, and declare the court shall have jurisdiction over the offenses."

This legal opinion should now belong in the past. The judgment of the Nuremberg Tribunal, which is supported not only by the four Great Powers of the world but also by nineteen other states which have signed the agreement of August 8, 1945, on the foundations of the Nuremberg trial, has promoted the development of international law in a magnificent manner. It sprang from the desire to prevent that terrible danger which threatens human civilization with destruction—war. It is immaterial whether the Charter and the Judgment of Nuremberg created new international law or whether existing international law has only been clarified. At any rate, the direct effect of international law on the individual implies a welcome weakening of the sovereignty of the individual states. Only by the removal of this sovereignty can a collective order be created which guarantees to all states and men security and peace.

It has been asserted by the Nuremberg defense counsel that the direct application of international law still did not create a possibility of the pronouncing of sentences, as international law had hitherto not contained any penal regulations. The Tribunal stated on this point that this was not necessary in accordance with common law; the Hague Convention, for instance, prohibits certain methods of warfare without affixing penalties to them—and yet, for many years military tribunals have called to account and punished persons who were guilty of violating the specified rules laid down in the Hague Convention.

This is true, but it must be confined to the sphere of virtual war crimes; for, of course, not every insignificant violation of a regulation of international law during peacetime constitutes a punishable crime. But frequently an act in violation of international law will simultaneously violate the national penal law; then punishment is undoubtedly warranted. The precedent case of Nuremberg makes clear that acts against the peace are punishable as crimes under international law, while the pertinent nations are competent to establish the procedural prerequisites, as has been done by the Declaration of Moscow and the Charter of Nuremberg.

2. Contrary to the German opinion upheld until World War I, England has never since hesitated to try before British courts-martial citizens of enemy states who had been captured by her for earlier war crimes. It may have justified these measures by the remark that the native state may for psychologically understandable reasons tend either to leave offenses of a citizen which were directed against the enemy state or its population unpunished or to punish them much too lightly. We shall not enter here into the consideration that on the other hand the trial by the offended enemy state—equally from a psychologically understandable attitude—may easily bring with it the danger of judgment that is not objective and thus of too severe punishment. At any rate, it is a fact that this practice is legal not only in England but in the whole Anglo-Saxon sphere of law. The continental enemy states of the Middle Powers followed the same procedure during World War I.[7]

As the maintaining of its own legal opinion proved to be unfavorable, the German Reich and its military tribunals changed their position on the issue during World War I. German military tribunals tried in accordance with the legal practice of the Allies—not only in World War I, but particularly also during the last World War—all prisoners who had made themselves guilty of disregarding the Hague Convention on land warfare during the time prior to their seizure. In the same manner in which many German soldiers are today tried before English, American, French, and Russian military tribunals, many Allied soldiers were tried before German military courts a few years ago. This is easily overlooked when today the war crimes trials of the present are criticized in this country with slashing opinions. And yet, this trial of citizens of the defeated state by judges of the victorious states corresponds absolutely with international law as it has developed in the last twenty-five years. The fact that Germany has made use of this practice, which it had originally denounced, has to a certain extent concluded the development of a complex of common law in international law.

The establishment of the Nuremberg Tribunal is also in correspondence with this custom of international law. For when a war crime is directed against several states, then it is customary to form mixed tribunals with the participation of judges of the offended nations. Correspondingly the Declaration of Moscow of October, 1943, states that the major war criminals are to be tried in common, since their crimes were directed simultaneously against all of the four major powers; but as soon as war crimes of regional significance were concerned, the trial was to be left to the state solely concerned.

Independent of general international law, we Germans cannot raise any objections against these proceedings—from the legal standpoint—because with the unconditional surrender we have agreed to all measures of the Allies which are compatible with the commandments of humanity and that part of the principles of international law which is indispensable as a moral minimum.

3. The opinion prevailing at the beginning of World War I in Germany and Austria-Hungary that measures like the shooting of francs-tireurs, spies, and other such war criminals can be effected without judicial judgment now belongs in the past, too, and will scarcely still be taught by any law teacher. The Anglo-Saxon opinion that in such a case sentences in the meaning of the law are concerned and not acts of war necessity or war expediency has successfully asserted itself and thereby led the international law of war in the direction of improvement.

At the beginning many may have thought the Nuremberg

judges were not fit for the task because as citizens of the victorious states they would not face the defendants free from hatred, passion, and national prejudice. Many may therefore have thought of a trial by German judges as more just. But today, when the judgment of Nuremberg and the reaction to it among the German population is known, only malevolent persons and hardened National Socialists can doubt the real objectivity of these judges. Many, if not the majority, tend even to the assumption that the objectivity was carried rather too far. But those who had called for German judges have meanwhile fallen silent; for today there emerge well-founded doubts as to whether in view of what the German people had suffered from the defendants the German judges could have been capable of such objectivity and dispassionateness, and whether they could have shown such a degree of independence as was shown by the judges of Nuremberg. Such a trial would be worthless, however, without this objectivity and this judicial independence; and the judgment would then have to be taken not as an act of justice but as a political measure. But justice is not apt to pass its vestment to politics.

The Judgment of Military Tribunal III in the Nuremberg Trial of Justices

HERBERT THIELE-FREDERSDORF

1. On December 3 and 4, 1947, the judgment against the fourteen accused officials of the *Reichsjustizministerium* (Ministry of Justice), state attorneys, and judges was pronounced.

The bill of indictment was handed down on January 4, 1947; the major proceedings were opened on February 17, 1947; the hearing of evidence lasted from March 6, 1947, to October 13, 1947. The Tribunal heard 138 witnesses and received 641 documents in evidence from the prosecution and 1,452 documents from the defense. The indictment included the following four counts: (1) conspiracy for the purpose of committing war crimes and crimes against humanity; (2) war crimes; (3) crimes against humanity; and (4) membership of certain defendants in criminal organizations.

Through a predecision of June 1, 1947, the accusation of conspiracy as a separate offense was dropped on a motion by the defense because of incompetency of the Tribunal.

The Judgment comprises 330 pages apart from the appendix

First published in Neue Juristische Wochenschrift, *January, 1948.*
Translated by Dr. Georg Grimm.
Herbert Thiele-Fredersdorf was defense counsel before Military Tribunal No. I in Nuremberg.

and a supplementary argument by Judge Blair. It is divided into a general part consisting of fifteen chapters and a special part which comprehends the reasons for the conviction of the individual defendants.

For the establishment of its competency the Tribunal refers to Control Council Law No. 10 and Ordinance No. 7 of the American Military Government.

2. In its examination of the legal foundations of Control Council Law No. 10 the Tribunal arrives at the following conclusions: "It is . . . the complete dissolution of the government in Germany, followed by unconditional surrender and by occupation of the territory, which explains and justifies the assumption and the exercise of supreme governmental power by the Allies." In this case the occupation authorities were not subject to the restrictions imposed by the Hague Convention and the laws and customs of war. With reference to numerous sources of literature and the Judgment of the International Military Tribunal (IMT), the Tribunal compares and contrasts this occupation of Germany by the Allied Powers with that of Poland by Germany during the war at a time when forces allied to Poland were in the field and when the Hague Convention therefore had to be current as the most compelling criterion for the question of conduct in accordance with international law of the German occupation authorities. The Tribunal stresses the difference between these two utterly similar occupational affairs in international law, in order to show the principles of justice and morality on which Control Council Law No. 10 is based, although it would have to handle the Control Council Law in itself as an obligatory rule from the very beginning; for, as it declares at another place, a tribunal which owes its existence and competency only and alone to the provisions of a certain statute could hardly start exercising this competency in order to declare the act purposeless to which it owed its existence. The Tribunal furthermore concludes, to be sure, that the Control Council Law should confine itself to demanding sentences against German criminals

and that it should not introduce penal facts of international applicability, but that neither, therefore, did the Tribunal become a German tribunal, nor was it bound in any way by German law and German statutes. Since the Control Council Law represented a legislative act by an international authority, one could not appeal to the constitution of some state in order to invalidate the substantive purpose of such a provision of international law. On the other hand it followed from this that the customary regulations of American penal law and penal procedure could not be applied, but only the broad principles of justice and equity on which any civilized concept of law and legal procedure was based.

Since the majority of the substantive provisions of Control Council Law No. 10 corresponded, as the Judgment later states in greater detail, with already existing statutes of international law, it was to be regarded more as a codification of international law than as a creation of law. But insofar as the Control Council Law went beyond these existing statutes it assumed legal authority by the exercise of the sovereign legislative power of the Allied Occupation Powers and in this phase was also sanctioned by international law.

3. From the treatment of the material substance of the Control Council Law the Judgment proceeds to the examination of the rules of the proceedings. The universality and the title to supreme validity which were inherent in international law did not necessarily imply also a universality of its enforcement. Normally the sovereignty of a state prevents the exercise of sanctions within its territory by another authority than that of just this state. But in Germany an international body (the Control Council) took over for the reasons quoted above—and had to take over—the authority to establish a judicial apparatus for the punishment of those who had violated the rules of common international law. For the establishment of the penal responsibility of individual persons for violations of international law the Tribunal refers to the development of international common law recognized by the majority of civilized na-

tions, to the express consent of twenty-three states to the Agreement of London and the Statute of the International Military Tribunal, to the recognition of this Statute by the General Assembly of the United Nations, as well as to the literature, particularly Hyde's modern work, *International Law*. Special mention should be given the remark made in this connection, that confessedly the Germans were not the only ones who made themselves guilty of committing war crimes, but that the punishableness of other violators of international law depended upon the resolution of those states whose citizens they were or upon the question of whether the injured was in a position to obtain jurisdiction over their persons.

4. On the question of the construction of Control Council Law No. 10, the Military Tribunal starts out consistently from the statement that totally apart from the substantive scope of validity of common rules of international law, their enforceability in facts prescribed by the Control Council Law was limited. In regard to these facts it distinguishes between war crimes strictly speaking, which have been known in international law for a long time (they are committed by violating the rules of war against members of foreign states), and the more general crimes against humanity. These, it is true, could be in ideal concurrence with the war crimes, but existed also generally independent of violations of the rules and customs of war when interests of the civilian population—including the country's own population—guaranteed by international law were violated. And the bounds of individual crimes irrelevant in the meaning of international law and the Control Law are indeed to be regarded as transgressed when crimes against any civilian population as such are in question—crimes and inhuman acts as well as persecutions on a political, racial, or religious basis, which are either organized systematically or carried out by the government, or approved by it.

The legal development of international law is demonstrated by the Tribunal at another place in detail with historical examples and quotations from Hyde and other authors, in order to show that the fact of a growing world-wide mutual inter-relationship and the moral pressure of public opinion had brought about the knowledge that certain crimes against humanity which were committed by the Nazi authorities against Germans constituted transgressions not only of laws but also of common international law. As the most important illustration of such a crime against humanity was mentioned international murder, which recently was expressly denoted as an international crime by a resolution of the General Assembly of the United Nations.

5. In respect to the objection *nullum crimen sine lege*, raised also in the trial before the International Military Tribunal, the Judgment explains that international law is not a static statute, but—like common law—a constantly integrating customary law, the development of which would be made completely impossible from the beginning by a recognition of such an *ex post facto* prohibition. On the other hand, most of the acts the defendants are charged with were punishable also under German law, and even though the Tribunal could not apply German law, the defendants would nevertheless have to admit in reason that the evidence of their culpability under German law should also be considered in the determination of the question of guilt in the context of international penal law. In addition, the violations of international law by the defendants were preceded by several warnings that individual persons would be punished for crimes against international law, e.g., by the declaration of the Committee for the Establishment of the Responsibility of the Authors of Wars at the Conference in Paris in 1919, from which they should have known that they made themselves guilty of participation in a state-organized system of injustice and persecution and that they would be punished in case of their arrest.

6. In the next paragraph the Tribunal first considers an argument of the defendants that they could not be convicted because they had acted within the framework and on account of German laws and decrees. Against this objection the Tri-

bunal refers to the contrary decree of the Control Council Law
No. 10, Article II 1 c. It then states:

It is true . . . that German courts under the Third Reich were required to follow German law (i.e., the expressed will of Hitler) even
when it was contrary to international law. But no such limitation can
be applied to this Tribunal. . . . The very essence of the prosecution
case is that the laws, the Hitlerian decrees and the Draconic, cor-
rupt, and perverted Nazi judicial system themselves constituted the
substance of war crimes and crimes against humanity and that participation in the enactment and enforcement of them amounts to
complicity in crime. We have pointed out that governmental participation is a material element of the crime against humanity. Only
when official organs of sovereignty participated in atrocities and persecutions did those crimes assume international proportions. It can
scarcely be said that governmental participation, the proof of which
is necessary for conviction, can also be a defense to the charge.

Starting out from the remark that the Germans had developed under the Weimar Republic a civilized and enlightened system of law, at least on paper, the Tribunal gives a
thorough representation, then, of the legislation in the Third
Reich which it characterizes as a progressive degeneration of
the legal system which was transformed into a means of spread-
ing the national socialist ideology, of exterminating any existing
opposition against it, and of furthering plans for a war of aggression and of world conquest.

After the severe but still generally current national socialist
laws which gave the judges full scope for applying the severest
sentences, the Tribunal specifies as a second category that law
which discriminated expressly against minorities outside as
well as inside the Reich as a basis for racial, religious, and
political persecution. It stresses the extension of German penal
law to non-German occupied areas and enters into the development of the adjective law, the creation of Special Courts, SS
and Police Courts, the People's Tribunal, and Summary Courts,
as well as finally the centralization of the laws of pardon
and annulment under Hitler and his delegates.

7. In the next chapter the Tribunal comes to the conclusion

that in view of the dependence of the administration of justice upon interferences by Hitler, the Party and its organizations, and above all the police, and in view of the many measures which were taken apt to exercise pressure on the judges—as for instance the *Richterbriefe* (judicial letters)—judicial independence and impartiality had been totally destroyed, so that the claim of the defendants for judicial immunity in the meaning of Anglo-American legal doctrine could not be justified.

After a thorough consideration and evaluation of the major national socialist penal laws, the Tribunal distinguishes two different categories among them, of which it regards the first one—consisting of the penal laws concerning habitual criminals, plunderers, enemies of the people, criminals against the war economy, defeatists—as still compatible with the laws of humanity in view of the peculiar circumstances of the war. Nor could one see an incriminating fact in these martial laws and their application solely for their connection with a criminal war of aggression, since not every act which was legal in a defensive war became illegal *eo ipso* in a criminal war of aggression. The Tribunal arrives at another conclusion in relation to the second group of national socialist penal laws, i.e., those concerning high treason, those concerning the Poles and Jews, and the "Night and Fog Program."

The Tribunal sees a war crime and a crime against humanity in the extension of the concept of high treason to acts of aliens which, in the opinion of the Tribunal, were lawful in international law (as, for instance, the flight of Poles from the territory of the Reich for the purpose of joining the Polish legion).

8. Before the discussion of the "Night and Fog" program, the criminal organization is considered rather briefly and generally. The Tribunal confines itself almost exclusively to quotations from the Judgment of the International Military Tribunal, among other things that passage in which the criminal organization is compared with a criminal conspiracy "in that the essence of both is cooperation for criminal purposes," with-

out entering into the consequences inferred from this by the defense.

The most space (pp. 105-49) in the Judgment is taken by the factual and legal interpretation of the "Night and Fog" program, according to which "civilians of occupied countries accused of alleged crimes in resistance activities against German occupying forces were spirited away for secret trial by special courts of the Ministry of Justice within the Reich"; while "the victim's whereabouts, trial, and subsequent disposition were kept completely secret, thus serving the dual purpose of terrorizing the victim's relatives and associates and barring recourse to evidence, witnesses, or counsel for defense"; and while, furthermore, "if the accused was acquitted, or if convicted, after serving his sentence, he was handed over to the Gestapo for 'protective custody' for the duration of the war." The Tribunal describes the origin and development of proceedings in the *Reichsjustizministerium* (Ministry of Justice of the Reich) and the practical handling by the state attorneys, judges, and execution officials, and concludes as a result of its argumentation that the leading men of the Wehrmacht and of the Nazi Party, several Reich Ministers of Justice, and other high officers of justice, as well as the judges at the tribunals of the Nazi regime and the state attorneys at these tribunals, had taken part in Hitler's Night and Fog plan in various ways.

The Tribunal finds fault with the legal supposition of the fact that the offenses punished in the Night and Fog proceedings were many times not concerned at all with the security of the German Wehrmacht in the occupied areas, and that the handling of the proceedings could not be warranted by military necessity. The transportation of the delinquents to Germany constituted a deportation of the civilian population of occupied countries which was forbidden by international law. Another violation of obligatory principles of international law and the law of war was to be seen in the secrecy of the proceedings and the modifications of a normal trial resulting from this. Especially, the object of special proceedings to have a deterring effect was terrorism against the whole civilian population of the occupied areas. The Tribunal regards the delivering up of acquitted persons and of those who had served their sentences to the Gestapo for the purpose of taking such prisoners into preventive custody and concentration camps, the use of such prisoners in the armament industry, and the final handing over of all "Night and Fog" convicts by the judicature to the Gestapo as particularly incriminating. It refers for the establishment of the contrariety to international law among other things to the reports of the Conference of Paris of 1919, which were considered in the Treaty of Versailles.

9. When examining the culpability of the defendants for racial persecution as a war crime and a crime against humanity, the Tribunal starts out from two factual requirements: first, the fact of the great pattern or plan of racial persecution and extermination; and second, specific conduct of the individual defendant in furtherance of this plan. Examining the first condition, the Judgment investigates national socialist racial legislation in detail as well as the practice of its application and compares it with the programmatic declarations which Hitler and other prominent persons of the Party and the state proclaimed in this field. It discusses thoroughly the history of the origin of the penal decrees for Poles and Jews. It concerns itself with the "Judenpogrom" of November 9, 1938, and the final cession of the Poles and Jews from the jurisdiction of the Ministry of Justice to the police by Minister Thierack. In relation to the second characteristic of the case the Tribunal arrives at this conclusion: "While the part played by the Ministry of Justice in the extermination of Poles and Jews was small compared to the mass extermination of millions by the SS and Gestapo in concentration camps, nevertheless the courts contributed greatly to the 'final solution' of the problem." In this connection the question of the defendants' knowledge of the cruelties which were committed by the Gestapo in the concentration camps is discussed. The Tribunal concludes from

the testimony of witness Behl that he thought it impossible that "anyone, particularly in Berlin, should have been ignorant of the brutalities of the SS and the Gestapo," and from the assertion of the defendants that they had endeavored to resist Himmler's evil encroachments into the field of the administration of justice, that they had known the true character of the forces against which they had shown resistance. It infers further:

Thousands of soldiers and members of the Gestapo and SS must have been instrumental in the processes of deportation, torture, and extermination. . . . The thousands of Germans who took part in the atrocities must have returned from time to time to their homes in the Reich. The atrocities were of a magnitude unprecedented in the history of the world. Are we to believe that no whisper reached the ears of the public or of those officials who were most concerned? . . . One man can keep a secret, two men may, but thousands, never.

The Judgment then concludes:

The evidence conclusively establishes the adoption and application of systematic government-organized and approved procedures amounting to atrocities and offenses of the kind made punishable by C. C. Law 10 and committed against "populations" and amounting to persecution on racial grounds. These procedures when carried out in occupied territory constituted war crimes and crimes against humanity. When enforced in the Alt Reich against German nationals they constituted crimes against humanity.

Nuremberg Problems

DR. CARL HAENSEL

THE procedure of the Nuremberg trial of the major war criminals is regulated by the Charter of the International Military Tribunal of August 8, 1945. Justice Jackson, who is one of the judges of the United States Supreme Court and who had been appointed by the President of the United States as Chief of Counsel of the American prosecution in Nuremberg, made a fine contribution to the accomplishment of the Charter, which has its origin in a suggestion by President Roosevelt. In his brief statement following the publication of the Charter in the Department of State Bulletin of August 12, 1943, he denoted as the most significant purport of the Charter, now for the first time realized, the resolution of the victorious nations to make individual responsibility for an attack on the peace of the world a law, and to punish this attack consisting of the preparation and initiation of aggressive war as an individual crime. The "principle of individual responsibility for the crime of attacking the international peace" is the soul of the Charter. It protects the international order and punishes the offender against this legal asset as a high traitor to mankind.

First published in Deutsche Rechts-Zeitschrift, *1st year (1946), Vol. 3, p. 67. Translated by Dr. Georg Grimm.*

Dr. Carl Haensel is a professor of jurisprudence, formerly attorney at law at Freiburg and defense counsel at Nuremberg.

It is worth while to indicate at least the problems which this bold and resolute charter not only considered but also solved. But for this purpose we would need considerably more space than we have at our disposal. Nor would a mere enumeration of these problems with a poor indication of the literature give us a satisfactory conception of the method of procedure used by the Nuremberg Tribunal. We can obtain this conception much more easily if we select one of the questions of doubt which emerged during the proceedings and try to give a lively impression of the facts through this example.

Since the beginning of the trial in November of last year, twenty-one defendants have been under indictment, the first one of them being Hermann Göring. But Article 9 of the Charter states: "At the trial of any individual member of any group or organization the Tribunal may declare . . . that the group or organization of which the individual was a member was a criminal organization."

The indictment read by Justice Jackson at the beginning of the Nuremberg trial charged the defendants with crimes against the peace, crimes against the law of war, and crimes against humanity, and that in the execution of a common plan within the meaning of the Charter. Further, it demanded that the *Reichsregierung* (Cabinet), the Leadership Corps of the Nazi Party, the SS, the SA, the SD (Security Police), the Gestapo, the General Staff, and the Supreme Command of the Wehrmacht, all of them being groups that were meanwhile dissolved, "be declared criminal"—"criminal" in the language of the text read by Justice Jackson—in connection with the punishment of the individual defendants.

Under the laws of all civilized states punishment has hitherto been directed as a rule against natural persons. Under some rules of penal law a majority of persons became relevant to criminal law—for instance, in the complicity, the plot, the gang, the conspiracy; but then the criminal proceedings were also administered against the individual persons, the rubric enumerating their names. In objective proceedings, and under the penal tax laws also, the property of juristic persons could be confiscated; but in these cases it is "liable" only for delicts which are established against physical persons. The Anglo-Saxon common law and the new draft recommended by the Latin-American Congress of Criminology in 1938 of the Chilean criminal code of 1907, article 59, knows also the punishment of corporations, but only with sentences directed against the property, i.e., confiscation of the means with the help of which the crimes were committed or aspired; it does not declare the corporation to be "criminal." But the latter possibility can be found in the Charter, which, I presume, may be interpreted only in its own terms.

Involuntarily one remembers the Treaty of Versailles and recollects that Part VII, Article 227 ff. of the treaty indicated only the former Emperor and other individual persons.

Many times, certainly, "criminal" organizations have been mentioned in many penal judgments; but always only within the arguments, while the individual persons were specified in the rubric. The Prussian penal law of 1851 knew, for instance, as a penal fact the "armed rod"; the Prussian provision was transferred as paragraph 127 into the German penal code. The establishment of the criminal character of a convicted gang did not become formal legal force. The inner facts had to be established in respect to every individual convict; the intention of each of the members of the gang had to be directed to the common accomplishment of the group delict.

In the Nuremberg trial, shall the guilt be established correspondingly against every individual defendant? Shall a number of persons be convicted without such proceedings? What are otherwise the suppositions and above all the consequences for the individual former member, if the whole organization be declared criminal!

Article 10 of the Charter states:

In cases where a group or organization is declared criminal by the Tribunal, the competent national authority of any Signatory shall have the right to bring individuals to trial for membership therein before national, military, or occupation courts. In any such case the criminal nature of the group or organization is considered proved and shall not be questioned.

During the Nuremberg trial Control Council Law No. 10 was signed in Berlin on December 20, 1945. This was to furnish a basis for the prosecution of war criminals outside the Nuremberg trial. Besides the three crimes named in the Charter for Nuremberg (crimes against the peace and preparation for war of aggression, war crimes strictly speaking, and crimes against humanity), it made punishable as a fourth fact the "membership in categories of a criminal group or organization declared criminal by the International Military Tribunal." The French wording is as follows: "Le fait d'être membre d'un groupe criminel ou d'une organisation ou catégorie déclarées criminelles par le Tribunal Militaire International."

Does this mean that the declaration of the Nuremberg Tribunal, that this and that "organization is criminal," creates only the supposition for the proceedings on the basis of which the local military tribunals can now proceed against the former members in completely independent proceedings, in which the defendants have full freedom of defense, also from the aspects of subjective guilt—i.e., that they may, for instance, raise the objection that at that time they had not been aware of the criminal character of the organization they joined? Or are the former members of the organizations deprived of this objection; has the guilt already been established in Nuremberg with the provision that the local courts had only to examine whether the defendant had been a member of one of the defamed organizations, whether his joining appeared perhaps to be void after all for want of will, as compulsion, while all other arguments besides those which prove from the beginning his nonmembership can influence the degree of the sentence within the extremely broad framework of sentences of Control Council Law No. 10 which extends from death penalty to fine?

The tremendous practical importance of this problem is

obvious. The theoretical consideration taking the second standpoint would have to view in the Nuremberg Judgment the
penal conviction of a limited number of persons which is only
determined by the fact of membership in an organization. The
violation of the penal norm would lie in this "plot" alone. Later
proceedings would merely fix the sentence already incurred.
But if we see in the declaration of the Nuremberg Tribunal
that an organization was "criminal" only the declaratory antici-
pation of a statement which would lead to the criminal conviction of the individual member only through later trial on
the basis of Control Council Law No. 10 in connection with
the affirmation of the subjective question of guilt, then the
Nuremberg Judgment, as far as it concerns itself with the organizations, would merely be some kind of incident-establishment as we know it in the civil proceedings in paragraphs 304
and 280 of the law of procedure in civil proceedings (ZPO).
In the local trials under Control Council Law No. 10 only the
criminal nature of the group or organization "is considered
proved and shall not be questioned" (Article 10 of the Charter
of the International Military Tribunal).

Whether we take the, let us say, "plot theory" or the "incident-establishment theory" is of importance in the Nuremberg
trial to the question of whether the member of an organization
is a defendant with the title to legal hearing, and whether it is
of importance for the evidence in Nuremberg that he was not
aware of the criminal nature of the organization which has
been proved in the trial, or that he became aware of it only
after he was prevented by force, that is by force relevant in
penal law, from leaving the organization.

The Tribunal repeatedly gave both the prosecution and the
defense opportunities to discuss these aspects and to arrange
the hearings in evidence accordingly. These discussions took
place particularly on December 14 and from February 28 to
March 2, 1946. Without predecision of the question whether
the Charter had to be interpreted under consideration of
Anglo-American or of continental or even of German law or

only from out itself when applied to German defendants within Germany—one of the many problems of international law mentioned at the beginning—the judgment of the former *Reichsgericht* (Supreme Court of Germany) in regard to the Security Law of the Republic was referred to. The judgment in Volume 58 on the inner facts of paragraph 7 (RGSt 58, p. 401) read as follows: "He who in cognizance of the particular facts participates, supports, or joins, makes himself culpable, may he approve or not approve of the objectives, efforts, tasks, or even only of the ways and means of the conspiracy." In support of the plot theory is, above all, the fact that the declaration of an organization to be "criminal" by the highest court established by the victorious states, and provided with all the esteem, represented already a condemnation of the members, and therefore was already a punishment. This stain would remain, even if the individual victorious states did not call all the members in their occupation zones to account under penal law before their courts, as the prosecution deemed possible. The condemnation of the group would even then constitute a conviction though no penalty of imprisonment or any other punishment of the individual member was connected with it according to the tenor of the judgment. Therefore the Nuremberg Tribunal was asked for an authentic interpretation in the Judgment by those who are more inclined to follow the incident-establishment theory.

The Tribunal determined by an order that the former members of the organizations be granted legal hearings. The official defense counsels appointed for their defense were then given opportunity to interrogate the automatically arrested members in their camps, and to summon those in Nuremberg who were able to submit important evidence. In this order of March 13, 1946, it is further stated what the Tribunal considers important in evidence. There are three counts:

1. Whether the accused organization or group consisted in particular of an aggregation of persons whose objective it was to put a common plan into practice which has been denounced

in the Charter as a crime; and in this connection, what the plans, the tasks, the activities, the methods, the structure, and the individual forces of the organization were.

2. Whether the membership in the organization or group was in principle voluntary, or whether it was the result of physical compulsion or legal orders.

3. Whether the purposes or activities of the organization or group, which are denounced in the Charter as a crime, were openly notorious or otherwise generally known to the members so that it must justifiedly be assumed that the members must have been aware of them at any particular time.

The Tribunal then states that the ignorance of one individual member of eventual criminal objectives was unimportant and that it did not want to prejudge with this decree. The decree and its execution in the hearing of evidence, meanwhile concluded, nevertheless seem to indicate that the Tribunal is inclined to follow the "plot theory." The Judgment to be expected in a few days will make this conclusively clear. The discussed points of view will perhaps contribute to the understanding of its importance.

At any rate, it is apparent again that the theory is not "obscure," but that it is the intellectual tool to illuminate, order, and organize a tremendous volume of facts. From the theories we derive the arguments which influence and help to support the final decision. The argument is only the servant of the law; and what is just is in the end decided not by logic but by conscience. General MacArthur said when the Japanese surrender was signed: "If we do not erect a better and greater system, death will be waiting in front of the door. The problem is after all a theological one."

Review

KARL S. BADER

THE Nuremberg trial, after more than ten months of almost uninterrupted proceedings, led to the conviction of eighteen of the twenty-one personally accused and to the declaring of the Leadership Corps of the Nazi Party, the SS, the SD, and the Gestapo to be criminal organizations—with certain restrictions. Three of the defendants were acquitted, and the criminal character of other national socialist organizations was denied against the demands of the prosecutors. With the greatest interest of the whole world the last, the decisive, scene of the great drama was unrolled. The relaxation of interest which had been taking place from time to time and the distance—only too frequently observed, particularly in Germany—kept by broad circles of the population, and also by the lawyers, gave way to an exciting attention toward the end. The breathless quiet of the last hours before the proclamation of the Judgment was soon followed, again also in our country, by loud, sometimes much too loud criticism. A journal which intends to serve the

First published in Deutsche Rechts-Zeitschrift, *1st year, No. 5, November, 1946, p. 140. Translated by Dr. Georg Grimm.*

Karl S. Bader is editor of the Deutsche Rechts-Zeitschrift, *in Tübingen, and professor of jurisprudence at the University of Mainz, specializing in history of German jurisprudence and law, and penal law; he was formerly professor of law at Freiburg and state attorney-general at the Freiburg Oberlandesgericht.*

law and which is as serious about this law as it is about the supreme principle of all academic observation, about the truth, is not called upon to follow this criticism in an open or concealed manner. We lawyers know (or ought to know) that the imperfection of men stands above every judgment men pronounce and that no judgment in this world can be right to everybody. Our present considerations will therefore not serve the criticism of a Judgment the consequences of which we shall recognize fully perhaps only after many years; but they will serve criticism at the point where on the occasion of this Judgment insufficiencies of our own legal thinking, for years so dreadfully endangered, became evident. One of the major effects of this Judgment will be that it gives the defeated an opportunity to review its own way once more and to adjust its thinking, above all its legal thinking, to strict standards.

The Tribunal in Nuremberg sifted in 403 public hearings material which was in fact overwhelming in its extent and purport. The German lawyers are not fond of long and "monstrous" proceedings. The German people meets judicial proceedings which are protracted unreasonably with more skepticism than ever. The truly German saying of "to make short work of" has scarcely ever in our history been used as often as it was in the months which were necessary for the Nuremberg trials. It is necessary to linger here for a moment and to ask ourselves about what stands behind the demand for "short work." Two wars with thousands and thousands of court-martial judgments, with other thousands of Summary Courts, evil times of Special Courts, years of arbitrary acts of all kinds have passed us. Everywhere and at every time "short work" was made. When, as after June 30, 1934, a farce of justification afterward gave the rudest injustice the appearance of justice, or when Himmler's SS shot the so-called "criminals," political and criminal prisoners without distinction, one after the other "on flight"— there also "short work" was made. It is a critical symptom which we thus recognize. A sign of false self-calming which does not want to know much about uncomfortable things. A symptom of the decay of the profound sense of justice which regards the *forma processus* as a necessary corrective of passion and which sees in thoroughness, that is to say in circumstantiality, the supposition of true legal knowledge. To all those who assert loudly or quietly that one had better "make short work of" the Nazi leaders, we might recommend that they think this over again later. If they are honest they will encounter motives which will frighten them about themselves.

Certainly the trial lasted a long time; with the short memory peculiar to us, we nearly forgot the premises. It is likewise certain that strictness in the procedure of the trial was also necessary for thoroughness. But do not let us forget something of which perhaps only the historian will have a final understanding: that here, besides the sifting and evaluating, a securing of material took place which is hardly less important for our future recovery than the quick perception of the objectionableness of a system which has been removed. Nobody who considers the years 1933 to 1945 will in future times be able to pass by this material, which is tremendous in its extent and tremendous in its value for the perception of the errors of men. When the Tribunal decided to make all the material of the trial accessible to the world, and above all again to the German people, we do not want to and must not put this off with a disdainful gesture as "counterpropaganda." We, every one of us who claims to face the time fully, must occupy ourselves with this material. Not only, as many of us lawyers are accustomed to do, with the legal foundations on which the Charter of the Tribunal was based, with the principle *nulla poena sine lege*, which is now suddenly on the tongues of so many and all those who until April 1945 firmly despised it; not only with the acts of the others whom we should like to see convicted as accessory. We must occupy ourselves with just this historical material which we have to cut out of our own bodies if we want to think of recovery.

The accompaniment which followed the conclusion of the trial also made the lawyer critical: the lack of inner readiness to recognize the Judgment as an obligation. While the sentences were taken as a matter of course (anyone who was perhaps of another opinion felt for near-by reasons a cause for silence), the acquittals of individual defendants caused many to come forth who perhaps would have done better to remain silent. Nobody should be prevented from having his own political opinion. Nor are we Germans debarred from following world comment. But we do not wish just now to be the loudest ones. Our opinion should above all not violate that indestructible thing which we are called upon to protect: justice. When the reapprehension of the acquitted and their condemnation by a German "special tribunal" was demanded with wilful hastiness, we remembered, slightly ashamed, a not too far distant time at which the bailiff of the Gestapo waited at the prison gate which was opened to the acquitted or released prisoner of the Third Reich, in order to take the released into secure custody. The acquitting judgment of the Nuremberg Tribunal did not constitute a testimonial of complete innocence for the acquitted. That they were top-ranking activists of the Third Reich they will not be able to refute. This may and must find its expression in eventual denazification proceedings. But the acquittal which the Court Marshal executed on behalf of the Tribunal must be respected. That it was respected only when an order of the Occupation Authorities demanded it must make us think once again. "Hitler in us" is not yet dead as long as we are not willing to have an ear for justice. What high respect, on the contrary, our neighboring people showed when, in the Trial of the *Gauleiter* (regional leader) and *Reichsstatthalter* (governor) Robert Wagner, the tormentor of the Alsatians, they quietly left to those who were acquitted before the French Tribunal—German judges and public prosecutors who had pronounced and executed death sentences against Alsatians—the freedom adjudged to them by the Tribunal and released them to their homes in Germany!

A further sign of legal chaos made itself heard too loudly in those days: the lack of understanding of the duties of the defense. The German lawyer who had been forbidden on penalty of loss of his office and life to defend Jews, politically disreputable persons, and "troublesome foreigners" is free today. In the choice of the matter for which he may and should stand up he is bound only by his own conscience. I do not believe that any one of the Defense Counsel of the Nuremberg defendants was eager to take over the defense. Should he be prevented from answering in the affirmative the question of whether he is permitted to do it? The Nuremberg Defense Counsel served justice in their way. We do not have to decide here whether they did this with skill, with courage, or with extravagance. No doubt, considerable results have been achieved. There may have occurred offenses against duties of rank. But this violation of obligations of rank must not be seen in the acceptance of the defense of politically incriminated persons as such. *Audiatur et altera pars.* To call special attention to this legal right is the duty of the defense. At this time there was a note in the German press that the Cologne Board of Attorneys had decided to examine the behavior of the defense counsel in Nuremberg. We do not know what caused this decision, if it was really taken. Let us not believe that it was the defense of defendants as such. Or shall the defense counsel in trials with political backgrounds be a timid, humble echo of the prosecutor? But what an insight into the German mentality of our torn present we are afforded by the note, also published in the German press, that Lord Justice Lawrence found himself urged to protect the German defense counsel against offenses by Germans! "In the opinion of the Tribunal, Defense Counsel have performed an important public duty in accordance with the high traditions of the legal profession";[1] this statement of the Lord Justice must be put before all of us Germans, that may we recognize the functions of law again completely and that we may also destroy—in our appreciation of the achievements of the opponents in a case—the base "Hitler in us."

From the Nuremberg trial other trials will follow—proceedings against economic leaders of the Third Reich and others, and also proceedings before German courts. Control Council Law No. 10 created factual situations which place new tasks in the hands of the German judges. The crimes against humanity standardized therein will more and more engage German courts. From the Russian Occupation Zone various judgments founded on this legal basis have become known, and from the French Zone the first judgments of this kind have also been reported. From an utterance of the State Attorney General in Brunswick we learn that in the British Zone also, German courts are now to be entrusted with the punishment of these crimes. We know that among German lawyers there exist many objections; they will be discussed in this journal on another occasion. Today let us simply point out one thing: the much too loud emphasis upon the above quoted legal principle of *nulla poena sine lege* suits us very badly in this connection. Apart from the fact that Control Council Law No. 10 breaks this principle, restored in Law No. 1 by the same legislator with complete clearness and with stressed intention, we must tell ourselves: he who denied the importance of inhibited retrospectiveness can now appeal the least to it. We find this opinion represented also in other places, outside our ranks, by earnest men. Thus, Alfred Weber says in his treatise, *Freier Socialismus* (Liberal Socialism), in much farther reaching meaning:

Since in our present formation of life the practical alternative to democracy . . . is only the authoritarian regime with terror-dictatorship, the politic fundamental rights must remain suspended first of all for all those who took active part in the Nazistic or Fascistic terror-regime and therefore broke these rights.[2]

This is a slashing word and in principle not without danger. But when we call a Nazi activist to account on a clear legal basis, such as we receive from Law No. 10 which is binding for us, for an act prior to this law, we must not forget that it was this defendant who agreed to a system of complete defamation of numerous maxims of law and justice, including the principle of *nulla poena sine lege*. We do not wish to punish injustice with new injustice, but we may very well remind ourselves of an old German legal proverb which has seldom had a more timely significance than in our days: "He who enjoys the good things, also shall enjoy the bad things!"

The Judgments in the Nuremberg Trials of Economists

DR. HELLMUTH DIX

THE proceedings before the American Military Tribunals in Nuremberg were concluded with the judgment in the so-called Ministries Case in April, 1949. Almost all the judgments have already been examined and confirmed by the Military Governor and therefore have legal force.[1] To these judgments belong also those of the three trials of economists, against leading personalities of the Flick group, of I. G. Farben, and of Krupp. These proceedings were of fundamental importance to the whole German economy and granted an interesting insight into its hitherto existing structure and capacity. The four major counts of the indictment were in accordance with Control Council Law No. 10, Article II, 1: (1) crimes against the peace through wars of aggression, invasions of other countries and a conspiracy directed toward these; (2) war crimes and crimes against humanity, above all through the national socialist alien slave labor program; (3) the same crimes because of the looting of occupied areas; (4) membership in criminal organizations.[2]

First published in Neue Juristische Wochenschrift, *XVII (1 September 1949), 647-52. Translated by Dr. Georg Grimm.*
Dr. Dix is an attorney at law in Frankfurt-am-Main.

1. In the bill of indictment and in the material in evidence of the prosecution in the I. G. Farben Case—Case 6 of these proceedings—the indictment of crimes against the peace occupied the most space.[3] The Tribunal declared, under the presidency of Judge C. G. Shake—despite Control Council Law No. 9 on the confiscation of the I. G. Farben because of wilful participation in the completion of the German war potency[4]— that all the defendants were not guilty.[5] The Tribunal bases its decision in this matter, above all, on the Judgment of the International Military Tribunal in the first Nuremberg trial, since the acts of international law authoritative for it form the legal basis for all Nuremberg judgments.[6] The International Military Tribunal, however, required for this crime of a war of aggression and of conspiracy *wilful* participation in a *concrete* political plan and therefore acquitted numerous defendants in this respect because they had not stood in any demonstrable relation to Hitler's real plans of aggression. The I. G. Farben Judgment also takes this standpoint. It does not follow the opinion of the prosecution that there existed a common knowledge of Hitler's aggressive intentions in Germany, and in this regard remarks in particular:

The statesmen of other nations, conceding Hitler's successes by the agreements they made with him, affirmed their belief in his word. Can we say the common man of Germany believed less?[7]

As to the defendants' personal knowledge,[8] this decision too— in spite of the supposition of guilt to be gathered from Article II, 2 of Control Council Law No. 10 for leading men in politics, Wehrmacht, and economy—kept, in accordance with the practice of the Nuremberg courts, expressly to the principle of Anglo-American law in particular, that personal guilt must be proved. As for the rearmament, which according to the International Military Tribunal was not punishable as such, the I. G. Farben Judgment arrives at the conclusion that due to the relativity of its effectiveness to the armed strength of other nations and the strict secrecy of its total extent even from men in high positions, it did not, contrary to the assumption of the prosecution, afford reliable knowledge of Hitler's plans of aggression. To the benefit of the defendants the Tribunal considered that the essential materials produced on a large scale, especially by the I. G. Farben, e.g., nitrogen, buna, and gasoline, were necessary also for peacetime demand, and that according to the original documents the official construction and production plans for these products did not reach their ultimate goals, which in relation to those of other great powers were in no way immoderate, before the years 1942-43. Thus, the Judgment did not follow the prosecution insofar as the latter wanted to derive above all from the rearmament and the customary money contributions to Nazi organizations some sort of offensive alliance of Hitler with industry and particularly the I. G. Farben for the enslavement of other nations.

Since the counts of indictment of the joint planning of wars of aggression and of a conspiracy directed toward it are based on the same material of evidence, and according to the International Military Tribunal Judgment, are of equal nature, the Tribunal considered and decided the two together. The Tribunal in the I. G. Farben trial proceeded in the same way and therefore denied for all defendants any guilt for conspiracy against the peace.[9]

In regard to the reproach of "waging" a war of aggression after its outbreak the I. G. Farben Judgment arrived at the same conclusion.[10] It points to the fact that the fundamental Declaration of Moscow of October 30, 1943, proclaimed the punishment of German officers etc. only for "atrocities, mass-murder" and similar cruelties, but not for wars of aggression, and that in the proceedings before the International Military Tribunal only the generally responsible major war criminals were concerned. Since it rejected mass punishment, moreover, and even acquitted Speer and Saukel in this complex, the I. G. Farben Judgment sees no cause for extending the responsibility of individual persons in this respect beyond the number of leading personalities convicted by the International Military Tribunal. Above all it explains in this regard:[11]

It is, of course, unthinkable that the majority of Germans should be condemned as guilty of committing crimes against peace. This would amount to a determination of collective guilt to which the corollary of mass punishment is the logical result for which there is no precedent in international law and no justification in human relations.[12]

2. In all the trials against economists the defendants were furthermore charged with participation in the slave labor program of the Nazi regime as a war crime and a crime against humanity. This concerns the illegal employment and treatment of alien slave laborers, prisoners of war, and prisoners of concentration camps in Germany during the war, violating above all the Geneva Convention of 1907, especially Article 52 which confines the services of inhabitants of an occupied area to the necessities of the occupation forces and demands that the services be in proportion to the resources of the country and that they do not obligate the population to war measures against its own fatherland.

The Flick Judgment, supported by the decision of the International Military Tribunal rendered by the end of 1947 under the presidency of Judge Charles B. Sears, in principle affirmed the penal responsibility of private persons also according to international law,[13,14] basing itself on the decision of the International Military Tribunal. Under this it comprehends, like other Nuremberg judgments, the *principes generaux* not only of international law but also of penal law and adjective law which are expressed in the laws and customs of civilized states and in international agreements.[15] The Judgment acquitted the defendants in this complex insofar as they acted in a state of distress.[16] It observes that the slave labor program, i.e., the procuring of involuntary workers and the working and living conditions of these, had been organized in all details within the framework of the national socialist war economy by acts, decrees, etc. of the German authorities. Because of the want of German workers as a result of their conscription to the Wehrmacht, the defendants had to accommodate themselves in their fields of work to the official assignments of involuntary alien workmen if they did not want to make the fulfilment of their authoritative output duties impossible; any resistance and the endangering of the war-economy program connected with it would have had most severe consequences as sabotage. For this reason the Judgment referring to American literature[17] of penal law denied any penal responsibility on the part of most of the defendants because of a state of distress, although an order does not exclude the penal responsibility of the subordinate according to Article II 4 b of Control Council Law No. 10. It stresses the fact that the defendants took care that the alien workers were treated humanely, and that thus far they are free from guilt. Only two of the defendants were convicted because they had furthered of their own accord or tolerated the increase of car production and then employed Russian prisoners of war for this purpose. But in this respect the Judgment is not compatible with the prevailing doctrine which permits the employment of prisoners of war for the construction of cars, since the latter interprets strictly the prohibition of such employment and the concept of "war enterprises" according to Articles 6 and 52 of the Hague Convention[18] and "direct relation to acts of war" according to Article 31 of the Geneva Convention on the Treatment of Prisoners of war,[19] so that even the employment of prisoners of war at rear fortifications is recognized as permissible.[20]

Under the count of indictment of slave labor and other crimes against humanity the I. G. Farben Judgment,[21] at the beginning, declared all of the defendants to be not guilty of the reproach many times treated by the prosecution before the press that they had known that both the deliveries of means of decomposition (Cyklon B) by the *Deutsche Gesellschaft zur Schädlingsbekämpfung* (DEGESCH), in which the I. G. Farben had shares, and those of pharmaceutical preparations by the I. G. Farben itself to concentration camps served for the extermination of men. Nor did the Tribunal object to the employment of prisoners of war by the I. G. Farben, for the reasons discussed above. In respect to the forced labor of aliens and prisoners of concentration camps, also, the Tribunal acquitted most of the defendants because of the state of distress with the remark that they had, as far as possible, striven for a treatment of those workers worthy of human beings. In this regard it referred to the reasons for the decision in the Flick Case and the statements of the IMT Judgment on the terror of the Nazi regime, and finally quoted from that Judgment the following passage:

That a soldier was ordered to kill or torture in violation of the international law of war has never been recognized as a defense to such acts of brutality, though, as the Charter here provides, the order may be urged in mitigation of the punishment. The true test, which is found in varying degrees in the criminal law of most nations, is not the existence of the order, but whether moral choice was in fact possible.[22]

In this is obviously included not only the aspect of distress in the meaning of common criminal law, but also the insoluble conflict which the normal citizen faces when the acts and decrees of his government, to which he owes obedience for moral reasons, especially in war, are not compatible with international law.[23] The solution of this conflict and the collision of duties resulting therefrom is the harder for him since, as the I. G. Farben Judgment justly observes in its consideration of the war of aggression,[24] he possesses only an inaccurate knowledge of actual conditions, and since, according to the Judgment of the International Military Tribunal,[25] the development of international law and its difficult problems continuously follows the necessities of a changing world. Although the Nuremberg Tribunals, for which the statements of the International Military Tribunal are binding to a great extent, treated the deportations for work in Germany as inadmissible,[26] the critical examination of these problems was very difficult for the normal citizen not only as a result of the theory of the primateship of

national law, in any case hitherto prevailing,[27] but also for
other reasons.[28] In this connection the defense in Nuremberg
always pointed, above all, to the fact that in view of aerial warfare, which was incompatible with Article 25 of the Hague Convention, and also in view of the modern blockade,[29] which was
still contended during World War I, and in view of the destruction of private individuals and of private property effected
thereby, the compulsory use of these could be or seem to be
admissible in accordance with the preamble of the Hague Convention as the lesser evil in the interest of military necessity in
more developed and total economic warfare.[29a]

The conviction of some defendants in the complex of slave
labor at the I. G. Farben was pronounced especially because
they were responsible for the employment of concentration
camp prisoners in the building and operation of a buna factory
near Auschwitz and for the grievances there,[30] although the
Judgment recognizes that the prisoners were subordinated
chiefly to the SS and that the I. G. Farben had not intended
inhumane treatment, but had even taken measures for the improvement of the situation. A state of distress was denied by
the Tribunal because the convicted had thus far taken the initiative, and especially because at the beginning of 1941 they
had chosen the building plot in cognizance of the circumstances
that concentration camp prisoners were to be employed there.
Disregarding the fact that preventive arrest was as such eventually not inadmissible, according to penal law, after the repeal
of the constitutional guarantees in 1933[31] and during war also
in international law,[32] and that the major actions of arresting
and of exterminating were carried out only later, the convicted, and also other industrialists, were convinced at that time
that they had improved the fate of the prisoners through the
work in their factories.[33] Besides this, under the pressure of most
urgent construction and production orders from state authorities the directors depended, here as in other enterprises, upon
all accessible manpower. Later efforts to obtain this manpower
were, as in other similar cases, not really self-initiated but only

apparently voluntary actions forced by the pressure of the war economy as this is recognized, for example, in the case of such behavior under the domination of a collective compulsion, even within the scope of the restitution law.[34] But as far as an industrialist later heard rumors of top secret extermination measures, it was the harder for him to refuse the employment of prisoners who could thus be saved from the cruel end; he, then, faced to a particular extent the impossibility of a moral choice.[35]

The Krupp Judgment, the severest among these three decisions both in the proportion of convictions to acquittals and in punishment,[36] convicted all but one of the defendants in the complex of forced labor. It also denied the objection of the state of distress to those who in detail had had nothing to do with the execution of this program, since—even because of their own initiative—the burden of proof[37] incumbent upon them under American law was not sufficient. The aspect of the impossibility of any moral choice is not considered in the Judgment. But it also doubts especially that, considering Krupp's powerful position, resistance against the slave labor program was accompanied by any considerable danger for the defendants, and in this connection points to the fact that this firm had successfully refused the interruption of pregnancies of women laborers from the East, had produced milk cans in spite of the prohibition of peacetime production, and had cleared off in secret considerable sums of the national loan in the last years of the war. These considerations actually do not take adequate account of the situation under the Nazi regime during the war; and in the other two trials against economists similar occurrences were not evaluated in this manner either. An enterprise like that of Krupp was of course able to press its own opinion through in some matters and eventually at times to evade certain regulations of minor importance, among which belong those of finance. During the shortage of other manpower the rejection of alien slave workers during the war by one of the largest German armament enterprises would have endangered its production, so urgently needed for the continuation of the war, and therefore would certainly have led to the ousting of the managers and additional severe measures against them; but it would have changed nothing in the further execution of the labor and production program.[38] The statements of the Judgment on the inadmissible employment and treatment of the various categories of slave laborers are of a serious kind. But in this connection the German government regulations, for instance on the proceedings against the refusal to work or the initial treatment of workers from the East, and the frightening effects of these are only very generally considered in this Judgment—perhaps because of the fundamental standpoint of the Tribunal on the problem of the state of distress—so that an adequate legal consideration beyond that which has already been stated is hardly possible.[38a] When the Judgment declares a Franco-German government agreement during the armistice on the employment of French prisoners of war in the German armament industry to be contrary to the will of the French people and against good customs, we must consider that hitherto in such cases compulsion from state to state was in principle admissible.[39]

3. Of the war crime of "spoliation," i. e., an offense against property violating especially Articles 46 ff. of the Hague Convention, only the one authoritative defendant in the group was convicted in one case in the Flick Trial.[40] The subordinate participation of others in this matter effected no conviction. The conviction was for a trust agreement of the Friedrich-Flick-KG with the commissioner of a factory which had been left by the French management and had subsequently been confiscated by the German authorities, its operation thereby being transferred to the Flick group. Although the factory was improved by the latter and not acquired as property, and although the Tribunal recognizes that the first confiscation could be justified on account of Article 43 of the Hague Convention in the interest of military necessity and of public order, it sees without any detailed argument a violation of the Hague Convention in the

withholding of the factory from the lawful owner.[41] The Tribunal regards similar agreements with German authorities on state-owned factories in the East as not punishable because they served only a utilization of state property which is admissible according to the Hague Convention. The Flick Judgment, in accordance with the decision of the International Military Tribunal,[42] declared itself incompetent for the prosecution of crimes against humanity on account of an acquisition of Jewish property in Germany mainly effected before the war.[43] But it further points to the fact that in a strict and correct interpretation of Control Council Law No. 10 Article II 1 c, according to high opinion—especially expressed in the Eighth International Conference for the Standardization of Criminal Law, Brussels, 1947—offenses against property do not fall under this concept of crimes against humanity.

The I. G. Farben Judgment[44] followed this opinion and disregarded the prewar occurrences dealt with by the prosecution under the section on spoliation by which the I. G. Farben acquired property in Austria and Czechoslovakia, since they were neither crimes against humanity nor war crimes in accordance with Control Council Law No. 10 and the Hague Convention, and therefore the Tribunal, according to Article 1 of the Seventh Ordinance of the Military Government, was not competent.[45] Yet, supported by the International Military Tribunal[46] and the Allied Declaration of January 5, 1943, on the unlawfulness of direct and indirect methods of spoliation in the occupied areas by Germany, and rejecting the objection of *nullum crimen sine lege*, the Judgment believes that not only direct appropriation but also a contractual or institutionally legal acquisition—e.g., within a joint-stock company—in occupied areas may be a war crime according to Control Council Law No. 10, Article II 1 b, and a punishable violation of property rights particularly according to Articles 46 ff. of the Hague Convention. On this point it states:

Where private individuals, including juristic persons, proceed to exploit the military occupancy by acquiring private property against the will and consent of the former owner, such action, not being expressly justified by any applicable provision of the Hague Regulations, is in violation of international law. The payment of a price or other adequate consideration does not, under such circumstances, relieve the act of its unlawful character. Similarly where a private individual or a juristic person becomes a party to unlawful confiscation of public or private property by planning and executing a well-defined design to acquire such property permanently, acquisition under such circumstances subsequent to the confiscation constitutes conduct in violation of the Hague Regulations.[47]

It emphasizes the fact that criminal responsibility attaches to a transaction only if it can be declared invalid in civil proceedings for being actually involuntary. The judgment adopts the denotation "spoliation" used by the prosecution for such acts of systematic expropriation or looting as a synonym for the hitherto customary expressions "plunder" and "pillage" of Control Council Law No. 10 and the Hague Convention. It rejects, however, on account of the Hague Convention the theory of the prosecution, represented supposedly also by the Krupp Judgment,[48] according to which injurious encroachments upon the economy of an occupied area, which in violation of Article 52 of the Hague Convention exceed its resources and the necessities of the occupation forces, constitute also a punishable spoliation even if admitted by the proprietors. Therefore it is of the opinion that truly voluntary legal property transactions between the inhabitants of an occupied area and citizens of the occupation power are admissible, since any other view would aggravate the maintenance of public order according to Article 43 of the Hague Convention. The Judgment observes in this respect:

The mere presence of the military occupant is not the exclusive indication of the assertion of pressure. Certainly where the action of private individuals, including juristic persons, is involved, the evidence must go further and must establish that a transaction, otherwise apparently legal in form, was not voluntarily entered into because of the employment of pressure. Furthermore, there must be a causal connection between the illegal means employed and the result brought about by employing such intimidation.[49]

Affirming the penal responsibility of private individuals for such offenses, the Tribunal rejects here an alteration of international law in consequence of the character of modern wars. The objection that these occurrences served the obligation and will of the occupation power to maintain the economy and thereby the public order in the meaning of Article 43 of the Hague Convention was rejected. Departing from the Flick and Krupp Judgments, this Tribunal expressed the opinion that it could be of importance, if only temporary measures, e.g., management during hostilities, were in question. Accordingly it desisted from a conviction in the case of the lease of an enterprise in Alsace, in spite of an eventually intended appropriation.[50]

The occurrences for which the I. G. Farben Judgment proved any guilt in this complex are divided into two groups. The one comprises contracts of sale by which the I. G. Farben acquired factories confiscated or expropriated in the course of German government measures from the commissioners appointed by German authorities and then operated them properly. The Judgment observes that these acts represented a violation of Articles 45 ff. of the Hague Convention and its regulations in regard to private property and the prohibition of its confiscation. Here, too, the limitation of the circle of persons responsible under penal law for these consequences of the German policy in the occupied areas may cause doubt at least for the past. The normal German citizen, even if he occupied an economically leading position, could scarcely judge, in the view of the foregoing statements of the I. G. Farben Judgment on the war of aggression,[50a] whether the proceedings of his government were admissible, for instance, on the strength of Article 43 of the Hague Convention or by reason of the cessation of the sovereignty of the occupied country by *debellatio*.[51] Thus, even leading officials of the former German occupation authorities

who carried out such measures were now not only exempted
from punishment but were also permitted to resume their pro-
fessions. In view of the uniformity of treatment of all offenses
recommended by the International Military Tribunal,[52] however, this is important also to industrialists who acquired from
these authorities estates[52a] of the possession of which the lawful
proprietors had already been deprived by authoritative confiscation or expropriation.

The second group of occurrences penally objected to as
spoliation in the I. G. Farben Judgment consists of transactions
in which the I. G. Farben did not face the commissioner of the
German occupation authorities but negotiated, under German
government programs for the requisition of the economy of the
occupied areas, directly with the firms of these areas on the
re-establishment or the increase of the capital of foreign companies with the participation of the I. G. Farben, while the
character and result of the negotiations were determined by
measures of those authorities.[53] The objection of adequate
returns by the I. G. Farben was declared to be legally incon-
siderable by the Tribunal. This standpoint of the Tribunal
exceeds both the concept of spoliation generally prevailing in
the Nuremberg trials and that of extortion prevailing not alone
in Germany, since there is no enrichment of the perpetrator.[53a]
The circumstance that the conclusion of a transaction is co-
determined by the pressure of state measures and of political
conditions and that the effects of these and the negotiations for
the conclusion—as frequently for large transactions—mutually
influence each other is therefore, in the meaning of the *principes généraux* of the civilized nations, not in itself sufficient for
the assumption of an extortion. But Control Council Law No.
10 is the foundation of the Nuremberg jurisdiction as a codification of common and already prevailing principles.[54] As to contracts on factories in unoccupied France, the I. G. Farben Judgment too declared, in accord with the foregoing explanations,
that any pressure of legal or economic kind was criminally

irrelevant and to this extent did not arrive at a conviction.[55] It indicates a particular limitation of private economic activity for the time and the area of a warlike occupation, which in this form does not find expression even in the earlier Nuremberg Judgments, when the Judgment represents expressly,[56] within the new concept of spoliation and on account of the Hague Convention, a more severe standpoint on occurrences in occupied areas. Judge Powers is moreover of the opinion that the German-French government agreements on armistice and co-operation had a priority over the principles of the Hague Convention on the *occupatio bellica* and that occurrences and transactions resulting from these special agreements could not be treated as war crimes in accordance with the Hague Convention and Control Council Law No. 10. This opinion, which is not shared, of course, by other Nuremberg Tribunals, shows how difficult the legal qualification of such transactions carried out with the co-operation of the Vichy government is.

The Krupp Judgment, in its broader apprehension of the concept of spoliation, also considers temporary lease-contracts with commissioners of confiscated factories in the occupied French areas as punishable violations of international law,[57] while the I. G. Farben Judgment, as already discussed above, arrives at another result in a similar case and recognizes in principle, under such circumstances, the possibility of a justification of temporary measures by the interest of public order according to Article 43 of the Hague Convention.[58] The convictions in the Krupp Trial in this complex are based, however, essentially on the removal of machines which was done on demand of the German authorities, particularly in Holland during the last phases of the war.[59] Although a Dutch court decision of April 1948 had not objected to such a removal of machines necessary for war in 1944 according to the Hague Convention, the Krupp Judgment in all cases recognized neither any military necessity nor even any state of distress of the convicted. For it sees in the co-operation of the Krupp firm and its employees in the selection and the removal of the machines a punishable initiative, while on the other hand it repeatedly emphasizes the impossibility of any resistance on the part of the Dutch companies whose property the machines were. But no more could the German businessman refuse his co-operation in these measures considered by his government to be necessary for the war in view of the destruction of German industry by air bombardments, and any active or passive resistance would have been regarded and treated by the military authorities as sabotage. Nor was co-operation of a similar kind in the execution of the forced labor program conceived as deliberate and punishable personal initiative in the other two trials of economists.

This different evaluation of the factual and legal evidences of this new state of distress in international law, so to speak, and of the impossibility of moral choice in these three Judgments gives cause for the question often discussed in Nuremberg, whethe.: another delimitation of the responsibility for the consequences and programs of a government policy violating international law is perhaps possible. The Anti-Slavery Agreement already mentioned above[60] establishes in Article 5, paragraph 3 the responsibility of the central authorities for the employment of slave labor. The Judgments in the I. G. Farben Case and in Case 12[61] confined the responsibility for crimes against the peace to the politically leading class. Judge Powers wants on principle to make only those responsible who are able to cause or prevent a measure. At the Eighth International Conference for the Standardization of Criminal Law in Brussels, 1947, it was suggested by the French delegation that the responsibility for crimes against humanity be limited according to international law to the "*gouvernants.*"[62] Although common criminal law knows a particular responsibility of the management of juristic persons, too, this suggestion was not followed. In the U.N., on the other hand, a right of resistance on the part of the normal citizen against the exercise of the supreme power in violation of international law, as a correlate to the duty of obeisance demanded now in international law, was not recognized.[63] The problems of a possible conflict between the two orders and the citizen's position of constraint and a collision of duties resulting from it, therefore, remain unsolved; this will be the case as long as and as far as the more general order is not in a position to protect him according to the ancient principle *protego, ergo obligo*—the foundation of any legal coercion. May we then avoid in international law, in view of the problem of the citizen's state of distress, limiting in the interest of justice and clarity the number of persons who are responsible for a state policy in violation of international law and the necessary consequences thereof? For otherwise there might be in the future an open door for a legislation of collective guilt and mass punishment for which there is "no justification in human relations."[64]

It is not possible here to enter into the various problems, already many times discussed,[65] which were the same for all the Nuremberg trials, and which, in view of the firmer jurisdiction in the trials of economists, were treated and decided only casually. But it may be said that the defense, which under Anglo-Saxon law was charged with the procurement of the total defense material, was, in comparison to the prosecution, often at a great disadvantage in preparing the proceedings in regard to time and because of general conditions. In particular, the necessary journeys to foreign countries for the procurement of defense material about earlier transactions mostly met with insurmountable difficulties in spite of support by the Tribunal. Also, the summoning of foreign witnesses was often impossible. But of great—and for the defense frequently very favorable—significance before the Tribunal were above all the far-reaching powers of the representatives of the prosecution and the defense in the interrogation of witnesses, which under Anglo-Saxon law rests almost totally in their hands. In these trials, in which the judges were confronted with personalities and conditions of a foreign country, the interrogation of the defendants as witnesses of the defense especially formed not only good professional training for the counsel but also a moral and intellectual probation and, for a judicious tribunal, an excellent means of exploring the truth. By these proceedings the myth of the complicity of German industry and its most significant representatives in the initiation of the war and its inhumanities has been destroyed, and thus the way has been cleared for its peaceful reconstruction.

The Nuremberg Judgments

DR. KURT BEHLING

THE answer to the question of international penal responsibility of individuals in the matter of war crimes and crimes against humanity is extremely delicate. To be sure, the War Crimes Tribunals emphasize again and again that their jurisdiction was founded upon "generally recognized principles" of international law; but anyone who carefully examines the hitherto existing international judicature, especially the Nuremberg Judgments, will realize how the courts have struggled with these "generally recognized principles" of international law. This is not too astounding, when the judgments as such in no way concur with each other on important points and thereby confirm the words of Edward Grey: "The law of nations has always been very flexible."[1] Indeed, there is considerable doubt about the question of whether there exist at all—especially in the sphere of international law—"generally recognized principles."

Certainly exaggerated is the assertion that of the "generally

---

First published in Juristische Rundschau, *XVI (November, 1949),* *502-5. Translated by Dr. Georg Grimm.*

Dr. Kurt Behling, an attorney at law in Berlin, is author of various other articles on Nuremberg and on the Judgment against General von Falkenhausen in Brussels.

recognized principles" of international law only the one was recognized, that nothing has been recognized. But there is still a little truth in this sentence. That the penal aspect of the problem has hitherto not been given particular attention as compared with the other disciplines has mainly been due to the fact that the results were limited and that individuals were either not affected or only indirectly so. By the creation of almost unlimited responsibilities under the international war crimes legislation this question has been brought very much into the foreground, not only of pure aspects of international law, but also of aspects of penal law.

Hitherto there has been agreement on the fact that for violations of international law only the responsible state was liable, and that persons acting as organs of the state were not acting for themselves, and therefore received in principle no rights and duties.[2] Even Hans Kelsen, the head of the so-called Viennese School, in spite of his monistic attitude, has not come to the conclusions laid down in the laws against war crimes. He rather explicitly advocates the standpoint that violations of international law by state organs were to be attributed to the state, but were not to be attributed to the acting organs.[3]

It means a change of incalculable importance when the laws against war crimes now demand the punishment of individuals. Above all, it is in contradiction to the famous passage in Rousseau's *Contrat Social* according to which war is not a relation between men but only between states, and therefore can justify only a liability of the state.

This, of course, does not mean that persons participating in war measures are free from any responsibility. They can act, of course, relevant to penal law and commit, for instance, facts of killing, injuring, theft, and robbery. But it is then a matter of national penal law to establish adequate principles in order to call the culprit to account. In cases of this kind, the same facts would constitute a violation of international law for which the state—and only the state—is liable, and at the same time a penal offense for which the individual is to be called to account under penal law as the offender according to the provisions of the law of his country. Therefore the right of the victorious nations to summon German nationals, especially after the conclusion of hostilities, before foreign tribunals and to try them according to foreign laws is still repeatedly contended, even today. In accordance with this theory only the German courts, which have to base their jurisdiction exclusively on German law,[4] are declared competent for judgment.

After the conclusion of World War I attempts were already being made to create, for certain delicts, a general basis of international penal law. No notable resolutions were reached, however.[5]

In this point the practices of the Nuremberg and other war crimes tribunals deviated, as in other points, from hitherto current rules of international law. As early as the IMT Judgment the responsibility of individuals for violations of international law was confirmed.[6] In one of the later judgments — that in the Flick Case — the Tribunal drew up the following sentences:

International law, as such, binds every citizen just as does ordinary municipal law. Acts adjudged criminal when done by an officer of the government are criminal also when done by a private individual. The guilt differs only in magnitude, not in quality. The offender in either case is charged with personal wrong and punishment falls on the offender in *propria persona*.[7]

These statements are then found equally or similarly formulated in all the other Nuremberg and other foreign war crimes judgments—which is not so surprising, since to deny this question would mean to saw off the branch upon which the tribunals rest.

If, in spite of lasting scruples, an immediate international penal responsibility of the individual be assumed, most particular care will have to be exercised in a penal judgment of the individual's conduct. It should be a matter of course that any punishment may be executed only when individual guilt has been established and insofar as a considerable chain of causation between the act declared to be a crime and the conduct of the culprit has been proved. This is also true, in principle, in regard to crimes of organizations, although for the latter different measures must be applied.[8]

In the practice of the War Crimes Tribunals these suppositions have unfortunately not always been fulfilled. To a great extent, this is due to the dispersion of the legal foundations and jurisdictions and also to the many times unsatisfactory (historical) ascertainment of the facts.

1. The one codification best known in Germany is Control Council Law No. 10, enacted on January 31, 1946. Besides this there exist in almost every state, however, particular war crimes laws; we only need to refer to the French, Dutch, Romanian, Polish, Norwegian, Belgian, and Luxemburg codifications.

All these regulations are based, in thought, on the Statute of London (St. James Declaration) of June 12, 1941, and the Declaration of Moscow of November 1, 1943, respectively;[9] but they deviate from each other not inconsiderably on individual facts and legal constructions. In spite of the special facts enumerated in them, they remain more in the nature of frames clarified by instances[10]—which is not so astounding, since they are politically determined rather than juridically thought over.

(a) If we disregard the purpose to which they owe their creation and the spirit which they breathe, there remains the regrettable impression that the legislator or legislators failed to formulate obligatorily the general principles which are authoritative for the application of these facts. At that time, it is true, questions of more general juristic-political character were discussed, which are reflected in part in the Charter of the International Military Tribunal. But no final resolutions have been reached so far; the settlement of all these questions has rather been left to the internal legislatures of the victorious nations.[11] Apparently the great differences existing in the doctrines of guilt in Anglo-American penal law, as compared with the concepts of all continental laws, have not permitted any agreement.[12] At any rate, the laws of the victorious states are confined in general—mostly to the disadvantage of the defendants —merely to touching in a few regulations (as, for instance, on the question of superior orders) upon problems which appear to them to be important, leaving their further interpretation to the jurisdiction of the tribunals. During the days of Moscow and London there may perhaps have been thought of an international jurisdiction uniformly determined at least in its fundamental questions. Whether the question of a conveyance of the jurisdiction to German courts was discussed by the Allies seems to be more than doubtful; for in the Declaration of Moscow of November 1, 1943, it is expressly stated that the culprit was to be tried under the law of the (foreign) *locus delicti* and by the respective competent courts. Consequently, nothing was said of a German jurisdiction. Only through Ordinance No. 47 (*Amtsblatt*—Bulletin—p. 306), e.g., the German ordinary courts were authorized by the British Military Government to try persons who made themselves guilty of crimes against humanity (and only of these) insofar as the act had been committed by Germans against Germans or against stateless persons.[13]

But neither has a common international jurisdiction, save the IMT trial and the Tokyo trial, been arrived at. Apparently there had been in these trials such essential disagreement among the American, English, French, and Russian judges on the basic questions of law, that in further trials common proceedings were avoided and left to the tribunals of the individual victorious nations. All other trials took place before tribunals of the individual victorious nations, with the occasional presence of members of interested states as judges or observers —as, for instance, the Röchling trial in Rastatt, or the Rath trial in Hamburg.

Since the courts regarded the facts exclusively or prevailingly from the standpoint of the substantive and adjective laws of their respective countries, there arose therefrom considerable differences on fundamental points—completely independent from the controversy on the individual legal figures in the respective legal systems—which, as a rule, were again to the defendant's disadvantage. Thus the tribunals in Nuremberg considered primarily continental-American law,[14] the French courts based and base their jurisdiction on the general principles of French penal law,[15] and the other states clung and cling to their respective codifications in force,[16] even at the risk of thereby disregarding or contradicting an already existing jurisdiction or procedure of other War Crimes Tribunals. Sauer's opinion,[17] that for instance the general part of the *Reichsstrafgesetzbuch* (Reich Penal Code) must be applied to Control Council Law No. 10, is not affirmed in international practice. Sauer evidently has in mind only the German development and disregards the non-German proceedings. The character of the material (special facts of international law) permits, however, only a uniform legal consideration apart from the laws of the individual states. At any rate, neither the American tribunals in Nuremberg when applying Control Council Law No. 10, nor the French courts in Rastatt, nor the British tribunals in Hamburg have attributed any importance to the general part of the German penal code.

I do not think it unobjectionable either, when the German courts—as is understandable from the German perspective, it is true—proceed from German penal law without reservation when applying Control Council Law No. 10.[18] At any rate, I can derive neither from the construction of Control Council Law No. 10 nor from the history of its origin any obligation of the German courts to apply German law as Wimmer demands it.[19] Control Council Law No. 10 is certainly a law with a special purpose of the victorious states, based on various foreign legal systems, which, in addition, bears the signs of an international compromise solution created in the most turbulent times of world history. In its specifications of the facts it contains legal figures which hitherto have been unknown to German legal thinking; one thinks only of the facts of conspiracy and of group criminality. But it differs otherwise in many essential regulations, too, from the legal figures known and familiar to us, where we may, for instance, refer to the various modern forms of participation. It would therefore mean to constrain the matter if one forced them into German law, just as I consider it a failure when the individual states apply the principles of their, and only their, general penal law in the determination of the law. In order that a just judgment may be reached in this Babel-like legal confusion, a reform of the general principles of penal law on an international basis seems to be indispensable above all. As long as this uniform starting line does not exist, contradictory judgments of the various tribunals, in spite of equal facts, will be inevitable. The regrettably not always fortunate judgments of the Supreme Court in the British Zone are a remarkable example of this. The equality of all before the law requires a uniform judgment; for, as Constantopoulos is justified in saying, one cannot set national frontiers to legal consciousness. It is simply the consciousness of man, and therefore is human and international.[20] For the future we must attain a certainty that the same facts will be judged under the same legal suppositions wherever trials of this kind may take place.

It is concealed from nobody with insight that the jurisdiction of the War Crimes Tribunals shows inner gaps with no uniform development. I only remind you of the utterance of the presiding judge in the Nuremberg Hostage Case, Judge Charles F. Wennerstrum, upon his return to America: "The supreme ideals which had been denoted for the creation of this tribunal have not been perceptible. . . . If I had known seven months ago what I know now, I would have never come here."[21]

Such a regrettable utterance would certainly have been avoidable if the general principles had been dealt with prior to the establishment of the individual facts.

The Nuremberg experiment has shown that in the course of time a number of fundamental questions which in the IMT trial and in the first succeeding trials had been dealt with by the tribunals with a certain liberality—if not even frivolity—could be developed, though not satisfactorily solved. If this way had not only been followed consistently in spite of the difficulties in the beginning, but beyond this a really impartial tribunal had been entrusted with the judgment, an excellent foundation for future international legal development could have been laid. This could at the same time have become a future international legislature, perhaps within the framework of the Council of Europe. Unfortunately, the creation of these generally binding principles has not been arrived at either in Nuremberg or at other focuses of the War Crimes Trials, although the Nuremberg Military Tribunals had been fully aware of this necessity. In this connection, the following programmatic statement can be found in the Weizsäcker Judgment:

... We are here to define a standard of conduct of responsibility, not only for Germans as the vanquished in war, not only with regard to past and present events, but those which in the future can be reasonably and properly applied to men and officials of every state and nation, those of the victors as well as those of the vanquished. Any other approach would make a mockery of international law and would result in wrongs quite as serious and fatal as those which were sought to be remedied.[22]

In the interest of the development of international penal law the hitherto prevailing discordance of the development is to be regretted, as otherwise the now many-sided and in part contradictory jurisdiction would have been directed into uniform ways not only on fundamental questions, but also in respect to the interpretation of the individual penal decrees. I remind you, for instance, of the jurisdiction of the victorious nations of Western Europe in Article 118 of the *Code pénal*. The Brussels court of cassation declared expressly in its judgment at the end of 1948, in the Mons War Crimes Trial, that this provision was inapplicable to Germans who were on duty in Belgium during the war.[23] The neighboring country of Luxemburg nevertheless affirmed, in the judgment of first instance of the Jurist Trial there, the applicability of the same provision, which is also contained in the penal law of Luxemburg, to German judges and attorneys of state without reservation.

(b) What is true for questions of substantive law is also true for adjective law. To this extent care should have been taken that all proceedings were administered, if possible, according to uniform rules of procedure before a central tribunal, and not according to special regulations, in part quickly formulated, before an immense number of local courts in the individual states. But to this extent, too, the legislators withdrew behind the comfortable bulwark of the "generally recognized" rules of international law, as is proved, for instance, in the unpublished official Norwegian argument already mentioned, which reads as follows:

International law does not contain detailed regulations of adjective or substantive law for the prosecution of war criminals. This is left to the national legislators with the limitations which result from the generally recognized principles of civilized jurisprudence.[24]

Indeed a flexible definition. We are in want of an "Esperanto of adjective penal law," which would exclude not only the uncertainties of law but also the other sources of error (use of foreign languages, foreign legal definitions, unprecise translations) of an international penal jurisdiction. The hitherto existing dispersion of the law is in this respect very great. Thus, the Nuremberg Tribunals based their proceedings on Ordinances Nos. 7 and 11 of the American Military Government.[25] The British courts in Germany worked according to the English Military Ordinance 69 and the ordinance of procedure of February 17, 1947, and the French tribunals when applying Control Council Law No. 10 used the regulation of the Military Government of May 21, 1946,[26] while the French tribunals in France apply exclusively French penal law. The Luxemburg tribunals refer to the *Code d'instruction criminelle* of 1806, which has been amended in essential regulations by the War Crimes Act of 1947; Norway proceeds according to the tempo-

rary regulation of February 16, 1945, which is provided mainly
for the Landsviker (followers of Quisling), and in the Hamburg Manstein trial the English labor representative and acting defense counsel Paquet demanded—and from his standpoint
was justified in doing so—that the bill of indictment against
Feldmarschall von Manstein had to correspond with the principles of English jurisprudence. The questions of doubt emerg-
ing because of this different procedural treatment of the same
facts are very serious. They touch practically all questions of
penal proceedings from the preliminary proceedings to the
instance of pardon, and render a regular preparation and administration of the proceedings more difficult for the defense
counsel. Besides the creation of generally obligatory principles
of the substantive penal law, it will therefore be indispensable
also to attain generally obligatory rules of procedure of international penal law.

2. Besides these legal difficulties, which are merely to be
indicated here, those of a factual kind must not be overlooked.
In normal local proceedings the court and all parties to the
proceedings generally start out from precisely outlined facts.
In the Nuremberg trials as well as in similar cases this positiveness of foundation is, however, lacking. Starting-point of the
proceedings is the bill of indictment drafted at the discretion
of the prosecution, based on individual facts, in part incomplete, which were selected at random. Many times the defense
was unable to examine the documents in time and to a sufficient extent. I remind you, for example, of the case of Dr.
Mettgenberg and Dr. v. Ammon in the Nuremberg Trial of
Justices. In accordance with American practice in proceedings,
the prosecution reported in both cases on parts of the complete
documents on the persons which were in their possession from
the former *Reichsjustizministerium* (Reich Ministry of Justice)
insofar as it deemed this necessary for the argument of their
thesis. An application of the defense for cession of the personal
documents was rejected. The German and above all the foreign

archives, almost exclusively confiscated by the occupation authorities, were generally inaccessible in Nuremberg without the help of the prosecution. In this connection it must be emphasized, however, that in the course of the later proceedings a certain growing liberality of the American authorities could be increasingly noticed. Thus in the High Command Case the OKW documents kept in American archives were placed at the disposal of the defense and returned to Nuremberg; in the Weizsäcker Case the defense was permitted to procure material in London and in the central document office in Berlin. Unfortunately no final evaluation could be made, since because of the extent of the complex and the complicatedness of the material the time was too short for the defense. A collection of the complete historic events, the final comprehension of which alone could have formed an incontestable basis for the proceedings in international law, was practically impossible because of the destruction or blockade of the documents, and becau e of the fact that the most important witnesses were interned or were prisoners of war. But it was not only the defendants who had a lasting interest in the greatest possible comprehension of the facts, but also the German public and above this the commonwealth of nations.

Here a broad field of activity has opened itself for historic research in the future. With an objective revision of the individual facts it will certainly reach in some cases—such as, to mention only a few, the case of v. Weizsäcker, Schlegelberger, v. Kuechler, and Loeser—results essentially different from those in Nuremberg.

In the future it will become necessary to subject the judgments rendered throughout the whole world to a careful scientific historical revision. Beyond this, we will have to endeavor to create an instance for legal measures in all the cases in which such a legal instance had been lacking, i.e., mainly for the judgments rendered in Nuremberg and in Poland, and finally to create a Supreme International Court of Appeal which, with foreign and German judges, is competent to render the final judgments. In this respect a profitable field of activity will open itself to the planned Supreme Court for the Protection of Human Rights.

The Conclusion of the Nuremberg Trials

DR. CARL HAENSEL

With the judgment in the case of Weizsäcker and others, the proclamation of which was concluded on Maundy Thursday, April 14, 1949, the Nuremberg trials, which began on October 18, 1945, with the proceedings against Göring and others before the International Military Tribunal, came to an end. Altogether, twelve trials were administered before American Military Tribunals besides the IMT (International Military Tribunal) trial. Military Tribunal III (the Justice Case) stated expressly on December 3 and 4, 1947, that it had to carry out the law which had been laid down in Control Council Law No. 10 and in the Statute of London; it had to enforce international law, which represented law superior to any German law.[1] Therefore, international law, rather than German or American law, was applied.

Military Tribunal IV, which, among other things, had to decide the case of Weizsäcker, took this same position. Sup-

First published in Neue Juristische Wochenschrift, *May, 1949, pp. 367-70. Translated by Dr. Georg Grimm.*

Dr. Carl Haensel *is a professor of jurisprudence, formerly attorney at law at Freiburg and defense counsel at Nuremberg.*

porting this position is above all the following statement of the Judgment:

... We are here to define a standard of conduct of responsibility, not only for Germans as the vanquished in war, not only with regard to past and present events, but those which in the future can be reasonably and properly applied to men and officials of every state and nation, those of the victors as well as those of the vanquished. Any other approach would make a mockery of international law and would result in wrongs quite as serious and fatal as those which were sought to be remedied.[2]

In this statement the Tribunal expressed its position on the demand, discussed during the proceedings as well as in public, that there must not be two different kinds of international law for the victorious and for the defeated. In connection with this the objection was also discussed in public that in the Nuremberg trials, as proceedings of international law, neutral judges or German judges should have participated. As my statements are to be confined solely to the results for practical lawyers, I do not want to discuss this problem any further, but I do wish to point out that today it is perhaps more important to the development of international law that international law be given validity under the authority of the American flag rather than that an international group pronounce legal principles for which the American world power does not feel responsible. The military judicial competency has been proved since the IMT Judgment by the international legal practice of sentencing members of enemy states for crimes against the customs of war and of issuing laws in the occupied German areas after the capitulation.[3]

This international law is "not statutory":

In determining whether the action of a nation is in accordance with or violates international law, resort may be had not only to those treaties and covenants, but to treatises on the subject and to the principles which lie beneath and back of these treaties, covenants, and learned treatises; and we need not hesitate, after having determined what they are, to apply them to new or different situations.[4]

Legal sources for this international law are therefore the literature and rational considerations of the Tribunal. The Judgment contains broad passages with such considerations, in part even in the style of rhetorical questions. To answer the questions raised by the Tribunal in another meaning than the questioner expects would mean "to shroud international law in a mist of unreality."[5]

The Judgment in Case 11 is based upon Control Council Law No. 10, which consists of but five articles. Like other tribunals, it takes the position that Control Council Law No. 10 "merely defined what offenses against international law should be the subject of judicial inquiry," but that the facts had already been developed in existing international law.[6] Among these facts it counts the crime against the peace, the initiation of a war of aggression—for the reason, among others, that the war of aggression had already been outlawed in the Kellogg-Briand Pact and even before Napoleon's wars of aggression were made the cause for his banishment to St. Helena.[7] From this standpoint follows also the rejection of objections based on the principle *nullum crimen sine lege,* as well as on the formula *tu quoque.* Even if the Soviet Union, through the secret clauses of German-Russian agreements of 1939, had become *particeps criminis* in the war of aggression against Poland, which the Tribunal leaves undecided, the facts standardized in Control Council Law No. 10, which was cosigned by the Soviet Union, would not be contendable; since the law here was taken from existing international law its validity could not be questioned.[8]

Judge Powers signed the judgment with the following reservation: "I reserve the right to file later, separate dissenting views as to some convictions."

Accordingly he filed a 123-page Dissenting Opinion to the 824-page Judgment. He, too, starts out from the opinion that at the time of the formulation of Control Council Law No. 10, ". . . the obvious purpose was to provide machinery for the punishment of crimes which were thought to be crimes under international law existing at the time."[9] But he turns against

the opinion of the Judgment drawn up by the other two judges
that the Tribunal was "to lay down rules of conduct for the
guidance of nations in the future." He furthermore made his
position precise to the effect that Control Council Law No.
10 "has no effect in limiting international law generally, but
only limiting the particular type of crime with which we are
authorized to deal."

By this he can supposedly only mean that international law
as such had to show forth still other facts, but that the Control
Council Law had taken from these and delivered up to the
jurisdiction of the Nuremberg Tribunals only part of them.
With this position no positive basis was therefore attained,
but the "not statutory" law in the meaning of the above quotations was to be developed from the principles which result from
the practice of the states, from the literature, and from "their
own character."

"He who does not want to abandon the positive law must
drop totally the law of nature," said Berolzheimer in 1906 in
his major work.[10] He thereby outlined the positivistic opinion
of the prewar time. The Nuremberg Tribunals place us anew
before the problems of whether positivism really represents the
final conclusion of wisdom and the coronation of jurisprudence,
or whether we have again entered a new cultural period and
thus also a new period to be comprehended in legal history, in
which in the practice of the courts an argument emerges which
is not based solely on positive norms and their interpretation
according to the opinion of the lawmaker. The problem becomes the more urgent when we notice that the Nuremberg
Tribunals do not stand alone in this argumentation. A number
of German courts have recently tried to establish the application of principles of natural law by a general clause immanent
to positive law.[11] For the pure positivist it may be easier to
enter into the inevitable discussion of these problems if we
take an expression of Berolzheimer from his speech delivered in
Darmstadt in 1911 against the "dangers of a jurisprudence of
sentiment," and—turning away from the law of nature founded

by the philosophers and state critics in the eighteenth century
—talk of cultural law which includes the "temporal-national-
local conditions."[12]

These considerations indicate the limits of the prejudicial
effectiveness of the Nuremberg Judgments. Not German Control Council law was pronounced there, but pure international
law which the German judges could apply within Germany
only after a transformation. But for the judge who has to apply
Control Council Law No. 10 against Germans according to British Military Government Ordinance No. 69 and the ordinance of
procedure of February 17, 1947, or the ordinance of the French
Military Government of May 21, 1946, the handling of a concept like "knowledge," for instance, is of great importance on
account of the judgment in Case 11. Here it is stated even for a
state secretary holding office "that mere knowledge of aggressive war or of criminal acts is not sufficient" for a conviction.[13]
Or in another passage on another defendant:

The evidence would indicate that he was advised of what was trans-
piring. The evidence does not indicate, however, affirmative acts on
his part or such contributions to the plan or the execution thereof
as to justify finding him guilty with respect to the aggression against
Czechoslovakia.[14]

Knowledge that a crime is proposed is not sufficient. A defendant
may only be convicted because of acts he has committed or his
failure to act when it was his duty to have done so.[15]

The much contended formulations in Control Council Law No.
10, Article 2, paragraph 2 c and d, according to which any person is deemed to have committed a crime against international
law if he "took a consenting part therein or was connected with
plans or enterprises involving its commission," are interpreted
to the effect that only a person who takes part therein or abets
it commits a crime against humanity.[16]

The following sentences of the Judgment are characteristic
of the view of the Tribunal, which is by far less positivistic and
systematic than orientated by natural law:

One cannot give consent to or implement the commission of murder because by so doing he hopes eventually to be able to rid society of the chief murderer. The first is a crime of imminent actuality while the second is but a future hope.[17]

A troubled conscience is not a defense for acts which are otherwise criminal. Nor can we hold that he who signed, cosigned, executed, or administered measures which violate international law, because he thought that acquiescence would enable him to maintain and safeguard the integrity of his department and the career of his officials or even the life or liberty of individuals whose cases came to his attention, but who by his actions condemned the great inarticulate mass to persecution, mistreatment, brutality, imprisonment, deportation, and extermination, escapes responsibility for his conduct.[18]

Inner resistance, even if it can be proved by participation in a resistance movement, does not exculpate an act of participation or a failure to intervene in spite of the obligation to do so. But this obligation never goes so far as to inform the enemy of expected acts of aggression; the Tribunal expresses its firm conviction that such high treason would not be in conformity with either common sense or moral law.[19] However, the "resistance" was considered at the determination of the sentence. The Tribunal, it is true, declared that it was not understandable "how a decent man could continue to hold office under a regime which carried out planned and wholesale barbarities," but it does not yet see an act of participation in such acts alone;[20] there must be an additional "active participation."[21] But active participation does not presume execution, and "those who in the comparative quiet and peace of ministerial departments, aided the campaign by drafting the necessary decrees, regulations, and directives for its execution are likewise guilty."[22] The reference to the state of distress founded in the pressure of the regime cannot be conceded to any of the defendants: "'We find that none of the defendants acted under coercion or duress."[23]

At many places the Judgment gives interpretations of special regulations of international penal law. Interesting is the con-

troversy between the Judgment and the Dissenting Opinion of
Judge Powers on the question whether even the invasion which
does not encounter armed resistance—Austria in 1938 and
Czechoslovakia in 1939—or only the completely developed war
fulfils the fact of the crime against international law in the
wording of Control Council Law No. 10, Article 2, 1. The Judgment answers the first part of the question in the affirmative
and pronounces sentences accordingly; Judge Powers answered
it in the negative.[24] Judge Powers bases his opinion, among
other things, upon the fact that "there was no possible basis
for claiming that a mere invasion was contrary to international
law, prior to the adoption of Law 10."[25] Articles II and VII of
the Geneva Prisoner of War Convention of August 27, 1929,
are thoroughly interpreted in order to make possible a decision
on the question of at what time a belligerent power may trans-
port away P.O.W.'s and when it has to withdraw them for the
sake of their security from areas which are threatened by acts
of the belligerents.[26] At another place the opinion of Military
Tribunal V in Case 7 is confirmed that guerrillas are not entitled to the protection of the Geneva Convention.[27] The Judgment not only rests in this individual case on the previous decision of a Nuremberg Tribunal, but endeavors throughout to
adopt the legal opinions of the International Military Tribunal
and the Military Tribunals which rendered judgments before;   ·
nevertheless, there are deviations at hand, too. A great part of
the evidence had already been introduced in these proceedings.
But in Case 11 it was supplemented to a great extent by the
authorities of the prosecution and defense which were given
the opportunity to let someone from their ranks work in the
document center in Berlin and later on in London.

The prosecution had classified the material into eight counts
of accusations, of which counts 2 and 4 were eliminated by the
Tribunal. The bases for the sentences were only count 1,
waging of wars of aggression; count 3, war crimes strictly
speaking, particularly inadmissible treatment of prisoners of
war; count 5, crimes against humanity, among other things the

measures against the Jews and the inadmissible treatment of
inimi al civilian population; count 6, the looting of the oc-
cupi⸗ 1 areas; count 7, the so-called slave-labor program; and
coun⸗ 8, membership in organizations declared criminal by the
International Military Tribunal, mainly the SS and the Leadership Corps of the Nazi Party.

Among the defendants different groups were to be distinguished: seven defendants had been in the diplomatic service; five had been leading economists in banks or industrial
enterprises or in the Four Year Plan; the rest were ministers
or held high government rank with particular commissions.
With the exception of two, the former Reichsminister Meissner
and the Ministerialdirigent of the Foreign Office Erdmanns-
dorf, all of the defendants were convicted. The details, I suppose, are known from the newspapers. For legal criticism the
summarizing statement is of interest—that the sentences for
the group of diplomats were fixed, with one exception, at seven
years and less; and for three of the group of economists at
fifteen years, for two at less than that. For the diplomats counts
1, 3, and 5, and for the economists counts 6 and 7 played the
leading role.

Of symptomatic importance is the sentence pronounced on
one of the former State Secretaries of three years, ten months,
and twenty days. It corresponded exactly with the time of imprisonment served, which in cases of convictions were included
in the sentences. The defendant concerned was seriously ill;
there was testimony by German and American physicians that
it was an illness perilous to life and not merely an acute one.
The pronouncing of the sentence could have influenced the
condition of the heart catastrophically. The argument for the
sentence resulted in a judgment of guilty on counts 5, 6, and
8, so that a sentence lying under the limit stated above could
not be expected. The Tribunal, after including the time of imprisonment served in the sentence pronounced, ordered the
annulment of the warrant of arrest. The presiding judge later
explained: We did not want to be inhuman. This decision can-

not be established from positivistic argumentation, but it can very well be established from the standpoint of a tribunal which listens to the "consciences of mankind," which is not bound to the letter of a fixed law but which seeks its legitimation in natural law, or let us rather say cultural law. The leading event of the last day of the Judgment was the news of Judge Powers' Dissenting Opinion. Judge Powers declared that in his opinion the majority of the defendants should be acquitted, and founded this opinion on general legal considerations and an evaluation of the facts different from that of the other judges. In this review we cannot enter into the abundance of confusing details, but only into the fundamentals. In some fundamental considerations of Judge Powers there is a conformity with the statements of the Judgment, but the conclusions drawn on both sides in application to individual cases are different. On account of a sentence in a passage of the bill of indictment Judge Powers rigorously turns against a mentality which in some roundabout ways in the argumentation seeks to arrive again at a mass or collective guilt "under which men should be found guilty of a crime even though they knew nothing about it when it occurred, and it was committed by people over whom they had no responsibility or control."[28]

Continuing, Judge Powers comes to speak about the cardinal problem of all the Nuremberg trials, conspiracy, the joint planning of a crime:

Since conspiracy is out of this case, no sort of legal legerdemain can substitute for proof that the defendant as an individual committed some act either of omission or commission with the intent thereby to bring about a result which is a crime charged in the indictment, and which accomplished its purpose. If the evidence is insufficient to establish guilt beyond a reasonable doubt on the basis of such individual responsibility, as distinguished from a group responsibility, this Tribunal has no other alternative than to acquit.[29]

Conspiracy is a fact of Anglo-Saxon law which makes punishable combination for the purpose of criminal intent. Combination, joining together, is the gist of the offense, the essential characteristic.[30] Combination involves liability for the guilt of others, since every conspirator is liable for the acts of the others, even if he has not accepted them in detail in his will. It has been taken up as a penal fact in the Statute of London, paragraph 6, and in Control Council Law No. 10, but here in its wording only in Article II 1 a, Crimes against the Peace. The indictment before the International Military Tribunal is based on conspiracy:

All the defendants, with divers other persons, ... participated as leaders, organizers, instigators, or accomplices in the formulation or execution of a Common Plan or Conspiracy to commit, or which involved the commission of, Crimes against Peace, War Crimes, and Crimes against Humanity ...[31]

The argumentation on such an indictment makes possible proceedings which prosecutor Sidney S. Alderman, for instance, summarized in the following way:

May it please the Tribunal, the handful of selected documents which I presented yesterday constitute a cross section of the aggressive war case, as a whole. They do not purport to cover the details of any of the phases of the aggressive war case. In effect they do amount to a running account of the entire matter.[32]

In Case 1, the Medical Case, which was mainly concerned with the experiments with men by individual physicians, and in Case 2, against Milch, in which there was only one defendant, conspiracy was not the decisive part. In Case 3, the Justice Case, and in Case 4, the trial against the WVHA, against Pohl and others, the indictment was founded upon conspiracy for the commission of crimes against humanity. In the session of the Joint Nuremberg Military Tribunals, which met in public session only this one time on August 19, 1947, against the opposition of the pleading Chief Prosecutor, General Taylor, I succeeded after adequate preparation in establishing persuasively that Control Council Law No. 10 according to its wording knew conspiracy as a fact for wars of aggression, it is true, but not for war crimes and crimes against humanity; that the law to be applied was, however, pure international law, and that, therefore, the conspiracy of the Anglo-Saxon common law could not be applied.[33]

Military Tribunal IV as well as the other Nuremberg Military Tribunals did not, in Case 11, apply conspiracy to war crimes and crimes against humanity. Even for the war of aggression in count 2 it did not convict of conspiracy, but not for the legal reason that Control Council Law No. 10 did not create new law but only formulated existing law and that in existing international law the Anglo-Saxon conspiracy could not be proved, but only for want of sufficient evidence.[34] The judgment in Case 11 tried, in subtle work against every defendant, to establish personal guilt from individual evidence. The question is only whether this is persuasively possible with the documentary material of the state for individual defendants who acted not for themselves but as officers. After omitting conspiracy, which alone could comprehend the co-operation of many thousands of people who in part do not know each other at all, who many times also do not even know in detail how their laws and orders are later carried out and what series of causes become effective, one had to be (to speak with Judge Powers' words) in effect a magician in order to establish beyond reasonable doubt, except for the members of Hitler's clique, the international penal "individual responsibility as distinguished from the group responsibility."

On this point the opinions of the prosecution and defense and, as we learned from Judge Powers' Dissenting Opinion, also of the judges, differ. The fact that such a Dissenting Opinion of a judge against a judgment which he himself signed as all in order is possible, that it is even published, demonstrates the generosity and frankness of American proceedings. But such a discussion must not pass by the fact that dreadful things occurred in the Third Reich and that the world has a right to determine in the manner of a trial how far penal guilt extends. Different opinions about the composition of such a tribunal and the law to be applied are conceivable, and no human undertaking is totally perfect. I represented the opinion which in the end seems to coincide with that of Judge Powers: Considering its far-reaching effects, international law must be magnanimous; it must not be construed subtly and casuistically. The basic tendency of an international penal law must therefore be to concern itself only with great, serious, internationally important crimes and to exclude from the beginning all minor local offenses. *Minima non curat praetor* [35]

The Judgment in Case 11 states in its fundamental considerations:

These Tribunals were not organized and do not sit for the purpose of wreaking vengeance upon the conquered. Was such the purpose, the power existed to use the firing squad, the scaffold, or the prison camp without taking the time and putting forth labor which have been so freely expended on them, and the Allied Powers would have copied the methods which were too often used during the Third Reich. We may not, in justice, apply to these defendants because they are Germans standards of duty and responsibility which are not equally applicable to the officials of the Allied Powers and to those of all nations. Nor should Germans be convicted for acts or conducts which, if committed by Americans, British, French, or Russians would not subject them to legal trial and conviction. Both care and caution must be exercised not to prescribe or apply a yardstick to these defendants which cannot and should not be applied to others, irrespective of whether they are nationals of the victor or of the vanquished. [36]

Thoughts About Purport and Effect of the Nuremberg Judgment

RA. TH. KLEFISCH

THE Judgment pronounced in Nuremberg on September 30 and October 1, 1946, is the conclusion of a trial which up to now has no equal in the history of nations. The victorious nations charge the prominent statesmen and military leaders of the defeated nation, on the basis of a law drafted by themselves, with the initiation and waging of wars of aggression, with war crimes and crimes against humanity, and have judgment rendered over them by a Tribunal consisting of judges of their own states.

It is obvious that the trial and judgment of such proceedings require of the Tribunal the utmost impartiality, loyalty, and sense of justice. The Nuremberg Tribunal has met these requirements with consideration and dignity. Nobody dares to doubt that it was guided by the search for truth and justice from the first to the last day of this tremendous trial. According to world opinion, this endeavor has found its humanly possible realization in the Judgment. In the face of this common

First published in Juristische Rundschau, *August, 1947, No. 2, pp. 45-49. Translated by Dr. Georg Grimm.*
The author is an attorney at law in Cologne.

opinion the criticism here and there, from which important judgments of tribunals are seldom spared, must fade.

It is strange that the voices of criticism came preponderantly from within the country; it is even more curious that each and all of them object to the unjustified indulgence toward certain accused persons, and, therefore, object to an attitude which on account of the peculiarity of the trial and the composition of the Tribunal should be regarded as a sign of utmost objectivity. Though the right to criticize court judgments cannot be contended in principle, it seems to be unfounded in the present case even if this criticism originated from purely pertinent motives. As long as it exhausts itself in emotional considerations, as is true throughout, it cannot be remarkable anyway. Only he who knows the tremendous material of the trials from the proceedings or from the minutes, and who is able to value it in the factual and legal respect, can be entitled to objective criticism. He who was in a position to be present at the ten-month trial or part thereof and who could convince himself of the amazing command of the immense material of the trial and of the respective legal material on the part of the Tribunal, and of the high ethos and fairness with which the proceedings were arranged and directed, and he who was further able to notice the precise carefulness with which all the individual incriminating and defending evidences were collected can neither assert that any evidences important for the decision escaped the Tribunal nor that one little grain of the incriminating material fell under the table. When judges of the personality, rank, and reputation of the Nuremberg judges in the majority acquit the defendants Schacht, Von Papen, and Fritsche, nothing can be more absurd than to think that these acquittals resulted from some imponderable influence or even from a sympathy for these men. The reasons for the Judgment furnish irrefutable proof that the undeniably grave incriminating evidences as they were brought forth, for instance, by the Russian member of the Tribunal in his memorandum, were subjected to a thorough examination and that only the utmost carefulness and conscientiousness brought about the decision for the denial of the question of guilt, because for these defendants guilt did not appear to be completely proved in the meaning of the crimes enumerated in the Charter. Against such a Judgment—which, by the way, prohibits the prosecution of the acquitted only for these prosecuted crimes and not for other prosecuted crimes, e.g., under the Denazification laws—any criticism ought to vanish, if only in order to escape the danger, which is near at hand, that malicious tongues may impute to it other than purely objective reasons and particularly political motives and aims.

It cannot be the purpose of this treatise to discuss the Judgment thoroughly or to take a position on it. This is prevented by the extent of the minutes, consisting of 270 pages. In the meantime the text has been published as a book. This book ought to be distributed and read. There scarcely exists a more effective means of extinguishing whatever Nazi ideas and efforts may still exist among the people than the reading of this Judgment. For by means of almost exclusively German documents it opens the eyes of young people and of adults to a despotism which pressed for war by enslaving justice and freedom through terror, corruption, faithlessness, lies, and disregard for the most sacred human rights; which initiated war against the mightiest nations, violating international agreements, waged it with numberless and unparalleled cruelties, and by this criminal madness delivered the German people into inexpressible misery and its beautiful country into horrible devastation. The language of the Judgment is commonly intelligible, the construction is easy to survey, the factual observations are clear, and the legal explanations are intelligible even in the treatment of most difficult problems: advantages which increase the value of the Judgment and create a lasting effect.

The Judgment starts with the provisions on the creation of the Tribunal, a brief account of the course of the trial and the contents of the Charter on which the trial was founded. Then, the origin and aims of the NSDAP, the rearmament measures, the preparations for aggression, and the history of the initiation of the individual wars of aggression with reference to the international treaties violated by these wars are stated. Further explanations are concerned with the legal provisions of the Charter, with the concept of conspiracy, with the individual responsibility of the defendants, etc. Then follow the factual statements on the war crimes and crimes against humanity. In this chapter cruelties are revealed which exceed all imagination and which appear the more serious as they are told by eyewitnesses without any paraphrase. These statements are also subjected to abundant consideration in accordance with the rules of international law and the Charter. After a thorough treatment of the problem of organizations and of the question which of the seven accused organizations are to be declared to be criminal, the participation of every one of the twenty-two defendants in the crimes stated is examined, while at the same time the concession or denial of extenuating circumstances is decided upon. With this the argument for the Judgment closes. After its reading each one of the defendants was acquainted with the sentence in the absence of the other defendants without any further argument.

As already indicated, the Judgment brings the decision of a number of difficult and in part entirely new legal problems and questions of far-reaching importance. They will presumably occupy the minds of lawyers, historians, and statesmen for a long time to come. Some of the most important of these questions and their solutions may be treated here.

Within and outside of the trial scruples and objections were raised many times against the competence and composition of the Tribunal. The Judgment meets these objections by referring to the law of the Charter, which was decisive and binding upon the Tribunal. "The making of the Charter," the Judgment states,

was the exercise of the sovereign legislative power by the countries to which the German Reich unconditionally surrendered; and the undoubted right of these countries to legislate for the occupied territories has been recognized by the civilized world. The Charter is not an arbitrary exercise of power on the part of the victorious nations, but in the view of the Tribunal, as will be shown, it is the expression of international law existing at the time of its creation; and to that extent is itself a contribution to international law. . . . With regard to the constitution of the Court, all that the defendants are entitled to ask is to receive a fair trial on the facts and law.

That the defendants received a fair trial, the chief prosecutor of the United States of America, Justice Jackson, observed in his final speech against the major defendants in the following words: "They have been given the kind of a Trial which they, in the days of their pomp and power, never gave to any man."

One of the major attacks of the defense was directed against Article 6 a of the Charter which makes punishable the planning, preparing, initiating, and waging of wars of aggression or the participation in a common plan or a conspiracy with the aim of committing these acts. This was regarded as a violation of the principle of penal law recognized in all states: "No crime, no punishment without prior penal law," and it was maintained that the war of aggression hitherto has been threatened with punishment neither by the law of nations nor by national laws; that those international agreements condemning it were no longer regarded as valid and binding before the beginning of the war; that possibly the states contravening international agreements could be called to account and not the statesmen personally; and that the concept of war of aggression was extremely disputable and could not be determined unilaterally by the enemies.

These indeed difficult and incisive questions of law occupied much space in the statements of the prosecution and the defense. Their consideration forms an essential part of the Judgment, although the Tribunal did not consider the examination and decision of these questions as absolutely necessary because it was subjected to the Charter, and the latter declared wars of aggression and wars in violation of treaties to be punishable crimes against the peace. The Judgment derives from the Kellogg-Briand Pact of August 27, 1928, by which thirty-six nations, including Germany, condemned war as a means of future policy, as well as from its previous history in international law that the war of aggression, which, in the presence of the German delegation, had already been unanimously declared an international crime in the sitting of the League of Nations on September 24, 1927, violated agreements, was unlawful, and was a crime. The objection that the Kellogg-Briand Pact had not called it expressly a punishable crime with personal responsibility of the authors, and that no tribunal had been established for their prosecution, is put aside by the fact that war crimes strictly speaking have been punished for a long time by the military tribunals of all countries, although the Hague Convention of 1907 neither calls them expressly crimes nor makes them punishable, nor does it designate a tribunal for their punishment. It was therefore in no way unjust to punish war criminals; it was rather unjust to leave such evildoing with its horrible consequences unpunished.

Vehemently disputed was Point I of the indictment, which charged all of the defendants with participation in a common plan or a common conspiracy for the initiation of (previously undetermined) wars of aggression against neighboring states for the purpose of gaining *Lebensraum*. Besides this the defendants were charged under Point II of the indictment with the planning, preparation, initiation, and waging of the actually initiated wars of aggression against Poland, Denmark and Norway, Belgium, etc. These two separate accusations are based on Article 6 c of the Charter which defines crimes against peace as follows: "Planning, preparation, initiation, or waging of a war of aggression or a war in violation of international treaties, agreements, or assurances—or participation in a common plan or conspiracy for the accomplishment of any of the foregoing."

Indictment I of common conspiracy for the initiation of any previously undetermined wars of aggression, based on this second alternative of Article 6 c, ought also to include, in the opinion of the prosecution, the planning of war crimes and crimes against humanity of any kind, because the conspirators knew that the intended wars could only be successful if carried on in the quickest and most reckless way, i.e., without regard for existing rules on the conduct of wars and the population of the regions to be attacked. Consequently, the participants in the common plan or common conspiracy ought to be responsible for all crimes which would be committed by any one person in the accomplishment of this plan, or respectively, which were committed during the war of aggression later actually initiated. This extent of the responsibility is defined in the last paragraph of Article 6. The prosecution extended the common conspiracy according to Point I of the indictment to a period of time which began many years before the beginning of the war, and the roots of which are to be found in the Party Program and in Hitler's *Mein Kampf*. Most of the defendants had been informed of this plan from 1933 onward and all of them at any rate since 1937, and from there on they were convicted of participation in the common plan. Then, after the usurpation of power this plan entered into the stage of preparation of such criminal wars of aggression and was finally carried out by the initiation of the wars that were actually waged. All measures of the Party and of the state in the political, military, economic, and social spheres, as for instance the prohibited rearmament, the dissolution of the labor unions, the struggle against the churches, the persecution of the Jews, the seizure of Austria, Czechoslovakia, etc., were means for the realization of the conspiracy and at the same time signs of its existence. All persons who were aware of this plan and who supported the Party and the state and the essential aims of these—among these persons we must count the defendants and many other persons—were guilty of participation in this plan and responsible for all crimes that were committed in the accomplishment of it. The defendants and the defense contested the existence of such a plan, and at any rate the participation

of the defendants in such a plan, and for proof of the contrary
referred to the continuous affirmations of peace by Hitler and
his closest companions.

The Tribunal ruled on this divergence in the proceedings and
speeches, which was more and more intensified and supported
by numerous factual and legal reasons, on an impartial line.
First, it interpreted Article 6 to the effect that the common
plan or common conspiracy viewed as a particular crime applied only to crimes against peace, not to war crimes and
crimes against humanity, so that the indictment of participation
in the conspiracy for the accomplishment of these latter groups
of crimes was to be disregarded. Then in the Judgment the participation in the common plan or conspiracy for the accomplishment of the acts named before is limited not inconsiderably in respect to time and in regard to the circle of participants. The Judgment states, it is true, that the threat of war
and, if necessary, war itself had been an essential part of the
Nazi policy. However, it considers only eight of the defendants
to be convicted of participation in the common plan for the
initiation of wars of aggression of any kind, and that is for
the time beginning with November, 1937, after Hitler had
revealed his plans for winning *Lebensraum* to his closest staff.
As for the rest, the Judgment takes the position that according
to Point I of the indictment the conspiracy

must be clearly outlined in its criminal purpose. It must not be too
far removed from the time of decision and of action. . . . The Tribunal must examine whether a concrete plan to wage war existed,
and determine the participants in that concrete plan. . . . But the
evidence establishes with certainty the existence of many separate
plans rather than a single conspiracy embracing them all.

The eight defendants convicted of participation in the conspiracy were further declared to be guilty, in accordance with
Point II of the indictment, of participation in certain wars of
aggression in the World War. Besides these, four other defendants were convicted of this crime. It requires a deep penetra-

tion into the results of the proceedings and into the arguments for the Judgment to grasp completely the difference between Point I of the indictment and Point II in their structure and effect. Further considerations about this cannot be entered into here. But there can be no doubt that the foregoing interpretation of the Charter on the part of the Tribunal, which was indeed just, was in effect to the advantage of various defendants.

The same result arises from the circumstances that the Tribunal, partly in agreement with the chief prosecutor of Great Britain, further reduced the number of crimes against humanity. According to Article 6 c of the Charter, such crimes are to be prosecuted and punished as: murder, extermination, enslavement, deportation, or other inhumane acts committed against the civilian population before or during the war; or persecution for political, racial, or religious reasons, in accomplishment of a crime or in connection with a crime for which the Tribunal is competent. The Judgment relates the last part of the sentence "in accomplishment of a crime" to all of the delicts referred to above and concludes that those acts which were committed before the beginning of the war must have been committed in the accomplishment of a war of aggression or in connection with one or with war crimes strictly speaking, in order to establish the crime against humanity in the meaning of the Charter. "The Tribunal," the Judgment states,

is of the opinion that revolting and horrible as many of these crimes were, it has not been satisfactorily proved that they were done in execution of, or in connection with, any such crime. The Tribunal therefore cannot make a general declaration that the acts before 1939 were Crimes against Humanity within the meaning of the Charter.

This interpretation did influence the Judgment not inconsiderably against certain defendants and the accused organizations. This latter decision, which concerns the most difficult and, for broad circles of the German population, most important problem of the trial, will be discussed in a later treatise.

On the front page of the book *Das Urteil von Nürnberg*, which was published by the Nymphenburger Verlagshandlung, Munich, the Judgment is called the foundation of modern international law. This is true in so far as by the Charter and its application practical importance was given for the first time to the condemnation of wars of aggression, expressed already in earlier international agreements, by the punishment of the defendants. Herein and in the establishment of personal responsibility of the authors of such war crimes lies an essential development of international law. No state and no statesman will in future be able to deny the criminality of the acts enumerated in the Charter and the personal responsibility of those who violate these laws culpably. Another question is that of the preventive effect of the Nuremberg Judgment. Will it prevent further wars or, on account of its deterrent effect, contain them at least? According to common experience this deterrent effect of penal judgment must not be overestimated. It can hardly be assumed that a war criminal will take account of it or would shrink back from having to risk his neck. On the other hand, there is no doubt that the authors of a new war of aggression would face the same fate as those convicted in Nuremberg—if they were to be found on the side of the defeated.

But what would happen if the war criminals were members of the victorious nations? It must not be overlooked that this Charter, in accordance with the Agreement of London, decrees only the prosecution and punishment of the major war criminals of the European Axis of World War II, and therefore refers neither to crimes of future wars nor to those crimes for which members of the victorious powers were responsible in the last war. If the Nuremberg Judgment is to reach or at least to further its sublime aim, the prevention of new wars and the pacification of the nations, three postulates are indispensable. First, the Charter drafted for the defeated nations of the last war must be recognized, perhaps in a refined form, by all states or at least by the United Nations as decisive for all the future and for all states, above all the provision which makes the planning and the preparation of a war of aggression or of a war in violation of any treaties severely punishable. Then, an International Tribunal must be established or the existing one must once and for all be competent to prosecute and punish all persons violating the Charter. Furthermore, there must be a permanent authority of prosecution which summons those who violate the law before the forum of this Tribunal. Finally, —and this is most important—behind this court there must be a power which guarantees the prosecution and condemnation of all defendants, and the execution of the judgment against them, even when they belong to the mightiest and most completely victorious nations.

One cannot overlook the fact that such an arrangement to be made by the United Nations represents a tremendous task. However, it is worth the effort of the noble. The fate of mankind and especially of the European nations depends upon its solution. Everyone knows that another war would exceed by far the horrors and devastations of the last war and will most probably lead to the destruction of whole nations and destroy the civilization of the Occident for a time not to be foreseen. But even the most solemn and strong international treaties will not be able to secure the lives of the nations against the threat and scourge of war. Therefore the understanding and, above all, the good will of those men who are entrusted with the leadership of the nations is necessary. May the Nuremberg trial confer on them the knowledge that a future war will lead mankind into deadly ruin, and that it is therefore to be regarded as the greatest crime against it, a crime which cannot be justified by anyone who claims to be a human being.

Notes

Preface

1. The Plan, with some additions, was republished in 1946. The English text of the Plan may be found in the *Revue Internationale de Droit Pénal*, 1946, No. 3, pp. 249-62. In 1928 the International Association of Penal Law adopted the draft statute for the creation of a criminal chamber of the Permanent Court of International Justice, which was prepared by Professor Pella. This draft-statute was revised in 1946. See *Historical Survey of the Question of International Criminal Jurisdiction* (memorandum submitted by the Secretary-General), United Nations, Lake Success, New York, 1949, pp. 75-88. Also see V. V. Pella, "Towards an International Criminal Court," *American Journal of International Law* XLIV (Jan., 1950), 37. Also see Draft Statute for an International Criminal Jurisdiction, *Supplement to the American Journal of International Law*, XLVI (1952), Official Documents, pp. 1-11.

2. In 1937 the International Conference on Terrorism was held in Geneva. As a result of this Conference two conventions were opened for signature on November 16, 1937: the Convention for the Prevention and Punishment of Terrorism and the Convention for the Creation of an International Criminal Court. Neither of these conventions came into force because of the failure of the states to deposit their ratifications. The General Convention of November 16, 1937, was limited to cases involving terrorism, was optional, and only included the criminal responsibilities of individuals. "Nevertheless," in the words of Professor Pella, "it marked a decisive turning-point in the history of contemporary public law. For the first time the regular rendition of international judgments in criminal cases was contemplated, . . ." Pella, "Towards an International Criminal Court," p. 39. For the text of the two proposed conventions see Manley O. Hudson, *International Legislation*, VII, 1935-37 (Washington: Carnegie Endowment for International Peace, 1941), 862-93.

3. The Convention for the Prevention and Punishment of the Crime of Genocide was adopted unanimously by the General Assembly of the United Nations in Paris on December 9, 1948. On January 12, 1951, the convention became effective for certain states which previously had deposited their ratifications or accessions.

4. Article 11 (1) of the draft Covenant on Human Rights, as revised in 1950 by the United Nations Commission on Human Rights, appears to be based upon the existence of an international criminal code or the formulation of such a code in the future. This Article provides: "No one shall be held guilty of any criminal offence on account of any act or omission which did not constitute a criminal offence, under national or international law, at the time when it was

committed." A similar statement was included in Article 11 (2) of the Universal Declaration of Human Rights. There have been some regional developments in the field of human rights. For example, the Convention for the Protection of Human Rights and Fundamental Freedoms was signed at Rome on November 4, 1950. As a result of this convention, Members of the Council of Europe have taken "the first steps for the collective enforcement of certain of the Rights stated in the Universal Declaration" of Human Rights. The convention provides for the establishment of a European Court of Human Rights (Section IV, Article 38).

Introduction

1. Under the Code, "The king [was] advised to ravage the enemy's territory, 'and ever spoil his fodder, food, water, and fuel;' to 'burst tanks, enclosures and trenches;' to 'assail him and terrify him by night;' yet 'one should not, fighting in battle, slay enemies by concealed weapons, nor with barbed or poisoned (weapons), nor with fire-kindled arrows. Nor should one (mounted) slay an enemy down on the ground, a eunuch, a suppliant, one with loosened hair, one seated, one who says "I am thy (prisoner);" nor one asleep, one without armour, one naked, one without weapons, one not fighting, a looker-on, one engaged with another; nor one who has his arm broken, a distressed man, one badly hit, one afraid, one who has fled: remembering virtue (one should not slay) them.' " Amos S. Hershey, "The History of International Relations During Antiquity and the Middle Ages: International Law Impossible Before the Rise of the Modern European State System," *American Journal of International Law,* V (1911), 901, at p. 905.
2. Coleman Phillipson, *The International Law and Custom of Ancient Greece and Rome* (London: Macmillan and Co., 1911), II, 179.
3. Socrates and Glaucon were of the opinion that only a fight between Hellenes and barbarians should be called a war; "but when Hellenes fight with one another we shall say that Hellas is then in a state of disorder and discord, they being by nature friends; and such enmity is to be called discord." *The Republic,* Jowett's translation (New York: The Modern Library), BK. V, 470, pp. 198-99.
4. *Ibid.,* BK. V, 471, pp. 199-200.
5. Coleman Phillipson, *op. cit.,* II, 192.
6. The *Magister Fetialium,* a permanent functionary, presided over the College of Fetials. The latter, as guardian of the *jus fetiale,* was composed of twenty priests. Their term of office was for life, unless they committed a serious offense against the Senate and people. The Pater Patratus, who was elected by his colleagues, served as "chief of the fetials" or their spokesman when members of the College were sent abroad on diplomatic missions, or for negotiating the extradition of offenders, and for declaring war.
7. Other functions performed by the College of Fetials were as follows: (1) "In their priestly capacity they presided over the expiatory sacrifices and the performance of solemnities that were incidental to the commencement of war, the establishment of peace, the conclusion of treaties, and other interstatal affairs of importance" (Coleman Phillipson, *op. cit.,* II, 326). (2) If Rome wished to register a complaint or demand against another state, such was formulated and presented by the fetials. According to the *jus fetiale,* Rome was pro-

hibited from waging war until an attempt had been made to secure a peaceful settlement of the issue. (3) The fetials were employed to declare war and conclude peace, as well as negotiate treaties of friendship and alliances. (4) International claims which Rome had against foreign states, or claims by the latter against Rome, fell within the province of the fetials. (5) The latter negotiated the extradition of foreigners to stand trial in Rome, as well as the delivery of Roman citizens who had offended foreign states. (6) The fetials could give their opinion in regard to whether or not treaty-rights had been violated, and if so, they could demand restitution. (7) "They also took cognizance of offences committed against ambassadors, and investigated the transgressions of the generals with respect to the *sponsiones* they made with the enemy without the sanction of their government" (*ibid.*, p. 328).

8. In the early period, the vote of the senatorial majority in favor of war was considered final, but from about the beginning of the fifth century B.C. the question had to be considered by the *Comitia Centuriata* or assembly of the people, and if there approved it became a *Lex Centuriata*. Upon the approval of war by both the Senate and Assembly of the people, the fetials were dispatched to the Roman frontier, and issued a formal declaration of war.

9. If the analogy is not carried too far, the proceedings preliminary to war did approach the procedure evolved for ordinary actions at law consisting of a demand and deposit, formal notice, reply, oral pleadings, determination, and final settlement.

10. L. Oppenheim, *International Law: A Treatise*, ed. H. Lauterpacht (7th ed.; New York: Longmans, Green and Co., 1948), I, 72-73. Used by permission of the publisher. Cf. Amos S. Hershey, "The History of International Relations During Antiquity and the Middle Ages: International Law Impossible Before the Rise of the Modern European State System," *American Journal of International Law*, V (1911), 901, fn. 66, p. 920, and Coleman Phillipson, *op. cit.*, II, 182. For specific examples of the various causes of war see *ibid.*, pp. 182-91.

11. *Ibid.*, p. 332 (Liv. viii. 39).

12. Thomas I. Cook, *History of Political Philosophy From Plato to Burke* (New York: Prentice-Hall, 1936), p. 196. Used by permission of the publisher.

13. As quoted by Francisco de Vitoria in The Second Relectio *(De Jure Belli)*, on The Law of War Made by the Spaniards on the Barbarians. See James Brown Scott, *The Spanish Origin of International Law: Francisco de Vitoria and His Law of Nations*. "The Classics of International Law" (Oxford: Clarendon Press, 1934), Part I, Appendix B, 1i.

14. *Ibid.*, Part I, Appendix B, 1i.

15. Cook, *op. cit.*, p. 207.

16. *Ibid.*, p. 208.

17. James Brown Scott, *op. cit.*, *De Bello* (On St. Thomas Aquinas, *Summa Theologica*, Secunda Secundae, Question 40), Appendix F, P. CXVI.

18. *Ibid.*, P. CXVII.

19. *Ibid.*, Analysis of the Reading on the Indians Recently Discovered, Section II, p. 128.

20. See W. E. Benton, "Some Early Developments of an International Criminal Jurisdiction," *Southwestern Law Journal*, VIII (Winter, 1954), 65-86.

21. Josef L. Kunz, "Bellum Justum and Bellum Legale" (Editorial Comment), *American Journal of International Law*, XLV (July, 1951), 528, at p. 530.

22. *Ibid.*, p. 530.

23. New Jersey *v.* Delaware, 291 U. S. 361, at p. 383 (1934).

24. The Paquete Habana, The Lola, U. S. Supreme Court, 1900, 175 U. S. 677, at p. 700.

25. See Art. 12; Art. 13, par. 4; Art. 15, par. 6, Covenant of the League of Nations.

26. Claudius O. Johnson, *American National Government* (3rd ed.; New York: Thomas Y. Crowell Company, 1951), p. 696. Used by permission.

27. By permission from *Politics Among Nations* (New York: Alfred A. Knopf, 1948), pp. 374-75.

28. Frederick H. Hartmann, *Basic Documents of International Relations* (New York: McGraw-Hill, 1951), p. 115. Used by permission.

29. *Ibid.*, p. 115.

30. Quoted by Westel W. Willoughby in *The Sino-Japanese Controversy and the League of Nations* (Baltimore: The Johns Hopkins Press, 1935), pp 104-5. Used by permission of the publisher.

31. Ray Lyman Wilbur and Arthur Mastick Hyde, *The Hoover Policies* (New York: Charles Scribner's Sons, 1937), pp. 600-601. Used by permission.

32. Benjamin B. Wallace, "How The United States 'Led the League' in 1931," *American Political Science Review*, XXXIX (1945), 114, fn. 32.

33. Press release, Department of State, April 28, 1934. See also *Supplement to the American Journal of International Law*, XXVIII (1934), Official Documents, p. 79.

34. *Supplement to the American Journal of International Law*, Vol. 39 (1945), Official Documents, p. 108.

35. The brief analysis of the Judgment of Nuremberg follows very closely material presented by Dr. C. A. Pompe in *Aggressive War an International Crime.*

36. *Trial of the Major War Criminals Before the International Military Tribunal, Nuremberg, Germany*, 1948, XXII, 461.

37. *Ibid.*, II, 147.

38. Bergman *v.* De Sieyes, District Court, Southern District, New York, Dec. 30, 1946, 71 F. Supp. 334, at p. 337.

39. Dr. C. A. Pompe, *Aggressive War an International Crime* (The Hague: Martinus Nijhoff, 1953), pp. 248-49. By permission of the publisher.

40. *TMWC*, XIX, 460.

41. Christian von Wolff, *Jus Gentium Methodo Scientifica Pertractatum*, The Classics of International Law, published by the Carnegie Endowment for International Peace, Vol. II (Oxford: The Clarendon Press, 1934), Ch. VII, sec. 778, p. 402.

42. *Ibid.*, Ch. VII, sec. 789, p. 408.

43. *Ibid.*, Ch. VII, sec. 814, pp. 421-22.

44. E. de Vattel, *The Law of Nations or the Principles of Natural Law*, The Classics of International Law, Vol. III (Washington: The Carnegie Institution, 1916), BK. III, Ch. XI, secs. 184, 185, and 186, pp. 302-3.

45. F. B. Schick, "The Nuremberg Trial and the International Law of the Future," *American Journal of International Law*, XLI (1947), 770, at p. 779. A similar view has been expressed by Hans Kelsen, "Collective and Individual Responsibility in International Law," *California Law Review*, XXXI (1942-43), 530-71, p. 540.

46. *Report of the Commission on Responsibilities,* Carnegie Endowment for International Peace, Pamphlet No. 32 (Oxford: The Clarendon Press, 1919), pp. 65-66.

47. Pompe, *op. cit.*

48. Philip Marshall Brown, "The Legal Effects of Recognition," *American Journal of International Law,* XLIV (Oct., 1950), 617, at p. 618.

49. "Genocide: A Commentary on the Convention," *Yale Law Journal,* LVIII (1948-49), 1142, at 1157.

50. Statement of Dana Converse Backus, Hearings before a Subcommittee of the U. S. Senate Committee on Foreign Relations, 81st Congress, 2nd Sess., 1950, p. 77 (Hearings on the Genocide Convention).

Statement Before the Nuremberg Tribunal

1. Note of Secretary of State Kellogg to the French Ambassador of 27 February 1928.

2. Note of the United States Government to the Governments of Great Britain, Germany, Italy, and Japan of 13 April 1928.

3. "Considérée jadis comme le droit divin et demeurée dans l'éthique internationale comme une prérogative de la souveraineté, une pareille guerre est enfin destituée juridiquement de ce qui constituait son plus grave danger: sa légitimité. Frappée désormais d'illégalité, elle est soumise au régime conventionnel d'une véritable mise hors la loi. . . ." The speech by the French Foreign Minister is reproduced in The Department of State; Treaty for the Renunciation of War. United States Government Printing Office; Page 309.

4. Commentaire du Pacte de la Société des Nations selon la politique et la jurisprudence des organes de la Société. Paris 1930. (See especially Page 73 et sequentes.) Further in the supplements for 1931-35; 1er Supplément au Commentaire du Pacte (1931) Page 13 et sequentes; 2ème Supplément (1932) Page 17 et sequentes; 3ème Supplément (1933) Pages 18, 39; 4ème Supplément (1935) Pages 19, 99.

5. Congressional Record, Proceedings and Debates of the Second Session of the 70th Congress of the U.S., Volume LXX, Part. 2, Page 1333.

6. See Baker, Ray Stannard, Woodrow Wilson and World Settlement, New York 1922, passim.

7. See Kuhn, Arthur K., Observations of Foreign Governments upon Secretary Hull's Principles of Enduring Peace (A. J., Volume 32, 1938, Pages 101-106). Also: Wilson, Woodrow, War and Peace. Presidential Messages, Addresses and Public Papers, 1917-24 (edited by Ray Stannard Baker and William E. Dodd), New York 1927.

8. Commentaire, Page 74.

9. On the indisputable fact of the collapse, and the guilt of the great powers therein, cf. the bitter statements of Fenwick from the period immediately preceding the second World War. (International Law and Lawless Nations; A. J., Volume 33, 1939; Pages 734-745.)

10. Neutrality and Unneutrality (A. J., Volume 32, 1938, Page 778 et sequentes).

11. See also the Memorandum on the Signature by His Majesty's Government in the United Kingdom of the Optional Clause of the Statute of the Per-

manent Court of International Justice (Cmd. 3452, Miscellaneous Number 12, 1929).

12. It is the same train of thought developed by Brierly, Some Implications of the Pact of Paris (Br. YB 1929).

13. "Tout le mécanisme prévu pour le maintien de la paix s'est disloqué."

14. Parliament Debate, H. C., Volume 332, Column 226 et sequentes.

15. Parliament Debate, H. C., Volume 353, Number 198, Column 1178 (21 November 1939).

15a. See Jahrreiss Plea, Annex, Exhibit Numbers 35 and 36.

16. Resolutions of the Assembly and the Council of 14 December 1939.

17. Congressional Record, Proceedings and Debates of the Second Session of the 70th Congress of the U.S., Volume LXX, Part 2, Pages 1169/99. See also Ellery C. Shotwell, Responsibility of the United States in Regard to International Cooperation for the Prevention of Aggression (A. J., Volume 26, 1932, Page 113).

18. See also Brierly, J. L., Some Implications of the Pact of Paris (Br. YB 1929). He thinks that a violation of neutrality is impossible. In 1936 the same thought was expressed by the Englishman McNair: Collective Security (Br. YB).

19. See, for instance, Eagleton, Clyde, An Attempt to Define Aggression (International Conciliation Number 264, 1930). Cuten, A., La notion de guerre permise, Paris 1931. Wright, Quincy, The Concept of Aggression in International Law (A. J., Volume 29, 1935, Page 395 et sequentes).

20. Note of the United States Government to the Governments of Great Britain, Germany, Italy, and Japan of 13 April 1928; draft treaty of the 20 April 1928 drawn up by the French Government; Note of the British Secretary of State for Foreign Affairs of 19 May 1928 to the American Ambassador; Note of 23 June 1928 from the U. S. Government to all nine participants in the negotiations; Note of the British Secretary of State for Foreign Affairs of 18 July 1928; Note of the Soviet Commissar for Foreign Affairs to the French Ambassador of 31 August 1928.

21. Note of the Soviet Commissar for Foreign Affairs of 31 August 1928.

22. Note of the Soviet Commissar for Foreign Affairs of 31 August 1928.

23. See also Kellogg, F., The War Prevention Policy of the United States (A. J., Volume 22, 1928, Page 261 et sequentes).

24. Congressional Record, Proceedings and Debates of the Second Session of the 70th Congress of the United States, Volume LXX, Part 2 (5 January 1929 to 26 January 1929, Page 1169 et sequentes, Washington 1929).

25. International Lawlessness (A. J., Volume 32, 1938, Page 775).

26. Collective Security (Br. YB, 1936, Page 150 et sequentes).

27. Neutrality and Unneutrality (A. J., Volume 32, 1938, Page 778 et sequentes).

28. International Law and Lawless Nations (A. J., Volume 33, 1939, Pages 743-745).

29. See also Scelle, George, Théorie juridique de la révision des traités. Paris, 1936; further: Kunz, Josef, The Problem of Revision in International Law ("peaceful change"), (A. J., Volume 33, 1939, Pages 33-35).

30. International Lawlessness (A. J., Volume 32, 1938, Page 775).

31. Brierly, Some Implications of the Pact of Paris (Br. YB 1929, Page 208 et sequentes).

32. The well-known "Budapest Articles," International Law Association: Briand-Kellogg Pact of Paris, London 1934, Page 63 et sequentes.

33. Commentaire, Page 371.

34. Of 8 March 1930. See also Rutgers in the Recueil des Cours (Académie de Droit International), Volume 38, Page 47 et sequentes. Further: "Budapest Article 7" and Kunz, Josef, "Plus de loi de la guerre?" (Revue Génerale de Droit International Public, 1934). – Cohn, Neo-Neutrality (1939).

35. The Peruvian delegate, Senor Cornejo, in the Committee of the League of Nations Assembly in 1929 said (Assemblée 1929, C III J. O., Page 201): "Neutrality no longer exists!" Stimson, The Pact of Paris, Address 8 August 1932. Hull, Declaration on the Neutrality Law of 17 January 1936. Pact of Rio de Janeiro of 10 October 1933. Speech by the Swedish Foreign Minister Sandler of 6 December 1937 (see Jahrreiss Plea, Annex, Exhibit Number 27). 3 October 1939: Declaration of Panama; the exchange of notes by the 21 American Republics with Great Britain, France, and Germany (23 December 1939, 14 January, 23 January, 14 February 1940) is based completely on the classic Neutrality Law. The "Budapest Articles."—Literature: D'Astroy, B. (1938); Baty, Th. (1939); Bonn, M. J. (1936/37); Borchard, E. M. (1936, 1937, 1938, 1941); Brierly, J. L. (1929, 1932); Brown, Ph. M. (1936, 1939); Buell (1936); Cohn (1939); Descamps, de (1930); Eagleton, Clyde (1937); Fenwick, Charles G. (1934, 1935, 1939); Fischer Williams, Sir John (1935, 1936); Garner, James Wilford (1936, 1938); Hambro, Edvard (1938); Hyde, C. C. (1937, 1941); Jessup, P. C. (1932, 1935, 1936); Lauterpacht (1935, 1940); Mandelstam (1934); Miller, David Hunter (1928); McNair (1936); Politis, N. (1929, 1935); Rappard, W. E. (1935-1937); Schindler, D. (1938); Stimson, H. (1932); Stowell, Ellery C. (1932); Tenekides, C. C. (1939); Whitton, J. B. (1927, 1932); Wright, Quincy (1940).

36. Réserves de la Délégation Suisse (M. Motta) of 10 October 1935.

37. Udenrigspolitiske Meddelelser 4. Aergang, Numbers 4-5, Page 122 et sequentes (see Jahrreiss Plea, Annex, Exhibit Number 30).

38. Actes de la IIe Assemblée, séance des commissions, I, Page 396 et sequentes.

39. Actes de la IXe Assemblée, Page 75.

40. Department of State, Press Releases, 9 January 1932, Page 41.

41. Actes de l'Assemblée extraordinaire (J. O., Supplément special, Number 101, Page 87).

42. Jean Ray, 4e Supplément du Commentaire, 1935, Page 10: "Un homme d'État a dit un jour en parlant de l'article 16 que, s'il s'appliquait, il ne s'appliquerait sans doute, qu'une fois. On peut dire la même chose de tout le mécanisme quit doit faire obstacle à la guerre." – See also Fischer Williams, Sir John, Sanctions under the Covenant (Br. YB 1936) and McNair, Arnold D., Collective Security.

43. With reference to the Stimson Doctrine and the case of Abyssinia see also the works and papers of Borchard (1933), Fischer Williams (1936), McNair (1933), Sharp (1934), Stimson (1932), Wild (1932), Wright (1932, 1933).

44. With reference to the system of collective security see from the literature concerning the whole position in international law: Brierly (1932); Bourquin (1934); Brouckere (1934); Cuten (1931); Descamps (1930); Eagleton (1930, 1937, 1938); Elbe (1939); Fenwick (1932, 1934, 1935, 1939); Fischer

Williams (1932, 1933, 1935, 1936); Giraud (1934); Garner (1936); Graham (1929, 1934); Hill (1932); Hyde (1941); Jessup (1935); Mandelstam (1934); Politis (1929); Rutgers (1931); Shotwell (1928); Wickersham (1928/29); Whitton (1932); Wright (1942).

45. Parliament Debates H. L. 5th series, Volume 95, Cols. 1007, 1043.

46. Lauterpacht, The Pact of Paris and the Budapest Articles of Interpretation (Transactions of the Grotius Society, XX, 1935, Page 178), draws his conclusions from the fact that the states can accept or refuse, as logically established as law in Budapest. Jessup (Neutrality, Its History, Economics, and Law, Volume IV, Today and Tomorrow, 1936) finds that the states failed to accept the Budapest Articles.

47. See A. J., Volume 31, 1937, Pages 680-693.

48. See the concurring statements by Kuhn, Arthur K., Observations of Foreign Governments upon Secretary Hull's Principles of Enduring Peace (A. J., Volume 32, 1938, Pages 101, 106).

49. See Wright in A. J., Volume 34, 1940, Page 680 et sequentes; particularly Stimson's speech of 6 January 1941 should be mentioned here.

50. Fischer Williams also stresses this (Sanctions under the Covenant, Br. YB, 1936, Page 130 et sequentes). Also Kelsen, Collective and Individual Responsibility . . . 1943, Page 531.

51. An all too appropriate warning against mistaken conceptions in connection with the term "crime international" is given by Fischer Williams, Sanctions under the Covenant (Br. YB, 1936, Page 130 et sequentes).

52. Actes de l'Assemblée 1927, P., Page 153. Also Jean Ray, Commentaire, Pages 74/75.

53. Correctly Fischer Williams, Sanctions under the Covenant (Br. YB, 1936).

54. Collective and Individual Responsibility . . . , Pages 534, 538, 539, 540, 542.

55. Scott, James Brown, stresses the great merit gained by the American delegates at that time in the interests of law and justice (see House-Seymour, What Really Happened at Paris; New York 1921). — Williams, E. T., The Conflict between Autocracy and Democracy (A. J., Volume 32, 1938, Page 663 et sequentes). — Kelsen, Collective and Individual Responsibility . . . , Page 541. — Also Borchard, Edwin, Neutrality and Unneutrality (A. J., Volume 32, 1938, Page 778 et sequentes).

56. Kelsen seems to think that no such state exists (Collective and Individual Responsibility . . . , Page 543).

56a. Compare Jahrreiss Plea, Annex, Exhibit Number 42.

57. Kelsen, Collective and Individual Responsibility . . . , Page 546.

The Nuremberg Trial and International Law

1. *Der Prozess gegen die Hauptkriegsverbrecher vor dem Internationalen Militärgerichtshof, Nürnberg 14. November 1945 — 1. Oktober 1946* (Nürnberg, 1947), II, 40 (30). Citations to the official German edition were made by the author. Corresponding citations to the English edition have been inserted by the translator in parentheses following the German citations. The English edition is entitled *Trial of the Major War Criminals Before the Inter-*

national Military Tribunal, Nuremberg, 14 November 1945 – 1 October 1946 (Nürnberg, 1947).
2. V, 417 (370).
3. *Ibid.*, p. 479 (426).
4. Art. 3.
5. Art. 6, par. 1.
6. Art. 6, par. 2.
7. Art. 6, par. 3.
8. Art. 7.
9. Art. 8.
10. I, 30 (29).
11. I, 45 (42).
12. *Ibid.*, p. 46 (42-43).
13. *Ibid.*, p. 59 (55).
14. VI, 58, 59 (48).
15. I, 59 (55).
16. *Ibid.*, p. 60 (55).
17. *Ibid.*, p. 47 (44).
18. *Ibid.*, p. 56 (52).
19. I, 259 (232).
20. *Ibid.*, p. 70 (65).
21. II, 120 (102).
22. *Ibid.*, p. 128 (109).
23. *Ibid.*, p. 121 (103).
24. I, 188 (169).
25. II, 173 (147).
26. III, 120 (103).
27. *Ibid.*, p. 109 (94).
28. *Ibid.*, p. 124 (106).
29. II, 173 (146-147). Translator's note: The paper erroneously refers to Volume III.
30. II, 177 (150).
31. III, 121 (104).
32. *Ibid.*
33. *Ibid.*
34. II, 118 (101).
35. V, 418 *et seq.*
36. *Ibid.*, p. 438.
37. VII, 168 (148).
38. I, 244 (218).
39. I, 245 (219).
40. *Ibid.*, p. 246 (220).
41. *Ibid.*, pp. 246, 247 (221).
42. *Ibid.*, p. 249 (223).
43. II, 175 (148).
44. *American Journal of International Law,* Supp., XXVII (1933), 192, 194.
45. III, 121 (104).
46. II, 118 (101).
47. *Ibid.*, p. 182 (154).
48. III, 124 (106).

49. III, 605 (543).
50. II, 169 (143) (Jackson).

Nuremberg as a Legal Problem

1. "Das Kriegsverbrechen und seine Verfolgung in Vergangenheit und Gegenwart" in Jahrbuch fur internationales und ausländisches öffentliches Recht 1948, S. 283.
2. IMT Judgment, Nuremberg Edition, p. 81. In *Nazi Conspiracy and Aggression: Opinion and Judgment* (Washington, United States Government Printing Office, 1947), p. 48.
3. Militärgerichtshof Nr. III, Nürnberg, Fall 2. Milch-Urteil vom 16. April 1947, deutsche Protokolle S. 2518. (German record p. 2518.) *Trials of War Criminals Before the Nuremberg Military Tribunals Under Control Council Law No. 10* (Washington: Government Printing Office), II, 778.
4. Military Court No. III, Nuremberg, Case 3, Justice Judgment of December 3, 1947, English record p. 10648. *TWC*, III, 984.
5. U. S. Court of Appeals for the District of Columbia, No. 9883, Judgment of May 11, 1949.
6. Militärgerichtshof IV, Nürnberg, Fall 11, Weizsäcker-Urteil vom 11. bis 13. April 1949, deutsche Protokolle S. 27 616. (German record p. 27616). *TWC*, XIV, 317.
7. Militärtribunal V, Nürnberg, Fall 12, OKW-Urteil vom 27. Oktober 1948, deutsche Protokolle S. 9883. (German record p. 9883). *TWC*, XI, 510.
8. English record p. 10687.
9. Militärgerichtshof IV, Nürnberg, Fall 5, Urteil vom 22. Dez. 1947, deutsche Protokolle S. 10718. (German record p. 10718). *TWC*, VI, 1189.
10. E.g. Militärgerichtshof V, Nürnberg, Fall 7 (Südostgenerale) deutsche Protokolle S. 10300. (German record p. 10300).
Militärgerichtshof I, Fall 8 (Rasse- und Siedlungspolitisches Hauptamt called RUSHA), Urteil vom 10. Marz 1948, deutsche Protokolle S. 5121. (German record p. 5121).
Militärgerichtshof V, Nürnberg, Fall 12 (OKW) deutsche Protokolle S. 9883. (German record p. 9883).
11. IMT Judgment, Nuremberg Edition, p. 81. *NCA*, p. 48.
12. American Military Court No. III, Nuremberg, Case 3, Justice Judgment of December 3, 1947, English record p. 10622. *TWC*, III, 965.
13. Amerikanischer Militärgerichtshof IV, Nürnberg, Fall 11, Weizsäcker-Urteil vom 11. bis 13. April 1949, deutsche Protokolle S. 27907. (German record p. 27907). *TWC*, XIV, 527.
14. Rittler also talks about "revolutionary law." Rittler, Kampf gegen das politische Verbrechen seit dem zweiten Weltkriege (Fight Against the Political Crime Since World War II), Schweiz. Zeitschrift für Strafrecht, 64. Jahrg. 1949, S. 138-144.
15. International Law, 1944, Volume II, p. 451. (°,7th. ed., Vol. II, 1952, p. 567).
16. IMT Judgment p. 88. *NCA*, pp. 52-53.
17. German record p. 10722. *TWC*, VI, 1192.
18. Ex Parte Quirin 1942, 317 US 27.
19. Ex Parte Quirin 1942, p. 29.

20. German record p. 27618. *TWC*, XIV, 319.
21. Amerikanischer Militärgerichtshof V, Nürnberg, Fall 12, OKW-Urteil vom 27. Oktober 1948, deutsche Protokolle S. 9851. (German record p. 9851). *TWC*, XI, 990.
22. German record p. 9849. *TWC*, XI, 489.
23. Wendell L. Willkie, One World, New York 1943, p. 175.
24. IMT Judgment p. 61. *NCA*, p. 36.
25. IMT Judgment p. 63. *NCA*, p. 37.
26. IMT Judgment p. 74. *NCA*, p. 45.
27. German record p. 10315. *TWC*, XI, 1245.
28. IMT Judgment p. 113. *NCA*, p. 68.
29. English record p. 10646. *TWC*, III, 982.
30. English record p. 10641. *TWC*, III, 979.
31. The General Assembly therefore: "Affirms that genocide is a crime under international law which the civilized world condemns, and for the commission of which principals and accomplices — whether private individuals, public officials or statesmen, and whether the crime is committed on religious, racial, political or any other grounds – are punishable." (Journal of the United Nations, No. 58, Supp. A − C/P. V/55, page 485.)
32. Despite Nuremberg the Bonn Constitution apparently does not consider the punishableness of aggressive war to be applicable international law. For Art. 25 declares the general rules of international law to be a constituent part of the federal law. Art. 26 provides that the preparations for aggressive war should be made punishable, thus supposing that they are not yet punishable under international law.
33. De Menthon, IMT, Vol. V of Documents, p. 435 ff.
34. Südostgenerale-Urteil, deutsche Protokolle S. 10319. (German record p. 10319).
35. English record p. 10687.
36. 3rd ed., 1920, Vol. I, p. 26.
37. OKW-Urteil, deutsche Protokolle S. 9850. (German record p. 9850). *TWC*, XI, 489.
38. English record p. 10687. *TWC*, III, 1011.
39. English record p. 10854. *TWC*, III, 1128.
40. German record p. 13648. *TWC*, IX, 1346.
41. Urteil gegen Südostgenerale, Nürnberger Sonderdruck S. 38 and 59/60. (German Edition).
42. German record p. 28107.
43. British Manual of Military Law, 1929, Sec. 443.
44. German record p. 10302. *TWC*, XI, 1237.
45. German record p. 9884. *TWC*, XI, 510-11.
46. German record p. 10018. *TWC*, XI, 598.
47. German record p. 9934. *TWC*, XI, 543.
48. German record p. 9883. *TWC*, XI, 510.
49. German record p. 9885. *TWC*, XI, 511.
50. German record p. 10748.
51. IMT-Urteil S. 236. *NCA*, p. 140.
52. German record p. 27623. *TWC*, XIV, 322.
53. German record p. 10002.
54. German record p. 10736/10734. *TWC*, VI, 1200-1201.

55. Jurists Judgment: "International law is superior in authority to any German statute or decree." English record p. 10648.

56. Lecture before the Association des Études Internationales, March 1947.

57. Oppenheim-Lauterpacht, 1944, Vol. II, p. 458. (°, 7th. ed., Vol. II, 1952, 588).

58. Milch-Urteil, deutsche Protokolle S. 2533. (German record p. 2533). *TWC*, II, 791.

The Nuremberg Judgment: Penal Jurisdiction

1. S. Mendelssohn-Bartholdy in DJZ 1921, col. 446.

2. See the judgment of the Reichsmilitärgericht (Reich Military Court) of 23 August 1915 in DJZ 1915, p. 1235 and the consideration of the same case before the penal chamber of the Landgericht, explained by Gerbaulet in DJZ 1916, p. 184.

3. Many times proved by the extraterritoriality due to a foreign army. The question is contended less in its results than in its foundations. See above all Oppler in Zeitschrift f. Strafrechtswissenschaft 37, p. 849.

4. Many people understand thereunder only the customs of war of the German army, although it may have developed in common and in correspondence with the customs of war of other armies. (See Romen and Rissom, §160, note 18 before a.)

5. Friedmann: *Kommandogewalt, Kriegsgebrauch und Strafgewalt*, 1915 (printed only as a manuscript); Conference of judicial military officers in Brussels, 1915; ibid. Beling, p. 7; v. Staff, p. 31; v. Schlayer DStrZ 2 p. 7; furthermore see Romen and Rissom, Kommentar zum Militär-Strafgesetzbuch 1918, §160 note 11 d at the end.

6. After Oppenheim's death Lauterpacht took upon himself the editing of the newer edition of this work. Lauterpacht became councilor of the British Admiralty during World War II. He is at present a member of the British War Crime Commission.

7. See, e. g., Frankreich in Recht 1915, p. 3. The Swiss scholar in international law Bluntschli (Das moderne Völkerrecht, §602) regarded trial by the enemy state as unobjectionable, but demanded that the substantive penal law of the captured soldier's native state be applied. See also Olshausen, Berner Lehrbuch, p. 215.

Review

1. International Military Tribunal, *Trial of the Major War Criminals*, Nuremberg 1948, Volume XXII, Proceedings 27 Aug. – 1 Oct. 1946, p. 410.

2. Together with Alexander Mitscherlich, Verlag Lambert Schneider, Heidelberg 1946, p. 66.

The Trials of Economists

1. Art. XV ff. of Vol. 7, Amer. Mil. Reg. provides for no legal remedy. Cf. p. 176 in "Das Urteil im IG-Farben Prozess," Bollwerk-Verlag Karl Drott, Offenbach a. M.

2. In the trials of economists this count is not of fundamental importance; it is therefore not dealt with here. The Flick Judgment convicted in this respect not only an honorary SS leader but also one of Himmler's friends, who in most cases were rich and powerful industrialists; but in the corresponding cases the I. G. Farben Judgment arrives at acquittals even after an active SS leader had not been declared guilty in Case 4.

3. There was therefore no indictment in the Flick trial — Case 5. In the proceedings against the Krupp firm — Case 10 — the defendants were declared not guilty in this respect, however, even before the final judgment after the reading of the material of indictment, since the latter did not suffice for the proof of any guilt.

4. *Ibid.*, pp. 179 ff.

5. *Ibid.*, pp. 19-57; in accordance with Anglo-Saxon law guilt and penalty were always distinguished in Nuremberg.

6. See preamble and Art. I, Control Council Law No. 10.

7. *Ibid.*, p. 32.

8. The Nuremberg Tribunals require for the offenses under their jurisdiction in principle an intention, which, however, does not have to imply the particularly problematic consciousness of its illegality in general; e. g., Krupp Judgment, English text of the proceedings page 13300, German special edition, p. 68; dev., e.g., the judgment in Case 12 against the Generals, p. 10095 (p. 108); since the English text of the proceedings contains the authentic text it is quoted in the following as far as it was accessible to me.

9. *Ibid.*, pp. 19 and 50 ff.

10. *Ibid.*, pp. 52 ff.

11. *Ibid.*, pp. 54 and 55.

12. Continuation of the quotation — on the collision of the citizen's duties at a conflict of national and international law see NJW 49, 376. Judge Herbert in the I. G. Farben trial and Judge Wilkins in the Krupp case agreed in their "concurring opinions" to the acquittal because of the IMT Judgment, but they consider purely on principle a possible complicity of the defendants, especially because of their essential participation in the rearmament.

13. The "law of nations," strictly speaking, being the law governing the relations among the nations did not hitherto know a penal responsibility of individual persons in principle. See, e.g., Donnedieu de Vabres, "Droit Pénal International," Paris 1928, p. 3; one of the reasons for the objection of *nullum crimen sine lege.*

14. German text of proceedings, p. 10722.

15. *Ibid.*, pp. 10719, 10722 and, f.i., Judgment Case 12, English text of proceedings, p. 10032, German text, p. 33.

16. German text of proceedings, pp. 10725 ff.

17. E.g., Wharton, Criminal Law, vol. I, chap. VII, p. 126.

18. Oppenheim, International Law, 1921, vol. 2, pp. 230 ff.

19. *Ibid.*, 1944, vol. 2, pp. 298, and Rasmussen, Commentary to this Convention, Copenhagen 1931, p. 33.

20. Nuremberg Judgment in Case 12, Engl. t. o. proc., p. 10095, German text, p. 108.

21. Footnote 1, ibid., p. 107 ff.

22. *Ibid.*, p. 117; IMT Judgment official German text, vol. I, p. 250.

23. See also the moral-theological expert opinion of Pater Max Pribilla on

"Das Verhalten der Unternehmer im Dritten Reich," which was submitted by the defense in the I. G. Farben trial and published in "Stimmen der Zeit," 1948, vol. 3.

24. *Ibid.*, p. 55.

25. Official German text, vol. I, p. 247.

26. Also in principle the draft of a "Convention for the Protection of Civilian Persons in Times of War" which was concluded at the 17th Conference of the International Red Cross, Stockholm 1948.

27. Oppenheim, International Law, 3rd edition, vol. 1, art. 21; see also, e.g., "USA-Rules of Land Warfare" 1940, ciph. 202; also Hatschek, German and Prussian State Law, 2nd edition, vol. 1, p. 42 following art. 4 of the Weimar Constitution for the later Landrecht.

28. The internal compulsion to work, eventually even gratis and subject to a change in domicile — contrary to slavery, which founds property-like rights in men — is recognized by Article 5 of the Anti-Slavery Agreement of 1926 concluded by most civilized nations (in this count however with the exception of the United States of America). A large portion of the alien laborers were placed at the disposal of Germany during the last war on account of state agreements by their own governments, however, which were also recognized outside of the German sphere of control; therefore an offense against the principles of the Hague Convention and thereby of Control Council Law No. 10 does not come into question, according to the dissenting opinion of Judge L. W. Powers in Case 11, German text p. 96 and pp. 109 ff. — in deviation, however, from the prevailing opinion of the Nuremberg Tribunals. Any compulsion exercised for this purpose from state to state was hitherto admissible in international law. Cheney Hyde, International Law, Boston 1945, vol. 2, pp. 1380 ff.; Oppenheim, *op. cit.*, 3rd. edition, vol. 2, pp. 660 ff. — but compare the negotiations of the U.N. and new drafts of the convention of the International Red Cross which now aim for the protection of human rights, especially in regard to deportations abroad, at a limitation of the sovereignty of the signatory states; as for the rest, deportations from occupied areas to work were admissible according to the resolutions of the *Reichsgericht* of 1925-26, eventually in accordance with Art. 43 of the Hague Convention in the interest of public order, e.g., in unemployment; see Bell, Völkerrecht im Weltkrieg, 1928, vol. 1, pp. 193 ff. and 282; also the Nuremberg Judgment in Case 7, Engl. text p. 1047, Germ. text p. 29; in this respect furthermore under the aspects of reciprocity and of *tu quoque* the Russian ordinances in Poland etc. already in 1940 according to the Zeitschrift für osteuropäisches Recht, 1940-42 and ciph. VI of the procl. 2 of the Control Council of 1945; finally the theory of self-defense, Oppenheim, *op. cit.*, p. 601.

29. Cheney Hyde, *op. cit.*, p. 2177.

29a. See also Feilchenfeld, The international economic law of warfare of belligerent occupation, Washington 1942, pp. 18 ff.

30. Note 1, *ibid.*, pp. 121 ff.

31. RGUrt. of February 14, 1921, RGZ 101, 322.

32. See the quotation from Case 7 in footnote 28.

33. See Kogon, SS-Staat, 1946, p. 12.

34. Arndt, NJW 47-48, 162.

35. Judge Hebert in his "dissenting opinion" considers all of the defendants who were members of the IG management guilty in the complex of slave

labor. He denies the state of distress in view of the economic power of the defendants and the circumstance that their will and their initiative insofar coincided many times with that of the government, according to the documents; in this respect we point to the foregoing and following statements on the IG and Krupp Judgments.

36. With, however, a more lenient statement deviating therefrom by the Chairman, Hu. C. Anderson, who also rejects the forfeiture of the major defendant's property based on Control Council Law No. 10, Article II 3, which hitherto has not been declared in Nuremberg.

37. English text, pp. 13294 ff. and 13382 ff., German text pp. 62 ff. and 141 ff.

38. Therefore it is also doubtful whether the defendants' conduct was causal within the meaning of the law for alien forced labor; see Judge Powers, *op. cit.*, pp. 3 ff.

38a. A consideration of the attacks of the defense on the actual statements of the Judgment is not possible here for various reasons.

39. See note 28.

40. German text, pp. 10737 ff.

41. But hereto see also the I. G. Farben Judgment, note 1, pp. 73 and 81.

42. Official German text, vol. 1, p. 285 with reference to Art. 6 c of the Charter, see note 1, *ibid.*, p. 152.

43. German text, pp. 10753 ff.

44. Note 1, *ibid.*, pp. 58 ff.

45. *Ibid.*, p. 170.

46. German text, Vol. I, pp. 267 ff.

47. Note 1, *ibid.*, p. 63.

48. German text, pp. 19 ff.

49. Note 1, *ibid.*, p. 67; similarly Powers, *op. cit.*, pp. 104 ff.

50. *Ibid.*, p. 81.

50a. *Ibid.*, p. 55.

51. In the Nuremberg jurisdiction rejected, however, *in concreto*.

52. German text, Vol. I, p. 288.

52a. In view of the development that has meanwhile taken place, the uniformity of treatment demanded by the International Military Tribunal should in particular be a cause for a revision of the sentences in regard to the extent of their punishment.

53. Cases Norsk Hydro and Francolor, *ibid.*, pp. 77 ff.

53a. Any compulsion within the meaning of German penal law would require, however, that a criminal character of the threatened measures of coercion had been investigated and established.

54. See, e.g., preamble of Flick Judgment and Powers, *op. cit.*, pp. 12 ff.

55. *Ibid.*, p. 86.

56. *Ibid.*, p. 67.

57. English text, pp. 13260 ff.; German text, pp. 27 ff.

58. Judge Wilkins, in a "dissenting opinion" in the Krupp Trial, also calls the purchase of the Berndorfer Werke in Austria by Krupp a consequence of military aggression and a war crime of spoliation; also a.o. Krupp's contracts on the utilization of state-owned Russian industrial plants and the effects of these. Similarly Judgment Case 11, Germ. text p. 28204, but compare Flick Judgment, Germ. text, pp. 10748 ff., and on Austria Germ. text pp. 10756 ff., and the IG Judgment, *op. cit.*, pp. 59 ff. and above.

59. English text p. 13281, German text p. 48.
60. See note 28.
61. English text p. 10034, German text p. 34.
62. Similarly the French prosecutor before the IMT, De Menthon, German text Vol. V. 5. 436.
63. In the interest of the positiveness of law, such a *ius resistendi* against the illegal exercise of government, which has always been contended altogether, is granted by the canonical and natural law majority only to particularly competent officials; thus according to Wolzendorff, Staatsrecht und Naturrecht in der Lehre vom Widerstandsrecht usw., Breslau, 1916, pp. 18 and 95, e.g., by Marsilius von Padua and also Calvin *magistratus* and *statuti ad hoc* as states. tribunes, ephores, etc.
64. See the foregoing quotation to note 11, Judge Powers, *op. cit.*, pp. 3 ff.
65. As, for instance, into the validity of Control Council Law No. 10 and the significance of the sentence *nullum crimen sine lege*; the same applies to the methods of the preliminary investigation and the short apprehension of a part of the Krupp defense because of contempt of court, which was much discussed at that time.

The Nuremberg Judgments

1. Lord Edward Grey, *25 Jahre Politik 1892 bis 1916*, German edition, Munich, 1926, p. 17.
2. See Ehard, "The Nuremberg Trial Against the Major War Criminals and International Law," SJZ 1948, Sp. 358, as well as v. Waldkirch in his (unpublished) Legal Opinion read at the Luxemburg Meeting of Jurists.
3. Kelsen in *California Law Review*, XXXI (1942-43), 538, and in his (hitherto unpublished) lecture in Buenos Aires.
4. See Lummert, "Die Strafverfahren gegen Deutsche im Ausland" wegen "Kriegsverbrechens," Hamburg, 1949, pp. 31 ff.
5. V. Puttkammer, "Die Haftung der politischen und militärischen Führung des Ersten Weltkriege für Kriegsurheberschaft und Kriegsverbrechen," in *Archiv des Völkerrechts*, I, 424.
6. IMT Judgment, p. 59, Nymphenburger Ausgabe.
7. German text of proceedings of the Nuremberg Flick Trial, p. 10722; see also Dix, "Die Urteile in den Nürnberge Wirtschaftsprozessen," NJW 1949, pp. 647 ff.
8. See Haensel, *Organisationsverbrechen*, Munich, 1947, p. 53.
9. For detailed information see Kraus-Kommentar on Control Council Law No. 10, pp. 9 ff.
10. See Wilhelm Sauer, *Völkerrecht und Weltfrieden*, 1948, p. 242, and Jagusch, SJZ 1949, col. 620, who sees in Art. II lc CCL 10 a frame of facts clarified by instances; see also OGHST 1, p. 12.
11. Off. (unpublished) reasoning on the Norwegian regulations on the punishment of Germans, ciph. II.
12. Schönke, *Strafgesetzbuch* (penal code), Kommentar, 4th edition, Munich, 1949, p. 174.
13. See Frhr. v. Hodenberg, "Zur Anwendung des Kontrollratsgesetzes Nr. 10 durch deutsche Gerichte," SJZ, 1947, col. 114.

Notes

14. See Nuremberg Flick Tribunal, which declared expressly that it bases its judgment on "the generally current principles of Anglo-American law."

15. Jeschek, "Kriegsverbrecherprozesse gegen deutsche Kriegsgefangene in Frankreich," SJZ, 1949, p. 107.

16. See for instance Art. 6 of the Polish decree of August 31 and September 13, 1944; "To the crimes specified in this decree the regulations of the General Part of the (Polish) Penal Code are applied." Within this meaning also §1 of the provisional order of May 4, 1945, on the punishment of foreign war criminals in Norway.

17. Sauer, *op. cit.*, p. 243.

18. See Jagusch, *op. cit.*

19. Wimmer; "Unmenschlichkeitsverbrechen und deutschrechtliche Straftat in einer Handlung," SJZ, 1948, p. 253.

20. Constantopoulos, "Verbindlichkeit und Konstruktion des positiven Völkerrechts," Hamburg, 1949, p. 12.

21. *New York Herald Tribune*, Paris, April 9, 1948.

22. Judgment in Case XI, p. 338; see also Haensel, "Der Ausklang von Nürnberg," NJW, 1949, p. 367.

23. See Volkmann, "Kriegsverbrecherverfahren in Belgien," NJW, 1949, p. 659.

24. Official Norwegian argument, ciph. I.

25. Reprinted in *Gesetzliche Vorschriften der amerikanischen Militärregierung in Deutschland*, edition B, p. 10 a. C, p. 11.

26. Haensel, *op. cit.*, NJW, 1949, p. 368.

Conclusion of the Nuremberg Trials

1. *Das Nürnberger Juristenurteil*, Hamburg 1948, p. 42.

2. Judgment Case 11, p. 338. *Trials of War Criminals Before the Nuernberg Military Tribunals under Control Council Law No. 10* (Washington: Government Printing Office), XIV, 527.

3. IMT Judgment, ch. 5: "The Law of the Charter" – *Juristenurteil*, p. 11.

4. Judgment Case 11, p. 8. *TWC*, XIV, 318.

5. *Ibid.*, p. 15. *TWC*, XIV, 322.

6. *Ibid.*, p. 16. *TWC*, XIV, 323.

7. *Ibid.*, p. 13.

8. *Ibid.*, p. 16.

9. Dissenting Opinion, p. 10. *TWC*, XIV, 877.

10. Berolzheimer, *System der Rechts- und Wirtschaftsphilosophie*, 1906, III, 91.

11. Compare AG Wiesbaden of November 13, 1945, SJZ 46, 36; LG Berlin of August 12, 1947, in JR 48, 52.

12. Berolzheimer, *The Dangers of a Jurisprudence of Feeling*, Berlin, 1911, p. 14.

13. Judgment Case 11, p. 108. *TWC*, XIV, 382.

14. *Ibid.*, p. 127. *TWC*, XIV, 393.

15. *Ibid.*, p. 204. *TWC*, XIV, 443.

16. *Ibid.*, p. 465.

17. *Ibid.*, p. 291. *TWC*, XIV, 497.

18. *Ibid.*, p. 568. *TWC*, XIV, 674-75.
19. *Ibid*, p. 110.
20. *Ibid.*, p. 251. *TWC*, XIV, 472.
21. *Ibid.*, p. 684.
22. *Ibid.*, p. 520. *TWC*, XIV, 645-46.
23. *Ibid.*, p. 45. *TWC*, XIV, 339.
24. *Ibid.*, p. 51.
25. Dissenting Opinion, p. 17. *TWC*, XIV, 881.
26. Judgment Case 11, p. 206.
27. *Ibid.*, p. 237.
28. Dissenting Opinion, p. 5. *TWC*, XIV, 874.
29. *Ibid.*, p. 6. *TWC*, XIV, 874.
30. Gibson, *Criminal and Magisterial Law*, London, 1934, p. 62.
31. IMT, official edition, II, 31.
32. *Ibid.*, p. 302.
33. Carl Haensel, *Das Organisationsverbrechen*, Munich, 1947, NJW 47/48, 35.
34. Judgment Case 11, p. 192.
35. Carl Haensel, *op. cit.*, p. 56.
36. Judgment Case 11, p. 7. *TWC*, XIV, 317.

Select Bibliography

Books and Pamphlets

Allied War Crimes and Crimes Against Humanity (Documents of the Second World War). Printed in German by the Duerer-Verlag, whose monthly magazine *Der Tag* was banned as Nazi in Germany and Austria, first by Allied occupation authorities and later by officials of those countries.

BAUER, F. *Die Kriegsverbrecher vor Gericht.* Zürich-New York, 1945.

German White Book Concerning the Responsibility of the Authors of the War. Translated by the Carnegie Endowment. New York: Oxford University Press, 1924. This volume consists mainly of the document entitled "German Observations on the Report of the Commission of the Allied and Associated Governments in the Responsibility of the Authors of the War," which was prepared by a group of German scholars.

GREWE, W., and KUESTER, O. *Nürnberg als Rechtsfrage: Eine Diskussion.* Stuttgart, 1947.

HAENSEL, CARL. *Das Organisationsverbrechen.* Munich: Biederstein Verlag, 1947. One of the most prominent of the Nuremberg defense counsel discusses the legal aspects of crime by organization.

JANECZEK, E. *Nuremberg Judgment in the Light of International Law.* Geneva, 1949.

KIPP, HEINZ. *Moderne Probleme Des Kriegsrecht in Der Spätscholastik.* Paderborn, 1935.

KNIERIEM, AUGUST VON. *Nürnberg: Rechtliche und Menschliche Probleme.* Stuttgart: Ernst Klett Verlag, 1953.

KRANZBUEHLER, VON OTTO. *Nürnberg als Rechtsproblem,* in *um Recht und Frieden, Festgabe Für Erich Kaufmann* (Stuttgart-Köln, 1950), pp. 219-37.

————.*Rückblick auf Nürnberg.* Hamburg: Zeit-Verlag E. Schmidt, 1949.

LANG, SERGE, and VON SCHENCK, ERNST. *Portraet Eines Menschheitsverbrechers; Alfred Rosenberg.* St. Gallen: Verlag Zollikofer, 1947. An analysis of defense material written by Alfred Rosenberg in the Nuremberg prison for the use of his defense counsel.

SCHMITT, CARL. *Die Wendung Zum Diskriminierden Kriegsbegriffs.* Munich: Schriften Der Akademie Für Deutsches Recht, 1938.

231

Articles

BALASZ, A. "Die Rechtliche Begründung Des Nürnberger Urteils," *Friedens-warte*, 1946, pp. 369-75.

BALMER-BASILIUS, H. R. "Nürnberg und Das Weltgewissen," *Friedenswarte*, 1946.

COMTESSE, F. H. "Betrachtungen Zum Nürnberger Prozess," *Schweizer Monats-hefte*, 1946.

FISCHLSCHWEIGER, H. "Zum Problem Der Kollektiv-Haftung," *Juristiche Blat-ter*, 1951.

MOSLER, H. "Die Kriegshandlung im Rechtswidrigen Krieg," *Jahrbuch Für Internationales und Auslandisches Offentliches Recht*, I, Hamburg, 1948.